ORIANA FALLACI

ORIANA FALLACI

The Woman and the Myth

Santo L. Aricò

SOUTHERN ILLINOIS UNIVERSITY PRESS

Carbondale and Edwardsville

01 00 99 98 4 3 2 1

Library of Congress Cataloging-in-Publication Data
Aricò, Santo L., 1938–
    Oriana Fallaci : the woman and the myth / Santo L. Aricò.
      p. cm.
    Includes bibliographical references and index.
    1. Fallaci, Oriana. 2. Women journalists—United States—
    Biography. 3. Women authors—United States—Biography. I. Title.
PN4874.F38A75 1998   97-14420
853′.914—dc21   CIP
ISBN 0-8093-2153-X (alk. paper)

To Julia Elizabeth. Have a great life.

Contents

Preface		ix
Acknowledgments		xi

	Introduction: In Search of Truth	3
1.	Florence	10
2.	Kipling, London, Hemingway	25
3.	Lights, Camera, Action	38
4.	On Center Stage	54
5.	Reaching for the Moon	71
6.	Movie Screen in Southeast Asia	97
7.	Superstar on a Balcony	116
8.	Performances of a Lifetime	126
9.	To Be or Not to Be	158
10.	The Man or the Woman	176
11.	Tolstoy, Dostoyevsky, and Fallaci	194
	Conclusion: Facing the Alien	225

Notes	235
Bibliography	259
Index	269

Preface

Oriana Fallaci, one of the twentieth century's most celebrated journalists, interviewers, war correspondents, and novelists has acquired an international reputation. Translators have made most of her books available throughout the world. Pro-life advocates and radical feminists alike study *Letter to a Child Never Born* and claim it as their own to justify their positions on abortion. While in Lapland for a news report, the writer's sister Paola discovered *A Man* in the modest home of a poor reindeer shepherd who had covered one wall with photographs of Fallaci taken from magazines and newspapers. Ordinary human beings examine her life with interest and invest it with a certain mystique. American professors use *Interview with History* to illustrate the Fallaci interview technique. When Khomeini received her in the holy city of Qom, he had editions of her books in Farsi translation. Some of Fallaci's formal honors include the Doctor in Letters Honoris Causae from Chicago's Columbia College; the Saint Vincent Prize for journalism, awarded on two occasions; Italy's Bancarella for *Nothing and Amen*; the Super Bancarella for her career as a writer; the prestigious Viareggio Prize for *A Man*; the Hemingway Prize for *Inshallah*; the International Antibes Award (also for *Insciallah*); the Messina Prize for best coverage of the Gulf War; and many more.

Fallaci has lived for more than twenty-five years in the shadows of New York City skyscrapers. Very few people know the address of her small but inviting brownstone with its minuscule rear garden and its few trees that welcome flocks of doves, pigeons, and sparrows. Her home abounds with souvenirs and old books for which she has an obsessive passion. A very rare illustrated edition of Shakespeare that dates from the eighteenth century represents just one of her treasures. She is one of this planet's most simple and yet most complicated persons and communicates with refreshing openness while never losing an air of mystery, hostility, and outright aggressiveness. For all intents and purposes, she remains a devoted American who has never regretted living in the country of her choice but frequently returns to her beloved Florence.

Acknowledgments

I thank Charles Conrad, Robert Frishman, James Marcus, and John Shepley, who allowed me to use material from my telephone interviews with them in the preparation of this book. I am grateful for the help and goodwill of my colleagues—too many to mention by name—and the staff of the John Davis Williams Library at the University of Mississippi. I am obliged to the College of Liberal Arts, the Graduate School, and the Department of Modern Languages, also of the University of Mississippi, for financial assistance. Above all, I wish to thank my family for their love and unqualified support. Without their sustenance, the journey from inception to publication would have proven unbearable.

ORIANA FALLACI

Oriana Fallaci with China's
Vice-Premier Deng Xiaoping.
Reprinted by permission of the
Xinhua News Agency.

In Search of Truth

Introduction.

I FIRST DISCOVERED ORIANA Fallaci in 1980 when a friend gave me her book *Niente e così sia* (*Nothing and Amen*). That moment marked the beginning of an intimate, emotional, and highly strained relationship that would ultimately culminate in the publication of *Oriana Fallaci: The Woman and the Myth*. Contact with Fallaci changed my life. Her views on American involvement in Vietnam so impressed me that I wrote an article entitled "Oriana Fallaci's Discovery of Truth in *Niente e così sia*."[1] Reading her interviews with such political giants as Henry Kissinger, Indira Gandhi, Muammar al-Qaddafi, Haile Selassie, and Golda Meir in *Interview with History* then motivated me to write "Breaking the Ice: An In-Depth Look at Oriana Fallaci's Interview Techniques."[2] After exposure to *Letter to a Child Never Born* and *A Man*, my attraction to the writer became even stronger. Explicating her books became a personal compulsion and led me to discover an intimate connection between them and her journalism. This insight influenced the composition of my essay "Oriana Fallaci's Journalistic Novel: *Niente e così sia*" and its inclusion in my edited volume *Contemporary Women Writers in Italy*.[3] The writer's magic had cast its spell and changed the rhythm of life of one individual living in America's Deep South. When she sent me a copy of *Insciallah* on 3 July 1991, no power on earth could have prevented my picking up a pen to ask whether she would assist me in researching her life.

What particularly characterizes Fallaci's career is her life's psychological journey. She is a journalist and a literary writer at the same time. The desire to write novels and free herself from journalism emerges as a dominant force in her life. However, the publication of her own images far surpasses this dynamic in power. Her greatest efforts have revolved around conscious attempts to create her own mythical status. As Fallaci herself indicates, she is born in each of her works like a wild mushroom in a forest. Her portraits are true, not invented. In succeeding articles and books, the mushroom—not a carefully cultivated rose—is born again with a slightly different shape. Fallaci is not a product of producers or agents, as are Michael Jackson and Madonna; she is the self that she, the writer, pours into every word put on paper.

After Fallaci wrote an encouraging letter to me on 3 October 1991, spoke to me on the telephone about her life's story, and met with me in New York, my attraction for the writer became stronger than a simple admiration for the way she wrote. I had to discover the reasons behind the Fallaci phenomenon. Her life was an outgrowth of her writing career and had determined the content of her works. Her lover, Alexandros "Alekos" Panagoulis, had literally written his poetry with his blood during his incarceration. Her accomplishment surpasses his, for she writes her books with her life. Fallaci reveals her intellectual, political, and philosophical journey in everything she has written. "It is all there . . . because I am a very sincere author. . . . Consequently, as I write, whether about Deng Xiaoping or Khomeini, I reveal myself."[4] Critics have never understood that she has consistently externalized herself as her own main character. In an ongoing manner, she transforms and, to some degree, distorts the objective world of reality, only to give it a shape and clarity that she could never achieve without the power of her Fallaci imprint.[5] Fallaci's material passes through the filter of her own individuality, becomes more memorializing with the passing of time, and, in the process, receives its highly personalized artistic edge. The end result is the creation of attractive, dynamic images.

In December 1991, Oriana Fallaci received me at her home in Manhattan and, with a warm, refined welcome, dissipated any nervousness. In the comfort of her living room, we talked about the reasons for her popularity and what she called the *click* and the *chemistry* of her life. Two on-site visits took place in Italy in July 1992: the first, shortly after her breast cancer operation, at the home of her sister Paola in Milan; the second at her apartment in Florence in the residential neighborhood above Porta Romana. We met again in New York for two days on the first weekend of March 1993. On 6 April, one month later, I called Fallaci in Florence and found her discouraged. Doctors could do nothing to relieve the discomfort caused by her cancer.

The telephone conversations and interviews in New York, Milan, and Florence, along with her writings and critical reviews, generated the impression of a woman who had turned her life into a series of carefully planned images and used her literary talent to ensure its effective communication. A British critic's definition summarizes the Fallaci dynamic. "Myth is a narrative connected with a rite."[6] In the case of Fallaci, she uses literary journalism as her communicative mode and projects herself into her own content. Her ritualistic performances allow readers to discover her, to watch her, and to experience pleasure as she takes delight in self-revelation. The combination of a powerful, realistic style and a continuous turning of the spotlight on herself fosters her myth. Her readers experience her adventures, love affairs, and philosophic anxiety. Fallaci has made herself a star and consequently represents mythmaking in process as surely as Ernest Hemingway's protagonists did in their time.

When Fallaci expressed a willingness to cooperate with the writing of a professional biography, I quickly discovered what she meant. She would edit her official image at every stage of my book. I would be her instrument, her tool. She would explain her works, correct my statements, affirm what was true, indicate what information was false, even though taken from documented sources, specify what she took from reality, and make known what she invented. In essence, she brandished a double-edged sword. On one side, she would carefully revise my manuscript. I would supposedly have only the freedom to interpret and analyze her style and ideas. On the other side, nothing dealing with her childhood could be touched, for she would treat this aspect of her life in her next novel. She wanted my book to be exclusively the story of her mind. I finally came to believe that my role was to embellish the only portrait she wanted her public to have.

Fallaci immediately set the parameters. All of the many stories she knew up to World War II, even though she might tell them to me, would be for her alone and her forthcoming book. She emphasized that she would read my drafts to make sure I used nothing that belonged in her forthcoming novel. Although I agreed to respect her wishes, my point of reference focused on her direct revelations to me during the interviews. I never agreed to ignore material about her youth that had already been published and formed such an integral part of her books and articles. Her "Nota introduttiva" to the Italian version of Jack London's *Call of the Wild* and interviews in an Italian magazine given to her sister Paola were filled with references to her mother, father, sisters, and childhood. For my purposes, insisted Fallaci, she was born the day she started to write for newspapers.

Fallaci wanted my book to be a professional biography and limit itself to literary analysis of her novels, nothing else. She wanted the world to remember her as a great author, not as a journalist. Any emphasis on her early books (collections of her articles) was degrading to her. (She later reversed this requirement and adamantly insisted that chapters deal also with her first books.) She provided pages from Yevgeny Zamyatin's aesthetic theories in *Tecnica della prosa*, which reflected how she had written her novels. She revealed her indebtedness to the American, British, and Russian literary traditions and relegated Italy's literature to secondary status with regard to the formation of her mind. She urged me to consult the Italian critic Giancarlo Vigorelli, who maintained that her fame earns comparisons with Hemingway and with André Malraux. She referred me to Bernardo Valli, who called *Insciallah* "Oriana's little Iliad" of modern times. She praised David Maria Turoldo, who indicated that, in *Insciallah*, Lebanon stands as a metaphor of contemporary society, as well as the universe of absolute irrationalism. She lauded Wolfgango Rossani, who compared Fallaci's creativity in solitude to Gustave Flaubert's secluded inventiveness.[7]

The image Fallaci demanded shone brightly before my eyes. She was an artist, a great writer, a learned person of refinement and culture. She had a right to take her place in the company of such great writers as Charles Dickens, Herman Melville, Jack London, Leo Tolstoy, Rudyard Kipling, and Fyodor Dostoyevsky. She consequently rejected my chapters dealing with her formative years on the grounds that they were not professional but personal. My information about her childhood had come from documented sources. Her love for travel and adventure connects, in large part, to her early admiration for Jack London. Are data about that time professional or personal? A further complication arose. Fallaci wanted me to include information about plasticity and panoramas in *Inshallah*, but when I mentioned the visual importance of Florence, where she was born, and the splendid view of the dome of the city's cathedral from her window, she bristled at the entry and called it her material.

Fallaci insisted that I record all of our meetings on tape and suggested that I logically divide into sections all of the material on the fourteen cassettes, which was her method after interviewing famous celebrities and political giants. Later, when Fallaci held the more than five hundred pages of my draft, she refused authorization, maintained that I had strayed from our agreement, and emphasized that my first two chapters were filled with errors. My explanation—that the manuscript did stress her writings—was futile. No matter what I said, she grew angrier, insisting that I had made her talk and that what she allowed me to record on tape was only background and never to be used in the book. In my mind, I envisioned her doing what my sixth-grade teacher, Sister Celine, used to do whenever she was unhappy with the notebooks she collected from her pupils. She would open the window next to her desk and hurl every one of them onto the pavement of the school yard below. On that discouraging day in Fallaci's Manhattan apartment, one window in her living room was, in fact, open; and, feeling much like a pupil whose teacher would have enjoyed thrashing him, I mentally imagined the famous Italian author rising, walking across her Persian rug, and hurling my pages onto the sidewalk below.

Fallaci objected to my writing about her mother, Tosca: how she had fought for her husband's safety after his imprisonment by Fascists and her miscarriage brought on by emotional stress. When I explained that the information about her mother was related to her own antifascism and that it came straight from her 1965 book *If the Sun Dies* (and not from the tapes), she challenged my accuracy and stared angrily. I tried to find the quotations in her book to justify myself in her eyes and finally found the references. "Here, Oriana, see. I am quoting from your own book, not the tapes." The point was important. If Fallaci said no to what I took from *If the Sun Dies*, she could just as easily say no to published articles and interviews, thereby controlling legitimate scholarship. In fact, she forbade me to use Paola's interview in *Annabella* magazine, stating that she had not had the opportunity to correct her sister's statements before publication. I felt myself in the presence of a celebrity determined to control absolutely my written words and her own official image.

The writer's insistence that I not mention her childhood or family life constituted an unreasonable and, at times, contradictory stipulation. Her books and articles, I soon discovered, are filled with references to her early years and her parents and recollections from World War II. One of the principal characteristics of her writing is its intensely personal nature. How could I ignore this aspect of her art?

Fallaci's disposition frequently turned in unpredictable directions. She stated that I needed to include in the book a short paragraph on Alekos Panagoulis's family. This from someone who stood ready to reprimand if the slightest hint of personal information appeared. She also wanted to write it with me because the subject of her lover's family was very sensitive. After I later reminded her of this, she simply said: *"Niente famiglia Panagoulis"* (Nothing about the Panagoulis family).[8] It was impossible to predict her moods and to meet her expectations.

I again revised the entire draft in an attempt to satisfy the writer. On two occasions, she had suggested a format for my work, stating that she was good at organization. I dutifully listened, recorded, took notes, and followed her instructions to the letter. Despite earlier admonitions not to touch her childhood, she startled me with her counsel to begin with the story of the schoolchild in Florence who read important books and wanted to write, essentially reversing her original restrictions. She suggested that I continue with her entrance as a sixteen-year-old into the newsroom of her first job with *Il Mattino dell'Italia Centrale* and then treat her entry into national journalism with *Europeo*. Her books would next summarize the various phases of her life.

Adhering to this new scheme, I completed another manuscript and mailed her the introduction and the first two chapters. I hoped this time to receive the much-sought-after authorization. She again rejected my work and, in an unnerving series of phone calls, candidly vented her indignation. According to Fallaci, the chapter sequence was utterly unsuitable; content was much too personal and poorly written; she felt *"tradita"* (betrayed). She bitterly objected to the inclusion of anecdotes about her first employers and family members but, at the same time, complained about the lack of information about her intellectual and emotional formation. When I timidly indicated her inconsistencies and my scrupulous adherence to her endorsed outline, her anger grew more intense. Mustering up my courage, I offered to read back my notes to her to prove my point and to reestablish my credibility. Fallaci took great offense at my desire to refresh her memory.

Fallaci returned my second-draft chapters and included her critique, which contained some positive suggestions. For the most part, however, it seemed designed to destroy thoroughly the fabric of my introductory sections. She dogmatically belittled endnotes and claimed that I had not verified information. She went so far as to order me to burn pages of what I had sent her. At that point, Fallaci had gone too far even for me. I communicated my objection in a harsh personal letter. "You ordered me to burn chapters. '*Da bruciare*.' Nazis burned books before World War Two. You place yourself in their company when you use their language—a language that sounds strange coming from a so-called champion of liberty and freedom and enemy of dictators."[9]

Again, I composed another draft. She insisted that I go back to the original project, the only one that she could authorize, provided that she approve the text. In my heart, I felt that nothing would ever satisfy her but started redoing the work anyway. When her last letter to me arrived in February 1994, she wanted to know whether I had abandoned the project. In my response, dated 16 February 1994, I admitted having fallen in love with her books and wanting to have the biography published. However, by that time, my good judgment had gained the upper hand. A red flag appeared whenever I was tempted to send Fallaci another manuscript. "A little voice in my head tells me not to place the completed work in your hands," I wrote.

Whenever people want to meet Fallaci, she wonders whether they simply want to see how she dresses, how she combs her hair, how many wrinkles she has or does not have, or how many cigarettes she smokes. The writer claims to be none of these things but insists that she is what she writes. To those claiming true affection for her, she unequivocally unleashes a warning. "Woe to those who personally meet a writer they love."[10] In most cases, admirers suffer a letdown; they expect too much. The writer they come to know differs dramatically from their ideal image. Fallaci tells the story of meeting a famous writer whose work she enthusiastically respected. Despite his politeness and favorable comments about her publications, he failed miserably as a human being in her eyes. "He so disillusioned me that now I have to force myself to continue loving his book."[11] It displeases me immensely to acknowledge the same frame of mind about Oriana Fallaci. I have evolved from a devotee, who would have gone to China and back to satisfy her slightest whim, to a disenchanted researcher, determined to speak truthfully and to tell my version of her professional life as I have discovered it—not as she wants me to tell it. This book tells the story of how one woman from Florence built her own myth.

Florence

1.

ORIANA FALLACI'S FAME IN THE WORLD did not occur haphazardly. An entire childhood laid the foundation for an exceptional career. She was born in Florence, Italy, in 1929 as daughter to Edoardo and Tosca Fallaci, the two most important people in her life. The somber-faced infant spent the early years of her childhood on the Via del Piaggione in a fifth-floor apartment that offered magnificent views of the Florence that she loves to this day. From the window in the living room, a postcard panorama of Filippo Brunelleschi's dome, Giotto's tower, and the old city filled the eyes of the reserved, pensive child. A short walk to the opposite side of the home exposed her gaze to a garden with a magnolia tree that she would later describe in *Letter to a Child Never Born*. Growing up in Italy's major Renaissance center provided daily contact with the masterpieces of such artists as Leonardo da Vinci, Fra Angelico, Michelangelo, Cimabue, and Botticelli. She paid little attention to sermons or services but instead stared hypnotically at murals and works of art in such churches as Santa Maria del Fiore, Santa Croce, and Santa Maria Novella. In this urban nucleus of rebirth, she came to feel the concrete manifestations of civilization in her blood and would later, as a writer, express this influence in the many visually expansive, realistic scenarios in her books.

Neither of Oriana's exceptional parents attended a university. After the death of Tosca Fallaci's parents, Tosca was raised by relatives and received limited formal education. Edoardo earned his livelihood as a craftsman and played an active role in the struggle against Italian Fascists. Despite their lack of schooling, they both read avidly and became addicted to the world of letters. Their passion for books so impressed Oriana that she would always view personal learning as more substantial than the shallow knowledge frequently acquired in classrooms. "When I see what students write, what they send me, I conclude that academic culture should be destroyed by a universal flood."[1] Her parents, on the other hand, never allowed anything less than near perfection in her scholarship and aroused in her holy awe before the accomplishments of authors. They talked about Alessandro Manzoni and about Dostoyevsky, Tolstoy, and Dickens as though they were next-door neighbors. Their daughter Oriana would reap the profits of this enlightened outlook through a covetous embracing of culture and, in turn, have her own life transformed by her ambition to become a writer.

Edoardo and Tosca Fallaci lived on a tight budget but allowed themselves one luxury—books. Lying on her sofa one night, Oriana overheard a strong discussion about finances in the next room. "Edoardo, that is enough with these books; we have to stop. We cannot allow ourselves to spend this money on books each month."[2] They habitually bought masterpieces on the installment plan, just as they would for a refrigerator, and then placed these treasures on a prominent glass-doored bookshelf in the living room. As a child, Oriana would fall asleep on a sofa staring at their red covers, experience their provocative impact on her imagination, and then awaken the next morning with them directly in her line of vision. The sight of these volumes day after day became such an integral part of her daily routine that she immersed herself in their vitality. A serious child who rarely smiled or played with other children, Fallaci reacted with great sensitivity to their presence. As soon as she learned how to read, she devoured book after book, setting the pace for her entire life.

As an adult, she would have bookshelves built in every nook and angle of each of her homes—in Manhattan, Florence, and Grevi in Chianti—to receive the precious collections gathered over the years. "You give me an old book and I tremble; it is a physical reaction."[3] She enjoys talking about the wonderful offerings of a bookstore in Manhattan near her home. On one occasion, she bought an archaic set of Molière plays there for only eighty-five dollars—an absolute bargain compared to the outrageous prices in Europe. She particularly treasures this Molière collection: it contains suggestive illustrations. She also found an antiquated edition of Emily Brontë's *Wuthering Heights* and feels a strong attraction to this British writer whom she read as a young adolescent. When she accidentally discovered the complete works of the Brontë sisters in a Brooklyn bookstore for only four hundred fifty dollars, she immediately staked her claim and savored the thought of making this acquisition. She possesses valuable, old, illuminated editions of William Shakespeare's plays and curiously questions why one of them has the English author's name spelled differently. She enjoys holding the volume and relishes revealing its price of one hundred fifty dollars. She religiously confesses paying just a little more for another treasured tome and then ecstatically enumerates its contents: *The Merchant of Venice, The Taming of the Shrew, Twelfth Night,* and *The Winter's Tale.*

Her copy of Jean de La Fontaine's *Fables* also raises sparks of excitement in conversation, particularly when she displays the artwork related to each poem and discusses the power of these sketches on her imagination. Illustrated books so fascinate her that she uses the comparison of jewelry to express her strong feelings. After the publication of *If the Sun Dies,* her sister Paola insisted that she celebrate by purchasing a diamond at one of the booths on Florence's Ponte Vecchio. However, she denies that she finds fulfillment in material acquisitions, affirming that books remain her most joyful possessions. "I did not grow up like Paola with the idea that richness is located in the eye of a diamond. No, no, books are precious objects."[4] She despises anyone who treats books badly. Whenever in need of a work copy, she always purchases two of them so that one remains untouched. The early spirit of reverence for the written word remains firmly intact in Fallaci's mind as she associates her collected volumes with past time and consequently with personal wealth. "An old book is the past; it is my love for the past."[5]

One of her earliest formative experiences occurred when Tosca Fallaci allowed her to discover Gustave Doré's *Illustrated Bible* and to revel in the sketches of the great nineteenth-century designer and sculptor. Biblical illustrations are inevitably tragic. God always punishes; Cain murders Abel; angels burn Sodom and Gomorrah; Lot's wife turns into a pillar of salt; Noah builds an ark and receives the creatures of the earth; a great flood destroys civilization. One of Doré's drawings particularly impressed the child. Land everywhere was submerged under the water of the great flood, while nude men, women, and children covered a protruding mountaintop. In the background, Noah's ark departed for safety across rising waters. This devastating perception of creation, along with family circumstances and Italy's ravaged condition in the 1940s, contributed to the cataclysmic outlook found in many of her future works. Fallaci's home in Florence contains all of Doré's illustrated books, except for *Don Quixote*, which she keeps at her Manhattan residence. After Edoardo's death, he left no money to his children because his financial standing, as well as Tosca's, had improved with their daughter's successful career. However, he did bequeath two personal possessions to her: Doré's *Illustrated Bible* and his old hunting guns.

After learning how to read, the child Oriana longingly stared at literary treasures in the family living room. On one occasion, she picked up the story of Casanova and, to this day, remembers the scene in which the celebrated seducer disrobes a nun. Her mother snatched it away and placed it on a shelf of forbidden books along with *Crime and Punishment* and *War and Peace*. "They are Daddy's books, big people's books; they are not for children."[6] On one day, Oriana lay sick with a fever on the sofa. Tosca opened the glass door of the bookcase, picked up one of the books with a red cover, and flung it at her. "You are sick; you are feverish; so you have time to read. Read!"[7] She greedily seized the long-awaited gift, one of the most important in her life—Jack London's *Call of the Wild*. Delicately turning its pages, she reached the first paragraph and began to read, as though hypnotized, this saga of life in the wild Alaskan Yukon. Poring over the story until nearly dawn, the young schoolgirl finally reached the moment when Buck followed the wolf pack into the wild and the call of nature. After finishing the story, she was no longer a child who believed in the pious, spellbinding stories of Edmondo De Amicis, Emilio Salgari, or Jules Verne. Now she was ready to deal with adults in their hard world of reality. Buck had taught her that life involved a daily struggle for survival, an unyielding combat for food and personal liberty.

> Woe to you if good faith or distraction causes you to lose your liberty. Your only alternative is slavery, injustice, shame, and leather straps that tie you to a gold seeker's sleigh: so that you pull it with its atrocious cargo across the ice, torn apart by a whip and insults.[8]

Fallaci agrees that traditional interpretations of London's chronicle emphasize the dog's rediscovery of repressed instinct and the inherent struggle between adherence to the hypocritical artificiality of modern civilization and receptivity to primordial spontaneity. However, she also recognizes that neither the explanations of critics nor the author's intention may fully elucidate the inner reality of meaning. "A book, above all when it becomes a work of art, is that which you discover in it through yourself."[9] On that day, during her twelfth year of life, she unknowingly sought an answer to what she considers one of life's principal dilemmas—the problem of liberty—and received a response that formed an adult conscience. Buck's loud howling symbolized the call to freedom and, to Fallaci during the Nazi occupation of Florence, active resistance against the enemy presence. The family no longer owns the original volume. Tosca Fallaci lent it to a kind Jewish teacher, Signorina Rubitchek, whom the Nazis sent to a concentration camp in Germany, where she died like Curly—"lacerated by savage wolves who then licked their lips."[10]

Fallaci never forgot the story of Buck, often referring to it as the source of her personal belief in radical individualism and the cause of her disbelief in the concept of romantic love. Praising the book as a great hymn to freedom, she also notes that the animal receives love from the hunter and cannot live without him. However, it grows fat, eats quietly as it attends its master, and becomes free only after his death. "And what I say in this preface is that no chains to freedom are as heavy as the chains of love."[11] Despite her stark view of the price paid for the ties of sentiment, Fallaci has never feared love and claims to have given a monstrous amount in her life. Nevertheless, she still refers to it as slavery, stating that the damage often "starts with parents" and infiltrates other affairs. "Once your heart—your person and your sentiment—are engaged to a creature . . . you're f——. F——! You are! It's a fact!"[12] After her liaison with Alekos Panagoulis, which lasted from 1973 to 1975, she still claims that all bonds are oppressive and refuses to plunge into sentimental reflection. Instead, she maintains the same opinion on the perils of romance. "Of course, any tie is oppressive, but no tie like the one called love!"[13]

The Call of the Wild was her introduction to the world of Jack London. Throughout her childhood and early adolescence, Fallaci devoured as many of his books as possible: *White Fang, Burning Daylight, The Valley of the Moon, The Mutiny of Elsinore, The Iron Heel,* and *The Little Lady of the Big House.* Although none of them equaled the powerful epic of Buck, she never tired of reading London's stories and admired the American writer's imagination and the mental richness that permitted him to write about everything from hunting to politics, from science fiction to sociology. In her youthful inventiveness, she toured unknown parts of America with him, searched for gold at the base of icebergs, fished in the Bering Strait, lived in London slums, foundered off the coast of Siberia, fell into rapture at the sight of the South Seas, and adventurously explored life as she would have enjoyed living it. Fallaci openly admits that she owes her craving for travel in large part to her childhood fascination with Jack London. His novels and wild, extraordinary life, which ended in suicide at forty, instilled within her the fine poison of adventure. "I read *The Call of the Wild*; I was nine; and I decided to become a writer."[14]

Fallaci's famous uncle, Bruno Fallaci, a learned man and an important literary critic, belonged to the ranks of those who thought London a literary dilettante. "Fifty books in sixteen years! Fifty divided by sixteen equals three with two left over! He wrote more than three books a year. Can they be good?!"[15] He impatiently reproached his niece for losing too much time on this novelist and recommended that she read Melville and Flaubert. He grew angry when she reminded him that he had secretly read all of London's works just as Antonio Gramsci had done in 1930 while in prison. Fallaci often followed her uncle's advice to the letter but obstinately rejected his view toward the American author. One of the salient characteristics of her life is active and adventurous journalism, which lends itself logically to an analogy with London.

Tosca Fallaci carefully selected her daughter's books and again exerted a strong influence when she literally ordered her to read Rudyard Kipling's *Kim*. "Who can forget *Kim*; it came after *Call of the Wild*, and I think it aroused in me my love for distant, exotic, and mysterious countries."[16] The Englishman's novel gave her a vivid picture of the complexities of India under British rule, bazaar mystics, the indigenous population, and military life, as well as a street boy's efforts to lead a Tibetan monk to the holy river of the Arrow that would wash away all sin. The narrative's dialogue, as well as much of the indirect discourse, made use of Indian phrases, translated by the author, to give the flavor of native speech—a technique used abundantly in *Inshallah*. A great deal of action and movement occurs in its vast, detailed, and occasionally ironic canvas. In retrospect, the writer acknowledges that Kipling's novel aroused an infatuation with India, China, and Afghanistan. Like her mother, she grew to adore Kipling, read his works, and espoused him as a model. His career as a journalist and adventurer resembled that of her first hero, Jack London. Instead of Alaska, however, Kipling voyaged as a reporter to the Far East. Years later, Fallaci would journey to these same regions as a journalist and correspondent, fulfilling her dream of encountering the lands of an early idol. "I wanted to go there; it was an excuse . . . and so, I went to India, to Kipling."[17]

Exposure to other literature also occurred. When she was sixteen, she began to read Russian novels. "We had these books at home. These were the books my parents bought on an installment plan."[18] She fervently devoured Tolstoy's *War and Peace* and refers to Natasha and Andrey as fully developed personalities. In *Inshallah*, she treats her many characters in like manner, revealing all of their psychological motivation and subconscious desires. In his masterpiece, Tolstoy revealed his craftsmanship as an author, as well as his personal vision of life. According to Fallaci, his characters embody an existential outlook, since they represent Tolstoy himself and consequently receive his total philosophic, artistic attention. As a writer, Fallaci would follow Tolstoy's pattern of pouring aspects of a personal ideology—existential doubt, despair, atheism—into many characters and then repeating in varied form in subsequent books the same basic message. In *War and Peace*, the story of five families and such other characters as peasants, aristocrats, and emperors appears against the background of Napoléon Bonaparte's invasion of Russia in 1812. All are brought completely alive in a unified narrative through the magic of Tolstoy's writing. Fallaci would similarly deploy a vast number of protagonists in *A Man* and *Inshallah*, placing their lives in the context of savage struggles but yet successfully consolidating them into a coherent plot and setting.

Prince Myshkin from Dostoyevsky's *Idiot* remains so unforgettable to Fallaci that she is inspired to impromptu reflection at the mere mention of his name. Seeing a Chinese vase at an evening party in St. Petersburg, he instinctively knows that, by approaching it, he will cause damage. His clumsiness fills him with premonitions and motivates his desire to remain distant. However, despite the resolution, he rises from his seat and walks near the vase, causing it to fall. Fallaci suggests that the incident exemplifies the functioning of destiny in life. The same atmosphere filters through *A Man* and *Inshallah*. Destiny led her to Alekos Panagoulis, the man who became her lover. The Arabic word *Inshallah* means "as God wills, or destiny"; the concept emerges as one explanation for conflicts in life, war, and man's inhumanity to man. Fallaci's spirit of existential introspection and self-analysis may be easily traced to the masterpieces of Dostoyevsky. Her characters would fanatically analyze themselves, revealing their inner conflicts. In

Crime and Punishment, a student commits murder to fulfill a theory that would enable him to be one of the strong men of the earth. The leading protagonist, Angelo, in *Inshallah* also kills and bases his decision on unremitting attention to a scientific formula.

As a student in *ginnasio* and *liceo*, she received a thorough grounding in classical culture and spent years translating Latin and Greek, reading Socrates and Plato, suffering through Virgil's *Aeneid* and Ovid's *Metamorphoses*, but also experiencing "the marvelous luck of having been persecuted by the *Iliad* and the *Odyssey*."[19] Both of these ancient works exerted an indelible impact. Agamemnon, Achilles, Ulysses, Penelope, Menelaus, Helen, and Ajax were as familiar to her as Mickey Mouse, Donald Duck, and fairy tales are to contemporary children. According to Fallaci, the *Iliad* reads easily and seductively. Homer so filled her with pleasure that she recites in Greek the story of Hector's death below the ramparts of Troy. She relishes the anecdotes that depict Paris's passionate love for Helen and their betrayal of the despairing Menelaus and ecstatically avows that the entire tale flows through her bloodstream. In *Inshallah*, the professor's desire to reproduce the spirit of the *Iliad* in his novel attests to the viable presence of classical culture in the writer's repertoire of literary influence.

Fallaci was also educated in Italian culture through the writings of Petrarch, Giovanni Boccaccio, and Dante Alighieri's *Divine Comedy*. Students in *liceo* labored through *Inferno*, then confronted *Purgatory*, and finally enjoyed the privilege of *Paradise*. Before taking college examinations, Fallaci rebelled against the restrictiveness of these studies and protested that the curriculum included no contemporary world literature. "Professor, how is it possible that we are about to take our examination of *maturità* in a few months and that it will include no questions on Goethe, Molière, and Shakespeare?"[20] Her professor agreed and provided the option of studying one of the neglected writers. She jumped at the opportunity and chose *Macbeth*, the Shakespeare play she loves best, while two other girls prepared reports on the French and German authors.[21] The bloodbath that ends *Inshallah* finds a direct source in the tragic endings of Shakespearean tragedies.

Fallaci's intensive readings aroused a love for writing, influenced her approach to literature, and left a salient imprint on her lifestyle. Growing up in a fiercely antifascist family, however, was an equally significant factor in the formation of her identity and dominant themes. Reflecting about her childhood, she often recalls how her father taught her to shoot, hunt, and fish but also remembers the war. On one occasion, she sat huddled in a

bunker as American bombs fell on Florence. Crying out of fear—not sob-
bing—she remembers Edoardo's anger at seeing the tears, his "tremendous
slap" in the face, and his firm admonition, "A girl does not cry!"[22] Repeating the story, her eyes narrow as she summarizes the lesson. "Strength!
Strength!" Unlike whining therapy patients who bemoan the crises of childhood, the writer today expresses gratitude toward both parents for their
strictness.

> Life is a tough adventure and the sooner you learn that, the better. I must
> admit that I am not generous with weak people. It's not in my nature or in
> my personality. My parents were not generous with weak people, see? I
> never forgot that slap. It was like a kiss.[23]

Fallaci's upbringing was in no way liberated or permissive. Both of her
parents demanded high standards of conduct and instilled in her a permanent spirit of discipline. Fully endorsing the cliché that things worked better
in the old days, she lacks tolerance toward the indifference of contemporary
youth and professes fright at today's generation gap. On speaking tours at
American universities, she turns aggressive whenever an audience fails to
give her its undivided attention. She thinks nothing of interrupting her lecture and, in a shrill tone of voice, calling someone ignorant. "What are you
doing? Listen to what I am saying."[24] Onlookers usually look back in amazement as she rejects a question as stupid, tells a student to sit down, calls for
the next query, or angrily and insultingly refutes someone, not least academ-
ics who might object to one of her statements.[25] Acknowledging that these
reactions are often unfair, she nevertheless justifies them by referring to her
scholastic training and background. Her parents so instilled in her the religion of education and discipline that she had no choice but to commit totally
to any engagement and accept nothing short of excellence.

In her view, young people fail to appreciate the value of sacrifice and
setting goals. Conceding that rigid routines, single-minded visions, and strict
adherence to work schedules offer little in the way of pleasure, she still regards these willful human actions as noble gestures. "I am absolutely convinced that we cannot live our lives without discipline and without the
strength derived from sacrifice."[26] As a young pupil, she studied intensively.
Tosca Fallaci wanted her daughter to understand her good fortune. "How
lucky you are to go to school and study! I was not able to study."[27] Repeating
these emotional words over and over again, Tosca thoroughly brainwashed

her own child into accepting their doctrinal veracity: "But look at my luck; I can go to school."[28] This attitude remained strong in the young girl's mind, carrying her on a wave of determination from primary grades to medical school at the University of Florence.

Fallaci's experience in the Resistance during World War II helped shape her future opposition to dictatorship and became the content of many of her articles and books. During the war years, Edoardo Fallaci was a member of the Resistance movement in Tuscany. As the eldest child in her family, Oriana took part in covert activities against German occupiers. Her experiences with the courageous, cultured, and patriotic heroes and heroines of the underground were some of her most privileged moments. She was thirteen and then fourteen years old when her childhood vanished and freedom fighters assumed equal and perhaps superior status to her beloved Jack London. Looking back, she labels herself a little Vietcong, struggling to liberate her country. She did not detonate bombs or shoot enemy soldiers but carried explosives to those who did and delivered messages to an underground newspaper. She received the nom de guerre "Emilia" and helped her father escort English and American prisoners to safety.

After Italy's surrender on 8 September 1943, the country's army disbanded, allowing detainees to escape from their concentration camps. The Action Party, which had contact with Allied forces, assumed the responsibility of helping them arrive at a safe haven. These activities involved heavy risks because the German military had already informed the local population that it would execute anyone found assisting the enemy. On one occasion, Edoardo brought home two escapees—Nigel Eatwell and Frank Buchanan— disguised as railroad workers. As Fallaci recalls their images, the twenty-six-year-old Nigel had a round face and a little red mustache; the twenty-two-year-old Frank had a long chin like Fred Astaire. At the time, Fallaci had tried to use her minimal English. Tosca had asked her to inquire whether they were hungry. Instead of saying "are you hungry," she asked whether they were angry and received a polite, negative response. As a result, the two men fasted until late in the evening when they could no longer resist. Bursting into the kitchen, they desperately asked for food as best they could: "*Mangiari! Mangiari!*"

Soon after, the journey to freedom began with a forty-kilometer ride to the Italian town of Acone and involved crossing German checkpoints. At one inspection sight, Nigel noisily fell from his bike. Unable to speak to him in English, Oriana used her Italian. "*Zio! Alzati zio!*" (Uncle! Get up, Uncle).

Upon arriving in the small mountain village of Acone, near Pontassieve, the local parish priest took charge of their safety until partisans could conduct them to the Allied lines. The return trip proved particularly uncomfortable for father and daughter. They had to ride back to Florence pulling the two other bikes, holding the handlebars of the empty one with the left hand and peddling at the same time. The incident ended on a tearful note. Nigel died along with members of the Justice and Liberty organization when German soldiers captured and executed them on the spot. Frank escaped; moments earlier he had gone into town to look for some food.

Three or four more trips to Acone took place. On the second, Oriana took a revolver with a silencer to an official of the British queen. In her mind, he looked like one of the guards wearing leather busbies standing in front of Buckingham Palace. Hiding alone in a cave, he had asked the parish priest for a weapon to aid him in reaching his regiment. Fallaci never discovered whether his plan succeeded but assumes that it did. "He forcefully pulled the revolver away from us without a word of thanks and then threw us out of the cave: 'Get out! Go away! *Fuori! Via!*' Mean scoundrels always seem to make out alright."[29]

The most difficult period occurred in March 1944 after Fascist authorities arrested her father. Taken to Villa Triste, he was severely tortured at the hands of Mario Carità's henchmen and condemned to death. His daughter's visit to Murate di Firenze prison left a wound on her soul. His disfigured and swollen face was unrecognizable. Bidding his family farewell, Edoardo Fallaci urged them to remain calm. "You'll see; they won't shoot me; they will send me to a workcamp in Germany."[30] Not knowing anything about Dachau, Mathausen, and Belsen, they rejoiced at that possible outcome. The detainee fortunately escaped the firing squad and remained imprisoned. However, Oriana would never forget the experience. She has remained unequivocally confirmed in her stance against fascism and all forms of totalitarianism and has incorporated many of these memories from the war years into her books.

Tension remained a constant right to the end of the occupation of Florence. In July 1944, Republican Fascists attacked the monastery on Via Giano della Bella, slaughtering many in the Resistance who had gone there to hide. Oriana, as directed by a high-ranking official, had hidden the names of the city's action teams in a pumpkin. Orders called for her to eat them in case of discovery. As soldiers rushed in with their guns ready, she tried to devour them but could not swallow the heavy strips. The taste of ink also caused her to vomit. Thinking quickly, she ran to the nearest bathroom to flush everything down the toilet. Only red armbands with the yellow words "Justice and Liberty" remained in the pumpkin. Somehow managing to escape with her precious merchandise, she prudently hid herself until the city's liberation one month later on 11 August 1944. Her orders then required that she quickly distribute the armbands to partisans before Allied troops marched into the city. She ran to Porta Romana in anticipation of their arrival but accidentally stumbled, dropping all of the armbands. An exultant crowd quickly seized the scattered insignia. Her youthful clumsiness infuriated resistance officials—one even smacked her—because, in most cases, people who had not joined the struggle and even Fascists themselves managed to confiscate and declare as their own the cargo.

The Resistance offered her an intense political education, strengthened her commitment to the dictates of personal conscience, and permanently imprinted on her spirit a hatred for the powerful who use their positions for personal gain. She had come into contact with courageous and refined patriots—writers, artists, artisans, historians, professors, and workers from all walks of life—who defied a totalitarian regime and an occupying army. Such people as Enzo Enriquez Agnoletti, Paolo Barile, Tristano Codignola, Margherita Fasolo, Carlo Furno, Maria Luigia Guaita, Ugo La Malfa, Emilio Lussu, the Rosselli brothers, Nello Traquandi, and Leo Valianti—all famous in the annals of the Italian Resistance—became her role models. She would never renounce her love for individualism in a free, democratic society and would remain unbending in her abhorrence to the powerful who succumb to corruption. She would also regard as idiots those who hate all politicians. Her youthful activity during the war years taught invaluable lessons about the true nature of government and inculcated in her genuine moral commitment.

After the downfall of Benito Mussolini and the end of the war, Fallaci approached her formal education with the same determination that characterized her struggle against fascism. She skipped two grade levels, graduated from the prestigious Liceo Galileo Galilei at the age of sixteen—earlier than the usual eighteen—and passed her examinations with high honors, earning a 9 in Italian (an irregularity even in normal times), 8 in history, 8 in philosophy, 8 in Greek, 7 in Latin, and 9 in art history. The only unsatisfactory mark was in mathematics. During the postexamination review, the committee of professors decided to award a 7: they realized her concentration in classics precluded continued study of mathematics at an advanced level. Little did they suspect that a mathematical formula would one day stand at the thematic core of her novel *Inshallah*. Filled with pride, she brought home her test results and boasted of having received superior grades. True to her stoic nature, Tosca Fallaci coldly stared at her daughter. "You did your duty."[31] She tempered her enthusiasm and further cultivated a disciplined attitude toward work and professional obligations.

Expressing the desire to become a writer, the *liceo* graduate received no encouragement at home, despite the family's affection for literature and culture. "What? A writer! Do you know how many books a writer has to sell to earn a living? And do you know how much time it takes to become popular and to start selling books?"[32] Tosca Fallaci even used Jack London, because he had to work as a waiter and go to Alaska in search of gold, as an example of a writer's self-martyrdom. She insisted that her impressionable Oriana read London's *Martin Eden* to understand the pain and suffering involved in the search for literary fame. The young girl immediately read the book and understood her mother's point. "I read *Martin Eden* and it frightened me; was it really so difficult to become a writer?"[33] Her uncle, Bruno Fallaci, already firmly entrenched in the Italian literary world as a critic, reinforced the idea that financial independence and experience alone provided the freedom needed to become a writer. "First you have to live and then you write! What can you say now if you do not understand life?"[34] The consequence of this onslaught of negative advice was the loss of valuable time that she could have dedicated to literary activity. "This idea remained with me and poisoned my very fabric; it caused me to lose precious years. Tens of years."[35]

Enrolling at the University of Florence, she chose to major in medicine, a profession that A. J. Cronin and many other writers had embraced. It was a way of entering the forbidden regions of the human body without renouncing her humanism. Science had always exerted a strong appeal despite her superior *liceo* performance in Italian, art history, philosophy, and Greek. In fact, she felt particularly drawn to the study of psychiatry and the human brain at the *facoltà di medicina*. Later in her career, this affection for science would motivate the inclusion of a large section about the human brain in her novel *Inshallah*.

During the initial months of study, financial pressures began to surface. Edoardo earned a modest salary and could not subsidize her education. "Listen, attendance at medical school is expensive. It lasts six years. I cannot finance this for six years. If you want to study medicine, you have to go to work."[36] She understood, found employment with a newspaper, and simultaneously continued her studies.

Italian critic and journalist Umberto Cecchi was Fallaci's classmate during that busy first year of medical school. He recalls that work and school combined placed quite a strain on her daily schedule and accounted for her rushed, animated movements. He remembers that, to fit everything into one day, she always arrived last to class and left before anyone else. Her schedule left little time for social intercourse. According to Cecchi, she rode "the oldest and squeakiest bicycle ever seen on the streets of Florence."[37] On one occasion, the youthful Oriana's classmates played a joke on her by inconspicuously placing in her pocket a brain preserved in formaldehyde. After discovering the prank, she searched for a handkerchief, grasped the organ, and quietly disposed of it without any show of emotion or change in composure. On the next day, she told Cecchi about the incident with a coy smile expressive of pride that would allow no one to enter the privacy of her thoughts.

Cecchi fails to mention, however, the story of Fallaci's initiation (the *corridoio*)—an incident that contributed to her disillusionment with higher education. Older students required first-year students to pay a specific sum of money to them for the privilege of attending classes or else insisted that they voluntarily submit to a beating. "I do not remember what the figure was to avoid the thrashing but I remember that my father thought it was disgraceful." As a compromise, Tosca scraped together her pennies and bought four packages of Macedonia Oro cigarettes with which to appease the upperclassmen. "But the pigs took the *Macedonia Oro* and then prepared the *corridoio* all the same." The *corridoio* was a long narrow aisle through which inductees ran while the initiators struck blows. During the war, Oriana had suffered several bouts with pleurisy that left her lungs in delicate condition. The poundings received on her back during the *corridoio* caused a great deal of discomfort.

> You know I have been hit by policemen many times in America, Paris, Teheran; God, what blows in Teheran the day on which I tried to enter the hospital in which Farah Deba had given birth to the heir of Iran's throne! I want to say that I could have gotten used to blows to my lungs with the passing of time. However, those that I received in the *corridoio* still today seem the worst to me. How they hurt![38]

The hazing episode not only forced Fallaci to take a hard look at the maturity of Italian university students but also reinforced important lessons. One had to have money and, to obtain it, a job was an absolute necessity. The incident strengthened her desire to work and earn a livelihood—an attitude that likely played a part in her decision to look for a job with a local newspaper, no small detail in the life of an internationally known journalist.

After a few months, Fallaci abandoned the much-treasured university career. The study of anatomy required many mnemonic exercises; she preferred reasoning and critical thinking to rote memorization. In addition, long hours working and studying had begun to take a toll on her health. Another event also contributed to her withdrawal by preventing the completion of her first year and placing at the forefront the necessity of earning a salary with which to support her family. Edoardo Fallaci decided to run for political office in Italy's first election after the war. But on the way to a rally, he had an automobile accident and fractured his skull. The catastrophic results of the crash left the battered candidate in a coma for almost two years, sitting in an armchair in an immobile, upright position. Realizing that someone had to take the initiative, Oriana resolved to find a full-time job. Her classical background, her thirst for reading and adventure, her spirit and discipline, and her desire to become a writer combined to foster a disposition that would allow only one choice—journalism.

Kipling, London, Hemingway

2.

ORIANA FALLACI CONSISTENTLY COMMUNI-cates a concept of journalism that never limits the press to a simple informative role. Lively ideas, intelligent discussions of cultural questions, and artistry characterize her articles. She regards her reports on Vietnam, investigations of the Arab and Israeli conflicts, and interviews of Henry Kissinger, Haile Selassie, and Giovanni Leone as being as important as a Françoise Sagan novel.

> I do not believe that my reportage on children in an elementary school or my portrait of Mastroianni is intellectually inferior to a Carducci poem. I regard this work as an extension of culture, I expend as much energy on it as I do on a cultural exercise, and I view newspapers as the most vibrant stimulators of intelligence. Do you not realize that they have taken the place of literary salons?[1]

Fallaci is a literary journalist in the tradition of New Journalism. Her opinions, ideas, and commitments permeate her stories, which she ap-

proaches with missionary zeal.[2] Her exposés are more than just a forum for
viewing and experiencing incidents through a reporter's eyes. They often illustrate accurate, nonfictional prose that uses the resources of fiction. Her
work stands as a classic example of what Seymour Krim labels "journalit"
and classifies as the de facto literature of our time.[3] William L. Rivers did
not have Fallaci in mind when he commented that this modernistic style
added "a flavor and a humanity to journalistic writing that push it into the
realm of art."[4] Nevertheless, without knowing it, he caught the spirit of her
articles. Fallaci's virtue lies precisely in showing the possibility of something
strikingly different in journalism and in furthering efforts to replace traditional reporting with a literary approach.

Oriana Fallaci's career began in 1946 at the age of sixteen and one-half
years. The slender adolescent actually intended to apply for a position with
the important Florentine newspaper *Nazione di Firenze*. However, things
worked out differently. She mistakenly went to *Il Mattino dell'Italia Centrale*, entering the busy newsroom without makeup, in pigtails, ankle socks,
and flats, wearing a dress sewn by her mother.[5] Thinking that Gastone
Panteri was news editor for *Nazione*, she asked to see him. "I want to be a
reporter," she said.[6] Fearing that the word *journalist* would have struck a
prospective employer as too presumptuous, she deliberately avoided it. "To
say *journalist* seemed a bit much to me."[7]

When Panteri asked about her age, she stretched the truth and responded that she was seventeen. Italian society regarded sixteen-year-olds
as children and would have frowned on anyone so young working for a newspaper. Although the editor did not believe her, he decided to give her a try
and assigned her to cover a new dancing spot on the Arno River. He asked
for the completed item in twelve hours. Embarrassed by the prospect of
entering a nightclub, she overcame all inhibitions and wrote a story describing how protective Italian mothers accompanied their daughters. The event
represented no exciting challenge and certainly could have been covered in
one brief paragraph; however, at that important moment, her literary instincts emerged and took over.

> Although very young, I did something smart and wise. I composed a little
> portrait of one aspect of postwar, summer society and described mothers
> who wanted a fiancé for their daughters but stood next to them in the night-
> club to protect their virtue. At that time, this was the custom and nobody

was surprised. But I saw the funny side of a man's asking a girl to dance with her mother's permission and made the whole thing very amusing.[8]

She proudly submitted the story in longhand on a lined sheet of paper as though it were homework. Bellowing, Panteri pushed her toward a monstrous object called a *typewriter*, which she had never used in her life but nevertheless manipulated for nine hours—from ten in the morning until seven at night. "Then I gave it to him and he said: 'Ah! Good!' And he published it. Then he hired me as a police and hospital reporter."[9]

Fallaci's early assignments illustrate her techniques as a literary journalist. She began to write some of her articles as though they were destined for inclusion in anthologies. She was no ordinary reporter but really a would-be author wearing a mask in the kingdom of the elect who die but yet attain immortality through books with red covers.

> To understand my case, it is necessary to think of persons like Kipling, London, and Hemingway, who worked as journalists but, rather than journalists, were writers lent to journalism. Look at Kipling's correspondence from India. Poor Kipling; he had to write journalistic assignments. But he constructed them as a story. He saw what a journalist does not see.[10]

Following in the footsteps of these authors, Fallaci began to write articles as though they were short stories. She imbues one composition about an old abandoned convent in Florence with melancholy by treating the courtyard cherry tree as the main character and then bemoaning the loss of its life when workers cut it down. She sketches a portrait of the convent by tracing the history of the tree—how nuns had planted it in 1800, how it had grown to great height by World War I, and how it continued to grow after runaways, spies, poets, painters, and sculptors began to inhabit the building. An ambience of despondency surfaces with the realization that they all have died and left the premises deserted and silent. The cherry tree's demise symbolizes the passing of an era, as well as its death blow. "The place was no longer a republic unto itself—full of freedom, full of fresh air. There is now a clear view of all the villas across the street."[11]

In another article, about the pigeons of Florence, Fallaci treats the birds as human beings and traces the history of a once-thriving community in decline. She points out their favorite hotel—the dome of the city's cathedral.

The portrait of their elderly leader, who dwells in the highest and most beautiful angle of the majestic structure, enriches the imagery. "He was a very respectable pigeon who supported with dignity the boredom of the cloister and, at sunset, when vesper bells rang, all the pigeons of Florence went to pay him homage." After two sources of food—the bell ringer and an old chef—retire and die, gradual deterioration of the community begins. A policy of extermination to save Florence's outdoor masterpieces from desecration then provides the coup de grâce and accounts for the defeated demeanor of the survivors. "They have the sad look and resigned, humble gait of foundlings." A series of comparisons reinforces the personification. "They do not possess the easy manner and the shrewdness of their fat colleagues in Venice and Rome and are not profit seekers like them." They are as disenchanted as retired generals, as poor as civil pensioners, and as worried as fathers of families. "They know very well that a sad and unjust destiny weighs on their shoulders."[12]

Fallaci turned many of her news items into narratives containing background, a story line, and a twist ending. These were the articles that, if collected in book form, would have become collections of short stories. They resemble works of fiction but contain verifiable facts. In the manner of literary writers, Fallaci early on sought out the story's built-in plot and instinctively *fished out* its sentimental, not necessarily psychological, overtones. The models for some of her best articles are humble characters, animals, criminals, and the working class. In "He Had the King's Feet in His Hands," she expresses her sympathy for the middle-aged Sicilian foot healer Carmelo Freni, who affectionately refers to his trade as an art. The introduction explains that he took a course in Berlin on body extremities and then, after trying to work in Florence, lived in poverty for many years. His good fortune begins after selling his ivory crucifix to an antique dealer for six hundred lire and using the money to open a pedicure office on Via Roma. After helping with his landlord's foot problem, others begin to come, including the Marquis d'Ajeta, master of ceremonies at the court of Victor Emmanuel III. In July 1942, the marquis summons Carmelo Freni to the king's residence. The use of dialogue, accompanied by a crisp description, one of the writer's hallmarks, develops the heart of the anecdote. After several hours of waiting in the Room of One Hundred Mirrors, the pedicurist finally has his audience.

> "Good day," greeted the king, as he smoothed his little gray mustache with
> one hand and caressed his heavy silk smoking jacket with the other.

"Good day."
"One of my toes hurts," said the king, without giving much importance to
the matter.
"Yes, Your Majesty."
"The little toe."
"Yes, Your Majesty."

Carmelo silently goes about his work, corrects the problem, and receives
great praise.

"But it is not possible, not even the pedicurist of the royal household is as
fast and gentle."
"I have finished, Your Majesty, and I thank you for the great honor that
you have granted me."

Although Queen Elena and the Princess Mafalda become his next cus-
tomers, no payment ever reaches Carmelo's hands. During his last visit on
9 May 1943, the king and queen look tired as they await the forthcoming
invasion.

"You who are so close to the people, tell me what they think."
"The people say that we must win, Your Majesty."
Shaking her head, she ironically uttered, "Yes, must win."

The conclusion depicts an atmosphere of disillusionment amidst Allied bombardment and then moves to a political finale on voting that reinforces the
atmosphere of a *conte littéraire*. "To whoever asks him whether he voted for
the monarchy, Carmelo Freni responds: 'My vote is a secret.'"[13]
    Many of Fallaci's articles, although based on actual occurrences, easily
pass for literary pieces. Some of her work resembles that of Charles Dickens
who, as a newspaper reporter in the early 1830s wrote feature articles for
the London *Morning Chronicle* and then published them in his first book,
Sketches by Boz, in 1836. Writing about the miserable, postwar life of shoeshine boys, she relates how they found hope in the loving care of Father
Bruno Fedi. This heartwarming narrative not only recalls Dickens's depiction
of poverty in *Oliver Twist* but also resembles *A Tale of Two Cities* in its
introduction suggestive of a bygone era.

Those were the times in which, because of the still-recent war, the city swarmed with Allied jeeps, with American soldiers (mostly Negroes), with black marketeers, women of evil deeds, with shoeshine boys who had come mostly from southern Italy with their mothers and sisters. The inhabitants of Pisa, even those who earned some money from it, now remember with naive horror and childish shame those hellish times.[14]

Fallaci's interview with the aristocrat accused of murdering and robbing Francesca Foglianti—a classic example of her crime reporting—reads like a detective story more than an objective summary of facts. The detainee's portrait immediately distinguishes the method.

Sergio Vanzini, was in a security cell next to the courtroom: he wore a plaid jacket and a pair of gray slacks in a kind of neglected elegance. He read newspapers and smoked. On the bench, not far away, sat a Thermos full of tea. Hearing my "good evening" from the little window, the long figure jumped up with a military movement, threw his paper and cigarette away, and brought his face up to the bars: a strangely ascetic face with sunken cheeks, very dark eyes, and a black, Mephistophelean short beard that ran right up to his earlobes. More than a face, it looked like a long comma. With an expression in the middle.[15]

After outlining his reasons for an optimistic outcome to the trial, he receives his sentence—fifty-seven years of incarceration—and, with a Guy de Maupassant ending, sees the crowd silently leaving the chamber amidst the noises of weeping women. The beginning journalist could have gathered these types of articles in the same manner as Dickens and invented an eye-catching title.

Even when reporting events that do not lend themselves to literary treatment, Fallaci enlivens the articles. Describing the women who participated in the Fifth United Nations Educational, Scientific, and Cultural Organization (UNESCO) Conference in Florence, she utilizes a serious introduction in which the American Myrna Loy, the Indian Sarah Chacko, the Philippine Geronima Peckson, and the Italian Maria Montessori deliver opening speeches. However, she unexpectedly injects humor into the narrative.

The most beautiful are the Indian women with their thin bodies wrapped in showy silk saris. The youngest and most numerous are the Americans: blond, quick, and happy. . . . The most gracious are the Filipinos: petite, round, and yellow like ripe tobacco leaves. The ugliest women (may God forgive me) are the English who, in everyone's opinion, look over fifty and like reform school instructors.[16]

In April 1951, after five years of reporting misdemeanors, medical news, human interest items, and covering the society beat, a local funeral unexpectedly added a boost to the young reporter's career. A waiter, Nello Casini, committed member of the Communist Party in the Florentine suburb of Fiesole, died without receiving the Sacrament. His funeral procession should have taken place at eight o'clock in the evening on 11 April and should have been Catholic because the deceased had not requested a civil burial. The local priest did not refuse to lead the ceremony but insisted that Communists pledge not to interfere by carrying their red flags. Their refusal caused the bishop to forbid the priest to accompany the dead man.

Fallaci went to cover the story and documented the actual event, but she also provides a description that communicates a distinct literary impression. She treats it with the seriousness of a historical chronicler and captures the charged atmosphere that engulfed the entire time after Pope Pius XII excommunicated the Communists. At the same time, she injects into the report the humor of a mock heroic epic. Factory worker Lorenzo Breschi, administrative council member for the Communist Party to the Department of Public Works of Fiesole and head guard of the town's Archconfraternity of Mercy, appeared at the home of the deceased with many of his comrades wearing the black robes of the Brothers of Mercy. Hoods covered their heads so completely that only their eyes were visible. They wore big rosaries on their belts and carried a crucifix, the coffin, and all the religious accoutrements required for funerals. When the church bells rang, the procession began to move.

The scene, a religious cortege without a priest, aroused seriousness and light humor because many of those in attendance could not read Latin. Breschi, a former sacristan, opened the ceremony, carried the cross, and solemnly recited the prayers of the dead. "Immediately behind, Brothers carried the coffin on their shoulders. In two separate lines along the sides of the street, one meter apart and with torches in their hands, around sixty Brothers of Mercy advanced, while chanting Psalms."[17] A crowd followed, including party comrades carrying eight red flags, the Communist mayor, the Communist municipal doctor, the deceased's family, and almost all of the town's inhabitants.

The burial took place in an atmosphere of religious veneration but also indicated the strangely contradictory personalities of those in attendance. They believed in their Communist Party but simultaneously accepted Christ and all of the saints. They attended party meetings but also attended mass, in spite of their excommunication by the Vatican. When the local bishop condemned the procession, their raising of the crucifix, the ridiculous ostentation of laymen in monks' garb, he threatened serious consequences if the deed ever occurred again. However, the Communist "guilty ones" attended the next general assembly at the headquarters of the Archconfraternity of Mercy and strongly debated the monsignor, who represented the cathedral. Arguments underscored their dualism as Communists and committed Catholics, engaged in an act of charity. "What harm is there if we pray for his soul?"[18] The entire article illustrates an early writing style—serious, accurate, subtle, humorous—but also projects a sociocultural context in which Italian Christians and members of Western Europe's largest Communist Party lived and attempted to worship side by side.

Fallaci understood that the incident deserved a larger reading audience than the one Florence had to offer. She also knew that *Il Mattino dell'Italia Centrale* favored the politics of Christian Democrats and would never have agreed to print the article. The paper's policy even called for prosecution and punishment of the guilty organizers of the funeral. She decided to send her account to *Europeo*, one of Italy's major newsmagazines, comparable in prestige to Milan's daily publication *Corriere della Sera*. Her narrative so pleased the anticlerical editor Arrigo Benedetti that he gladly published it one week later. At the time, *Europeo* resembled an oversized newspaper in format. On the morning of the issue, Fallaci had gone to court in Florence to cover a trial and, after its completion, left the courthouse in Piazza del Duomo, walked by a newsstand on the corner of Via Cavour, and saw the copy of *Europeo*. Her name in big letters on the first leaf above the title so moved her that she felt ill.[19]

Nervously returning to the news office of *Il Mattino*, she received a telephone call from *Europeo*'s Arrigo Benedetti. He wanted her to do a long interview with Cesare Cocchi, a famous pediatrician in Florence who successfully treated tuberculosis at the Mayer Clinic.[20] The completed article, which took up the entire third page, emerged later as a blessing: that news item, along with the report on the Communist funeral in Fiesole, helped her when she later lost her position with *Il Mattino dell'Italia Centrale*.

Despite the establishment of her first contact with *Europeo*, Fallaci continued to work for the Florentine daily in producing articles on celebrities.

She interviewed Clark Gable in Florence, wrote an account of the cold attitude Ava Gardner and Frank Sinatra had toward journalists during their trip to Italy, and did several human interest stories. She exhibited particular literary talent in her narrative portraits of Englishwomen, a series prepared in London. Her portrait of the tall, robust, twenty-five-year-old policewoman pursuing and apprehending a robber might have appeared in the pages of an English novel about modern London. The article focuses on the action in the manner of a film producer who projects a series of concrete images. The thief pushes her so hard that he sends her reeling back a few meters. She bounces back, grabs him, and locks her hands behind the nape of his neck. Her cap flies off; her blond curls fly into disarray; her white face turns completely red; her lips tighten as she struggles to subdue the culprit. They both roll down on the ground before the police officer finally scores her definite knockout and handcuffs him.[21]

In the article about aristocratic young ladies who for hours practice how to bow before the queen, Fallaci frames with her sense of humor and Florentine irony their hectic schedule during the debutante season, their efforts to meet eligible bachelors, and the mind-boggling expense involved in their reception into high British society. Her sarcasm surfaces when she attempts to meet the debutante of the year, Lady Rose Bligh, and soon realizes the futility of her aspiration. "The people to whom I addressed myself looked at me with ironic astonishment, as if you had said, for example, that you wanted to invite the Archbishop of Canterbury to lunch." The perfect curtsy before the queen becomes comical through Fallaci's exaggerated yet accurate description.

> Bend the left knee; move the right leg behind graciously grazing the point
> of the foot in a forty-five-degree turn until reaching the heel of the left shoe
> with the instep of the right foot; bend deeply the right knee but not to the
> point of touching the floor; lower the head maintaining the bust in a straight
> position and allow the arms to hang in an abandoned manner the length
> of the body while the head remains inclined as though in the act of looking
> for a penny, and the eyes looking up toward the queen.

The concluding remark reinforces the levity. "One of my friends tried to teach me, and for the rest of the week I felt like a cripple."[22]

Fallaci's articles on Iran, written early in her career, illustrate how she began to include herself as a main character. She wrote them as literary mosaics but, more important, they show that she had acquired enough confidence to inject herself into them. Her group consisted of four other journalists, three cameramen, and one radio announcer. She begins the first article as though she were a wide-eyed traveler and sustains that atmosphere through hyperbole, naïveté, and enthusiasm. "Meeting at Ciampino Airport in Rome, we greeted each other with a great outpouring of affection, as though we were leaving for the moon on a rocket ship."[23] As she traveled by air on LAI to celebrate the opening of a new flight from Rome to Teheran, she gave vent to romantic lyricism to describe the capital from the dark night sky. "Rome glittered below us like a bouquet of fireflies, palpitating with light, and was soon only a distant, luminous point, like a star flung from the infinite onto the earth."[24] At four in the morning, the plane landed in Istanbul for fuel and departed just as the sun began to rise above the Bosporus. Fallaci extended her emotional awe before nature's beauty by projecting herself as a mesmerized observer of the most stirring sunrise ever seen. "The horizon looked as though it were on fire, and red, purple, yellow, and violet flames broke through the blue sky disappearing toward the heavens in shiny pink tongues."[25]

The young journalist also proved her skill at juxtaposing the various parts of a total picture—all the sights from the Mahrabad airport to her hotel in the downtown area—in a manner designed to emphasize the single impression of an amazed Candide. Everything continuously astonishes the newcomer, especially the comic antics of the interpreter, the hotel manager, and the guards who all try to locate her lost suitcase.[26] In the article on Teheran's poor children, Fallaci once again resembles Dickens in his portrayal of undernourished ragamuffins roaming the streets of London. Five miserable wretches with red medicinal powder covering their bald, bumpy heads catch her eye. Fallaci greets their mother in their small hut, accepts a cup of tea, offers the youngsters chocolate, and then leaves for her hotel, where she experiences guilt before the good food of her evening meal.[27]

The story of her difficulties in arranging a meeting with the Empress Soraya reads like a comedy of errors and actually casts her—Fallaci—as the star who even overshadows royalty. The journalist at a party receives notice of the empress's acceptance of an interview and then forgets to ask about the time. Instead, she invites friends to celebrate her good fortune by touring the city with her the next day, thus missing the queen's eleven o'clock invitation. Reinforcing the element of humor, she calls her Italian-American friend Joe Mazandi, who rushes to her hotel with a throng of reporters for a

press conference. Every reporter in Teheran wants to interview her. After
questioning a despairing Fallaci for over an hour, they then print the entire
story under the headline "She Made the Queen Wait." Fallaci strengthens
her own centrality by taking on the role of an embarrassed, mortified reporter. The account takes an unexpected turn when the royal chamberlain
arrives with a second invitation and escorts the awestruck Fallaci into
Soraya's presence.[28]

Fallaci sustains and intensifies her stardom, even at the risk of disrespect,
when she visits the Sepahsalar Mosque into which only Muslims may enter.
She dresses as an Iranian wrapped in a black shawl that leaves only her eyes
exposed and begins her secretive adventure. Thousands of little tiles painted
in bright colors line the walls of the holy site. "Those yellow, green, red, blue,
and violet embroideries create the same effect as a flower in a desert of sand."
Blending into the crowd, she suddenly finds herself in the forbidden courtyard with an immense round basin in the middle. Perched like crows on an
eave, the faithful stand at the edge of the pool washing their faces, hands,
and feet. She naively questions her guide, who elaborates on the Muslim way
of praying in water in obedience to the precepts of Muhammad. She then
focuses on several niches along the walls of the courtyard where other members of the faithful enact such curious movements as stretching their arms
and legs, standing on the tips of their feet, bending their knees, and articu-
lating their fingers. In a state of greater surprise, she asks what they are
doing. When her attendant again responds that they are praying, Fallaci
changes from an acute observer and interrogator to a flippant commentator.
"I thought they were doing Swedish gymnastics."[29]

In her Iran articles, Fallaci never sacrifices accuracy, even though she
uses literary techniques. In her description of the shah's Golestan, her series
of hyperboles does not detract from an objective account of the sumptuous,
ancient residence. "It is an immense palace, entirely covered by majolica and
yellow and blue arabesques, and surrounded by a park, which . . . is the most
beautiful park in the world."[30] All of the articles in the series, "Voyage to
Iran" do not necessarily represent literary miniatures. "Petroleum Is Iran's
Arbitrator" depicts in documentary fashion the history of black gold in the
country since 1901.[31] Nevertheless, the overall tone of the collection indicates
that the reporter has formed a definite literary style at an early stage of her
career and has established herself as central in her own writing. In Iran,
Fallaci attempted to penetrate a culture, so different from her own, by total
immersion. Her personal voice continuously surfaced rather than stay hidden

to show her readers that she was at work. She brought her articles to life through the specific powers of feelings, dramatic moments, and literary techniques. At the same time, she convinced audiences of her respect for the basic journalistic questions *who*, *what*, *where*, and *how*.

In 1952, after six years on her first job, Fallaci's career had suddenly changed directions. When she was twenty-two, her editor, Cristiano Ridomi, fired her. He had insisted that she write a satirical story about a political rally organized by the Communist leader Palmiro Togliatti. Nothing ran more counter to her sense of fairness than attending his factional gathering with the intention of deriding him. She insisted on keeping an open mind. "First, let me hear what he has to say! And I will write a piece based on what he says." Her employer's reaction remained uncompromising. "There is no need to hear what he has to say." Fallaci's reply went right to the point. "Then, I am not writing anything." Two hours later, she received a verbal reprimand and severance papers from Ridomi, whom she describes as filled with arrogance and very fat. "One never spits at the plate from which one eats," he said. She unhesitatingly responded with typical brio, "I do spit on it, and I give it to you to eat."[32]

Suddenly without an income, Fallaci essentially found herself in dire straits. Bruno Fallaci had become editor of the magazine *Epoca* and could have easily lent a helping hand; after all, his niece had solid experience. Members of the profession had already taken notice of her interesting style. Even the publisher of *Epoca* recommended that he hire the proven journalist. Nevertheless, he still resisted, ironically fearing accusations of nepotism in a country that thrives on it. He elected to remain silent until forced to hire her.

As editor, he remained determined to avoid preferential treatment and delegated only such trivial assignments to her as stories about Italian ice cream, techniques for creating mosaics at the Academy of Fine Arts in Ravenna, the carnival at Viareggio, the tradition of Musical May in Florence, the history of the oldest pasta makers in Italy, the Palio of Siena, and the Passion play in Grassina. Oriana remained with *Epoca* for twenty months, from January 1952 until August 1953, when the periodical's management terminated Bruno Fallaci for his tense relations with the owner, Giorgio Mondadori. "And no one knows how or why but there were two severance letters. The second one was for me."[33] She had committed the unpardonable crime of being Bruno Fallaci's niece and sharing his propensity for calling a spade a spade, an idiot an idiot, and a scandal a scandal. Their honesty and integrity had not endeared them to many coworkers and editors in Italian journalism.

Fallaci's energetic involvement in what she wrote is not at odds with literary journalism but rather characterizes it. Ronald Weber explains that literature, as opposed to journalism, is always a refracting rather than reflecting mechanism and to some degree distorts life, if only to give it a shape or clarity that cannot otherwise be detected. "And the roots of literary distortion are always in the person of the writer himself, in the individual stamp he puts on his work."[34] As a professional, Fallaci blossomed the more she poured her own self into her articles. She not only reported on the world around her but, above all, injected her own temperament into the articles. She had become more conscious of herself as her own focal point and gave full vent to her journalistic theatricality in all of its forms. She maintained this style throughout her career, despite her self-proclaimed love of privacy. "A writer, even the most Greta Garboish of writers in the world, never remains secret because they reveal themselves through their books."[35]

Lights, Camera, Action

3.

FROM THE OUTSET OF HER CAREER, Fallaci's writing took on a flamboyant, memorializing character. Her attraction to acting further fueled this tendency. Michele Serra, editor of *Europeo*, recognized the dynamism of her style, invited her to join his staff, and sent her to Hollywood to write about the American city many Italians regarded as a twentieth-century El Dorado.[1] The assignment, perfectly suited to her performatory disposition, powerfully placed her image before the public eye. Oriana Fallaci, the young Italian lady from Florence, rubbed shoulders with the rich and famous and enjoyed every minute of it.

Fallaci felt very much at home in the company of celebrities, an ease perhaps the result of her attraction to an acting career. She had three opportunities to become an actress. When Hollywood crews filmed *The Agony and the Ecstasy* in Florence, its producer needed someone to play the role of Catherine de Médicis and offered her the job. "But you are Catherine de Médicis. You have her face."[2] When Michele Serra refused the necessary twenty-day leave, she turned it down. Then an Italian actor wanted her to play a part with him in a comedy, but she refused what she considered an undignified role. Finally, Luchino Visconti wanted her for the part of the Nun of Monza in *The Betrothed*. She once more felt disinclined. "At that point, I was too heavily involved in journalism. I was doing intellectual work. I felt it diminishing to do a single movie."[3] Fallaci later overcame this reluctance when she asked her producer friend Franco Cristaldi for the part of the empress in *Marco Polo*. However, the timing was not right. A Chinese actress received the role.

Fallaci found actors and actresses to be interesting and intelligent people and experienced pleasure in their company. Over the years, she developed a good rapport with celebrities, more so than with writers and journalists. She became friends with Ingrid Bergman, Anna Magnani, and Maria Callas. Perhaps she felt no rivalry with them, only affection. "I believe they understood the respect I feel for their work. I understand what a commitment it entails. It is a type of sensitivity that resembles that of a writer."[4]

Fallaci's flirtations with acting as a career partly explain her flair for visual, concrete descriptions in her writings. However, they are more indicative of a temperament that enjoys the spotlight and wants to be seen on her own terms. Not that she wants cameras to follow her in her private life. On the contrary, she claims to embrace seclusion with a passion and loses no opportunity to sermonize on her privacy. Her chance meeting with Greta Garbo in New York City's Dover Delicatessen exemplifies her obsession. She recognized the woman immediately, knew how she avoided publicity, and thus decided to make believe she did not recognize her. Since they both left the store at the same time, Fallaci held the door open for her, said, "Please, Ma'am," instead of "Please, Ms. Garbo," and was astonished when the retired actress responded, "Thank you, Ms. Fallaci." Still, Fallaci refrained from striking up a conversation, respected Greta Garbo's chosen lifestyle, and uses the chance meeting to illustrate how much she resembles the actress. "I belong to her type. My drama is that she could afford privacy, because she stopped making movies. I did not stop writing. Therefore, each time a book is published, the curse starts all over again."[5]

Fallaci explains her obsessive protection of her private life by two points of reference. She insists that professional jealousy is rampant in Italy among writers and defends herself from it through a shield of isolation. Then too, in spite of her success, she considers herself an unpretentious, reserved person who prefers solitary activities to company. "I never remember getting bored whenever I was alone. I always have a thousand things to do and think about. People, even friends whom I love, sooner or later always bore me."[6]

As a writer, however, Fallaci reverses her tendency toward withdrawal and makes no attempt to hide herself. Once she began her entry into national journalism with *Europeo*, she found it easy to insert her individual voice into her writings.

Right from the start of her tenure with *Europeo*, Fallaci wrote about such celebrities as Joan Collins, Vittorio Gassman, Gary Cooper, and Ava Gardner, as well as such vacationing celebrities as Jean-Paul Sartre, Simone de Beauvoir, and Graham Greene.[7] She reported on new films by Vittorio de Sica and Guido Salvini and profiled their stars. Music festivals, television personalities, love stories, and the history of Italian cinema in the memoirs of film director Augusto Genina constitute only a sample of the journalist's output. Fallaci enjoyed her contact with the rich and famous, found many of them emotionally and intellectually enriching, and illustrated her talent as a high-society reporter.[8]

Her first attempt to interview Marilyn Monroe exemplifies how Fallaci enlivens the facts of a report. She uses her articles as a stage for the dramatization of herself. The Marilyn Monroe frenzy, which was sweeping Europe at the time, ensured instant appeal. The way Fallaci writes further draws her readers. She first emphasizes the media's inability to locate the mysterious and elusive actress. Then she describes her determination to succeed where others had failed. The reader's desire to know whether Fallaci accomplishes her goal is sustained from beginning to end. According to Fallaci's account, she contacts such periodicals as the *Saturday Evening Post*, *New York Times*, *Look*, and *Collier's*, but she learns nothing about her whereabouts, aside from the fact that Marilyn changes apartments every twenty days. The tendency toward hyperbole—saying that she visited twelve restaurants, eighteen nightclubs, eight movie houses, and fourteen theaters, all of which the actress occasionally visited—is pardonable given the article's humor. Fallaci and her colleagues discover 60 Sutton Place as Monroe's probable address, rejoice, and go to bed early, only to discover that the furtive tenant had moved to a new location.

Fallaci's obvious injection of self into the article is most significant to maintaining excitement. Her reportage emerges as a first-person aria that centers the whole world on her attempts to meet the actress. The parading of her own personality became so important that facts exclusive of herself assume secondary status. She emerges as the lady who traveled to New York to interview Marilyn and catapults her personal image into the limelight. Italian readers reveled in the Fallaci—not Marilyn Monroe—extravaganza.

The biggest city in America focused on Fallaci's efforts; American reporters wanted to write about her and followed her everywhere; Louella Parsons even offered her assistance. "Will the Italian newswoman succeed in interviewing Marilyn Monroe?"[9] Had Fallaci given the facts-only variety of reporting, she would have drowned the long article in an endless flow of data. By injecting her personal voice and suspense into the account, she drew her audience into a setting more recognizable as the real world. Even her sarcastic invitation to Marilyn Monroe to visit her in Milan at any convenient time livened up the narration right to the end.

The amusing story of her frustrating efforts eventually surfaced again as the introduction to *I sette peccati di Hollywood* (*The Seven Sins of Hollywood*) but actually carries greater significance for other reasons. It provided exposure to America and a foretaste of her next visit to Los Angeles and New York. It demonstrated her ability to turn a story into a comedy, build suspense, and cast herself in a dazzling role. In addition, Fallaci maintained that Marilyn's behavior would one day resemble her own, when, as an author of several books, she would do everything in her power to avoid publicity. At the time of her Marilyn adventure, Fallaci was like the many anxious photographers, reporters, and writers who desperately desired to meet the star. Today, she looks back at the incident with an entirely new perspective. "Oh, how I understand why she hid from me."[10]

The trip to Hollywood was an enjoyable experience for Fallaci. California appeared utopian: "I felt like I was going on vacation."[11] Arriving in the famous section of Los Angeles with only fifty dollars in her pocket, Fallaci writes, she has to make the best of a poorly financed trip and accepts the hospitality of an Italian-American woman who has offered the free use of her garage apartment. Despite her penury, she survives and begins writing, losing no opportunity to make herself—not Hollywood's stars—the center of attraction. In one article, her own photograph is on the first page. Italians thus see her seated next to the actor Glenn Ford on the set of Columbia Pictures Studio during the filming of a Western.[12]

On a hot August afternoon, she accomplishes the difficult task of obtaining an invitation to a party at the Pacific Palisades home of the actor Joseph Cotten. Present on Cotten's sumptuous terrace overlooking the ocean is an array of stars: David Niven, Greer Garson, Alfred Hitchcock, Norma Shearer, Gregory Peck, Cole Porter, and the gigantic, solemn Orson Welles with his beautiful Italian wife, Paola Mori. In Fallaci's account, as soon as she enters the room, everyone stops talking and stares, as though the *devil* has just appeared. The guests become very reserved. During lunch, they drink mostly water and ice tea and watch to see whether she takes notes. When Fallaci downs a shot of whiskey, Greer Garson stares at her as though she is a filthy insect. "Not even Mamie Eisenhower or a tax agent would have been treated that day with such wariness on Joseph Cotten's terrace."[13] The impression given to Italian readers is that the eyes of Hollywood mistrust the young woman from Florence.

One unexpected fringe benefit derives from attending Cotten's party. At a certain point, Fallaci becomes bored and uncomfortable. Rising to leave, she notes that almost every person does the same, as if to create the impression that people of the cinema practice sobriety and go to bed early. However, she suddenly finds her path blocked by the towering presence of Orson Welles, who seems intent on befriending this young reporter from his wife's homeland and on explaining his colleagues' strange behavior. According to Welles, it is impossible to live anonymously in Hollywood. Homes have glass walls with implanted microphones; long-range telescopes spy on bedrooms. More than one thousand journalists work in the area for the specific purpose of gathering information on celebrities. Louella Parsons, the most important queen of gossip, and Hedda Hopper, the meanest of the lot, relentlessly menace the private lives of anyone fortunate enough to appear on a movie screen. The only way to avoid publicity is to hide. Fallaci concludes her visit with feelings of empathy and friendship for Orson Welles but also understands what a heavy toll the acting community pays for success.[14]

The friendship with Welles would continue and grow stronger over the years. He wrote a brief introduction to the original 1958 edition of *The Seven Sins of Hollywood*. The actor spoke highly of her and, according to Fallaci, became obsessed with her life. She claims to have learned later after his death that he had prepared a script featuring a young Italian female journalist. This not only flattered the writer but also proved that she had exercised a seductive appeal on his imagination. After the first meeting in Hollywood, they saw each other in Rome, Paris, and then in Los Angeles again where she had gone to promote her book *A Man* on the *Merv Griffin Show*. According to Fallaci, Welles, who was in the audience, let out a yell and gave her a warm embrace. His huge body engulfed the petite Oriana. They began to speak and just forgot about the embarrassed host. After Welles summarized many of her writing accomplishments and adventures, she nodded her assent and then illustrated her quick wit. "How disappointed I am in you, Orson. You have not succeeded in becoming president of the United States."[15]

The actor immediately burst into such a fit of hilarity that everyone in the auditorium also began to laugh. She maintains that he never forgot her clever retort.

Fallaci later developed a similar close friendship with Sean Connery when he starred in his James Bond movies. To this day, they call each other and occasionally visit. Fallaci maintains that intelligent people understood that she was different—not the typical journalist. "They recognized my talent and knew that one day I would become Oriana Fallaci. And so, not only did they agree to see me but we became friends."[16] According to Fallaci, her serious disposition prevented her from taking advantage of friendship with people like Cecil B. DeMille and Orson Welles. She never exploited their attraction toward her, felt they had given her a gift, and refused what she considers the presumptuousness of many of today's journalists, writers, and television personalities. "I, therefore, allowed so many occasions in my life to slip by. In addition and above all, I had no time. I always felt compelled to do things quickly, as though I were going to die the next day. So I never slowed down."[17]

On one occasion years later, the Italian writer Manlio Cancogni visited Fallaci at the Rizzoli publishing house's New York office on East Fifty-seventh Street. He had taught Italian at her Liceo Galileo Galilei in Florence and had also fought in the Resistance movement with her father. When the secretary refused to allow him into her office, Cancogni brusquely strode past, sat on her desk, and interrupted her writing.

"What are you doing?"
"I am working."
"I don't give a care. I am your ex-teacher!"
"Let me work, Cancogni."
"Oriana, how are you?"
"I am so tired."
"Tired just today or all the time."
"I'm always tired."
"Of course, obviously! You have lived one hundred and fifty years!"[18]

Cancogni understood the pace of life experienced by his former student. At the age of thirty or even forty, she had already accomplished what many people would never have completed in one and one-half centuries.

Like the party at Joseph Cotten's home, Fallaci's interview with Cecil B.

DeMille also produced its share of embarrassing but humorous moments. Of more significance, however, her article gives as much attention, if not more, to Fallaci as to DeMille. She had received specific instructions to arrive thirty minutes early, dress in a reserved manner for a dignified discussion, and ask only respectful questions. Wearing black and no makeup, Fallaci fearfully approaches the headquarters of "the king of Hollywood" at 5451 Marathon Street within the Paramount Studios compound. After meeting several inter-mediaries—a guard, a publicity director, a first secretary, another publicity director, a second secretary—she finally enters the inner sanctum, breathes rapidly as DeMille rises from his desk to greet her, and then realizes that she has committed a major diplomatic blunder before uttering a word. She has failed to see his most recent motion picture, *The Ten Commandments*, and is filled with fear and trepidation as the great producer initiates their con-versation. "I'll ask the first question. Speak to me about my last film." Ab-solute silence follows. The two secretaries taking notes wait for an answer. He anxiously draws closer to her and with a sweet smile on his face under-scores the request. "Tell me, tell me." She gulps twice before whispering the horrible truth. "I have not yet seen it, sir."[19] As both secretaries stare, he frowns, silences all attempted excuses, orders her to see the movie that evening, and makes a reservation at the Wilshire Theater for the eight o'clock show.

The next day, after dutifully completing her homework assignment, she anxiously arrives for the two o'clock appointment. DeMille begins with a long list of serious questions and shows not the least sign of any emotion. However, on discovering that his victim has enjoyed the production, he in-stantly assumes a new identity and expresses his appreciation. He provides so much information about his life to Fallaci that all of her inhibition and consternation evolve into sincere affection for the seventy-six-year-old pro-ducer. He tells her about the beginnings of his partnership with Jesse Lasky and Samuel Goldwyn, their move to Hollywood from New York, his first movie, *The Squaw Man*, the formation of his association with Adolph Zukor, the twenty-eight-month continuous run of the story of Christ in *The King of Kings*, the importance of the Bible in his career, and anecdotes about all of his films, including *The Crusades*, *The Plainsman*, *Union Pacific*, *Samson and Delilah*, and *The Greatest Show on Earth*. He speaks freely about his family and fifty-five-year marriage to Constance Adams. As the interview draws to a close, he reveals that he has seen *The Ten Commandments* two hundred fifty times and then offers her words of wisdom. "Since you are very nice, I want to give you some advice; do the same."[20] He gives this counsel so sweetly that she politely refrains from laughing. Before giving him time to present her with a second ticket, she respectfully bows and runs from the room.

Fallaci next studied the question of vice and scandal in the movie capital but learned that possibilities for a good life existed too. Fully determined to immerse herself in the city's world and, in the process, enthrall her readers, she went to view movie stars as they socialized in public. Wearing her most beautiful dress, she heads for the haunts of the rich and famous. She has a cup of saki at the Japanese restaurant Imperial Gardens, orders a martini at La Rue, and eats shrimp cocktail at Romanoff's. However, not a single celebrity graces any of these locations. She experiences the same disappointment after visiting a string of popular nightclubs. She finally considers a new strategy—attending mass the next day at "Our Lady of the Cadillac" in Beverly Hills. It works. Seated inconspicuously in a church pew, Fallaci watches in amazement a whole string of personalities in devout attendance: Van Johnson enters with his three children; Gregory Peck with his French wife, Véronique Passani, and his three children from his previous marriage; Loretta Young with her nineteen-year-old daughter and brother-in-law, Ricardo Montalban; Ann Miller, wearing a long black veil; Jeanne Crain with her three children and husband, Paul Brinckmann; Ann Blyth with her baby and nurse; Debra Paget; Vincente Minnelli with his latest wife; the Pierangeli sisters, Pier Angeli and Marisa Pavan; Louella Parsons; Margaret O'Brien; Anne Baxter; and Jane Russell. "Not even at a premier in the Chinese Theater would it have been possible to view such an assembly of personalities."[21]

Fallaci projected the image of a talk show host who really got to know her clever guests. The whirlwind of one interview after another flooded receptive Italians famished for her reports on the social dramas surrounding Hollywood's elite. She interviewed Burt Lancaster, discussed his films, and addressed his rise to international fame after his Brooklyn childhood. She also considered the success story of Kim Novak and wrote an article about Jayne Mansfield, whom she considered the nicest but most criticized woman in Hollywood. Fallaci visited William Holden at his home on a bright Sunday afternoon. Not surprised to see her as they had already met, he invited Fallaci for a swim and, afterwards, offered her a glass of whiskey in the living room. She described him as the boy next door and chronicled his career after discovery by a talent scout.

She also met the great one with gray hair—Frank Sinatra—in one of the highlights of her trip. In 1954, during Sinatra's Italian tour with Ava Gardner, he had brusquely refused to grant Fallaci an interview. She had angrily given him a piece of her mind, and they had parted on unfriendly terms. At the time, she had sworn never to speak to him again. However, three years later, she walked into the Wilshire Theater for the premier of *The Pride and the Passion*, sat with Sophia Loren and Cary Grant, and, by chance, found her old enemy occupying the next seat. "Fine, he will not remember an argument that took place years earlier with an Italian reporter!" She looks straight ahead at the screen, making believe that she does not see him. However, Sinatra has a mind like a steel trap. Right before the lights go out, he taps her shoulder and says, with the widest of his smiles, "Hello, still mad?"[22] Fallaci immediately succumbs to his charm and initiates a series of conversations about his career after *From Here to Eternity*, his many wives, his success with women, and his reputation as the Rudolph Valentino of 1957. On the evening of the premier, he politely poses for photographers, attended the gala after the film, and, during dinner, explains to Fallaci that she should not misunderstand the earlier dispute; it must have taken place on a nervous day for him. He calls himself a "simple guy." Two days later, however, when she accidentally meets him in a studio, he feigns not seeing her. Nevertheless, that same evening at Romanoff's, he affectionately greets her as though she is an ex-wife.

Fallaci took on the role of movie capital ethnographer when she wrote an article entitled "The Generation of Rebels in Blue Jeans"—including Montgomery Clift, Marlon Brando, Anthony Perkins, Sal Mineo, and Elvis Presley. She wrote another in which she relates that many actresses develop serious mental problems and deals with Judy Garland as a specific case in point. During her performance at the Greek Theater, Garland's nervous breakdown still seemed to plague her. After the show, Fallaci entered her dressing room, found the singer in a white bathrobe removing makeup, and felt a strong sense of attachment to her. Garland spoke freely and abundantly to her visitor that evening, as if in the presence of an irresistible talk show host. Fallaci closes her analysis by concluding that many in the acting community, including Gene Tierney, try suicide.[23]

Her Hollywood odyssey ended on a happy note. Fallaci was the special guest at a farewell dinner offered by Pier Angeli and Marisa Pavan. The two actresses' husbands, Vic Damone and Jean-Pierre Aumont, also graced the occasion, as did director Fred Zinnemann. Fallaci summarizes every detail of the evening and uses the opportunity to accumulate material on how the two Italian sisters live and what they do. The good-bye party takes place at their home in Beverly Hills. The friendly lasagna feast transpires amidst exchanges in French, Italian, and English. In her article, Fallaci emphasizes that good, bad, stupid, intelligent, happy, and unhappy people live in Hollywood, that life there requires hard work, and that the people there produce many of the world's best films.[24]

Fallaci continued on to New York before returning to Milan and wrote three more articles to include in the series on Hollywood. The first considers the career of actor Anthony Franciosa and his marriage to Shelley Winters. The second analyzes the Broadway entertainment industry. The third, however, deals with Arthur Miller and proves much more intriguing because it is an epilogue to the earlier Marilyn Monroe adventure. It depicts Fallaci at Miller's East Fifty-fourth Street home in an elegant, quiet neighborhood near Madison Avenue. It emphasizes how she had received strong advice from his very nervous press agent, Warren Fisher, who had insisted that she not ask the playwright indiscreet questions. Fallaci still longs to meet the actress and takes hope in Warren Fisher's words: "Marilyn will come after you have finished the interview with Miller. Arthur says that she is also anxious to see you after having read the article on your hating her like a jealous wife."[25]

Fallaci asks Miller one question after another about his recent trial and Marilyn's miscarriage. She delves into his modest background as a traveling salesman, his unsophisticated education, his accidental reading of *The Brothers Karamazov*, and his ensuing decision to write. A telephone call from Marilyn interrupts the final phase of Fallaci's conversation with Miller. The actress cannot meet her; a hospital appointment would make her late. Fallaci humorously ends the story with her first personism: "There is nothing to do. I am the one who does not succeed in seeing Monroe."[26]

After completing her reportage, Fallaci returned to the home base of *Europeo* in Milan, where Longanesi Publishers asked for permission to publish the Hollywood articles as a book. Fallaci happily agreed and allowed the production of *I sette peccati di Hollywood*. Its success came as no surprise because she had already acquired much experience writing about such celebrities as Tyrone Power and Clark Gable while employed by *Il Mattino dell'Italia Centrale*. The well-written communiqués violated all the rules of objective, serious reporting by spotlighting the author of the articles just as much as the Hollywood luminaries. Fallaci was on her way to becoming famous herself and seemed to belong in the company of stars. Italian readers vicariously sat in Cecil B. DeMille's office, drank coffee with Arthur Miller, had dinner at the Beverly Hills home of Pier Angeli and Vic Damone, and spoke with Jane Fonda, following Fallaci's itinerary, hypnotized by her every word and action.[27]

Later in life, after publication of *Inshallah*, Fallaci would only reluctantly consent to discuss *I sette peccati di Hollywood*. She even refuses to allow new editions. "I don't consider it a book. It's a collection of articles, something that everybody does and something I did when I was very young."[28] The later image she wanted to project was one of a committed author who had the courage to write serious novels. Any emphasis on her earlier, showy escapades detracted from her desired artistic image as a refined twentieth-century novelist.

In her string of reports entitled "America Seen by an Italian Lady," Fallaci continues her habit of casting herself as her own leading lady. She describes her arrival in New York in July 1965. She explains how, after obtaining clearance from customs, she accidentally met Shirley MacLaine at the airport and how her photographer, Duilio Pallottelli, went to meet her with flowers. She comments on the taxi strike and on one driver's refusal to take her trunk. She provides information about her apartment at 220 East Fifty-seventh Street—a five-by-four-foot room for two hundred fifty dollars a month—and her visit to NBC to thank a friend for finding her lodging. Fallaci met Eddie Fisher there, and together they went to Long Beach, on Long Island, where he performed at the Malibu Beach Club. He told Fallaci all about his ex-wife, Elizabeth Taylor. The article also has a photo of Fallaci talking to Fisher.

In the same article, Fallaci has a flashback to the year before, when Johnny Carson had interviewed her on *The Tonight Show* about *The Useless Sex* and had expressed disagreement about her thesis. He had rejected her opinion on American women, whose favorite food, according to Fallaci, was the American male. He had argued with her views on American men as defenseless lambs comparable to veiled Muslim women.

"My dear, I see no veil on me."
"You don't see it but I do."

Members of the audience had laughed, one crying out: "That veil looks great on you, Johnny."[29] Fallaci maintains that she and Carson had immediately become enemies, claiming that, one year later, he passed her in the NBC studio, did not greet her, and feigned not seeing Fallaci's hand extended as a peace offering. The article illustrates with crystal clarity how the writer produces a report not so much on America as on Fallaci's life in America. She constructs her own image—trendy, fast moving, fearless, having the last word, even with America's big shots.

Fallaci's trip across the United States with Shirley MacLaine intensified the impression of her stardom and stands as an exemplar of the Fallaci style—a journalist totally immersed in the writing of her article but also in living an exciting role designed to attract attention.[30] She literally bombarded audiences with one verbal picture of herself after another. She wrote about American teenagers, continued a nonstop string of interviews, reported on racism, and produced four humorous "Letters from America," which included pictures of a pensive Fallaci wearing a pearl necklace and smoking a cigarette.[31] The land of Florence's liberators was good to the young Florentine, and she fell in love with the idea of living here.

Fallaci had become the Sophia Loren of Italian journalism. Her next assignment strengthened the image. In the summer of 1959, Michele Serra's successor, Giorgio Fattori, asked Fallaci to take a trip around the world, spending time, above all, in the Orient. He explained that she would have to wait until the monsoon season was over and would leave in the winter or early spring of 1960. The term *monsoon season* impressed the eager journalist in the same way that such utterances as "The duke of Norfolk told me" or "I don't know if you are familiar with that little restaurant on Chekhov Street in Leningrad" would have. Even though Fallaci had already visited Turkey, Iran, and the United States, Fattori's proposal interested her. His specific idea—a report on the condition of women—diminished her enthusiasm. Fallaci has openly expressed uneasiness about researching her own gender and their problems. "Women are not a special kind of fauna and I can never see why they should be treated, particularly in newspapers, as a separate issue."[32] Treating them as though they reproduced through parthenogenesis has always struck her as illogical. However, her mother's advice to travel around the world helped her overcome any hesitation.

Tosca Fallaci never insisted that her daughter marry, obey a husband, or have children but instead emphasized the importance of having a profession in which she could travel rather than sew, wash clothes, iron, or supervise a household. The idea of housework invariably resurrects an emotional scene. "I am five or six and standing on my bed. My mother is putting a rough woolen vest on me. It pinches." In the recollection, she is as tall as

Tosca's shoulders, has to bend back to see her face, and notices angry tears. The words that followed leave a lasting impression. "You must not do like I am doing! You must not become a wife, a mother, an ignorant slave! You must go to work! To work! To travel! The world! In the world!" As an adolescent, Fallaci later discussed the vision with her mother and asked whether she considered her activity in the family household work. Tosca swiftly gave a categorical response: "No, it is slavery!"[33] Given this early indoctrination, Fallaci enthusiastically agreed to go on the journey. She received additional motivation when a successful acquaintance revealed her personal unhappiness and a desire to live in countries that relegate women to an inferior status. "Ours is a useless sex anyway."[34]

Fallaci, in the company of her Roman photographer, Duilio Pallottelli, departed from Italy during the winter of 1960 with ten cameras and a typewriter. She frames herself departing with a caravan to the Far East. A full itinerary begins with stops in Pakistan, then goes on to India, Hong Kong, Japan, Hawaii, and the United States. "The tale that follows is an account of what happened from the moment we touched down in Karachi to the moment we left New York; of what I saw, of what I heard, and of what I think I have understood."[35] In reality, her articles describe the voyage of Oriana Fallaci. Her strong personality prevails and acquires as much importance as her subjects.

Fallaci's odyssey across planet Earth interests from a cultural and sociological perspective. Many of her observations on Pakistani, Indian, Malaysian, and Chinese women attack the patriarchal system and predate feminist insights of the 1960s and 1970s. Even more interesting, however, is the playacting of the journalist herself. In one, in Pakistan at the Luxury Beach Hotel in Karachi, Fallaci notices a woman dressed from head to foot in free-flowing red silk. Fallaci's curiosity is piqued, and she discovers that a wedding ceremony had taken place. Somehow, she next manages to obtain an invitation to the celebration, uses all of her skills to obtain private time with the woman in red, and writes her story. The "woman" is only fourteen years old, has never seen her future husband, and dreads the idea of marriage. Fallaci thus takes on the role of a moralist shaking her finger at Muslim society. She confronts the practice of arranged marriages, as well as the subservient and functional role of young women as bearers of children.

Her interviews hold the seeds of her future exchanges with political leaders. Even at that early date, she tried to establish a reputation as one who dialogued mainly with interesting people and, as an intellectual person, discussed such controversial topics as birth control, sterilization, women's status in Hindu countries, and their political role during the struggle for independence from England. In her meetings with educated Indian women, she allowed their personalities and ideas to emerge through the words they spoke. Her first exchange is with Rajkumari Amrit Kaur, who discloses much about her country's history through her personal experiences. She had worked as Mahatma Gandhi's private secretary, had represented India at the Round Table Conference in 1928, had suffered imprisonment by the British on charges of public danger in 1935, and had acted as Minister of Health and Transportation in 1947. Kaur had also accentuated women's living conditions in India, their historical resistance to the English salt tax, and their adamant refusal to abandon saris in favor of a European style of dress. Fallaci describes her meeting such figures as painter, writer, and actress Jamila Verghese, stationmaster Anjani Mehta, hairstylist-scholar Veena Shroff, editor Leela Shukla, and physician Jaishree Katju.

During her visit with the maharani of Jaipur, Fallaci highlights herself strolling across a fountain-covered property, as Pallottelli takes pictures of the monarch's six hundred servants, young white elephants, and sacred dancers, who perform ceremonious movements across the green lawns. In Malaysia, Fallaci meets the famous jungle matriarchs who maintain their superiority through economic power and think nothing of sending a husband back to his mother. During her visit to the Asian mainland, she depicts herself as a knowledgeable sociologist by contrasting the attitudes of women in Red China with those in Hong Kong. In Tokyo, Fallaci maintains the same stance—a journalist investigating manners and customs. She reports on the freedom and promiscuity of many Japanese girls who wear blue jeans, as well as the rising rate of abortion, the use of birth control, and the fanatical attempts of working women to modify surgically their Asian features. After final stops in Hawaii and New York, the writer authoritatively concludes that women around the world live in gloomy, stupefying unhappiness and emphasizes this thesis in her preface. Her belief is that men experience economic, racial, and social problems but that women suffer from sexual discrimination. "I am referring to the taboos which go with that anatomical difference and condition the life of women throughout the world."[36]

In Italy, Fallaci's public admired her articles, as well as her ability to travel to faraway and exotic places. A photograph of her taken by Pallottelli appeared in one of her articles, reinforcing the strategy of keeping her figure in the public eye.[37] Rizzoli Editore published her articles in book form as *Il sesso inutile*, translated three years later as *The Useless Sex*. The publication was not well received by critics, who pointed out its unresearched superficiality and its lively but excessively emotional reactions. It frames Fallaci as a heroine on the side of freedom and enfranchisement of women, but it comes across somewhat damning of her because it is an unreliable source of information. Completely subjective and not profound, it also communicates humor because Fallaci did no editing. In the book, her audience keeps reading about Duilio Pallottelli taking pictures but never has the opportunity to see any of them. Perhaps the best pages pinpoint the differences between women in Hong Kong and those in Communist China. The passages on Hawaii and the historical fall of Polynesian women from innocence is perfunctory, while her attitude toward American women is too *anti* to have meaning, in contrast to the open mind displayed elsewhere. She unfortunately reports nothing on the condition of the Italian women on her own homefront.[38]

Fallaci is aware of the deficiencies of *The Useless Sex* and admits that her thirty-day trip around the world for *Europeo* provided insufficient opportunity to compose a serious report. She speaks with distaste of her early books and feels degraded when they receive too much attention. She chooses to disregard this aspect of her early career. "I have forgotten having done them. If you want to speak about them, do so only for a little, because I cannot bear it."[39] At the time, she enjoyed the assignment and succeeded in creating a unity of form through the framework of a voyage. She recognizes that its substance leaves much to be desired but, as a young reporter, gladly accepted her editor's assignment and looked forward to the whole project as an opportunity to visit distant lands and acquire experience. She admits her youthful enthusiasm for visiting India, the land of Kipling, but bristles when contemporaries focus attention on that work.

Fallaci currently refuses to allow new editions of *The Useless Sex*, regards it as juvenile, and speaks vehemently against the practice of journalists collecting their articles for publication. "I believe that half of today's books are collected articles. Having great respect for literature and for books as precious objects, I do not think that it is serious to make a book out of every article. As a matter of fact, I think it is highly grotesque."[40] Fallaci maintains that, had she collected all of her articles, she would easily have published many books.[41]

Although *The Seven Sins of Hollywood* and *The Useless Sex* increased Fallaci's popularity among readers at large, she explains time and time again that she experienced a void in her life. Becoming a writer involved more than composing articles or authoring a collection of commentaries. Her initial successes had confirmed more than ever her desire to live a life of adventure, to travel, and to become a novelist. The moment to abandon journalism had not yet come, however, and a retreat from society to write creatively was still far away. Nevertheless, nothing could have prevented her from incorporating her desire into her work. She knew she had the artistic personality to write literary books but could only direct aesthetic energy at weekly assignments and long investigative reports. In this context, Fallaci felt confined by the straitjacket of circumstantial truth and compelled to explore new horizons. She essentially tired of her Hollywood, celebrity status and wanted her public to see a new face. The right occasion soon came along and, true to form, she eagerly seized the opportunity to fashion a new image.

On Center Stage

4.

● DESPITE THE TIME REQUIREMENTS OF A demanding profession, Fallaci published her first novel, *Penelope alla guerra* (*Penelope at War*), in 1962. The book was an early attempt to compose a work of fiction but, nevertheless, continues her pattern of projecting performances of self-revelation. Outlining a young woman's internal struggle to arrive at emotional and professional maturity, the novel bears a striking resemblance to Françoise Sagan's 1954 *Bonjour Tristesse*. In *Penelope*, the protagonist, Giò, asserts her independence, matures, and pursues her career in journalism, not allowing emotional hurdles to block her way. Written long after the French author wrote hers, Fallaci's novel was an experimental, avant-garde attempt to express creatively her own life, while treating sensitive women's issues in Italian society.

The model for Giò's mother was Tosca Fallaci. "Women . . . counted for nothing, like her mother, and wept, like her mother."[1] Giò remembers her ironing shirts. "Her tears were rolling down on to the iron and sizzling against the hot metal; they left slightly opaque little marks on the iron, as if they had been drops of water instead of tears."[2] From that day on, Giò swears never to iron shirts and never to weep. Her resolution reflects the writer's own determination. From earliest childhood, Fallaci has always regarded work as a right rather than simply a need and never considered the possibility of becoming a housewife. She was indoctrinated in the importance of leaving the household and going into a profession. "What my mother intended when she told me that I had to go to work was not sewing, washing, ironing, or raising a family. It was being a career woman: outside, far away. Traveling."[3] The writer resembles the heroine Giò in that she never had any desire to become a wife but, rather, desired to love a man who in turn would love her.

> Love has always been part of my dreams and desires and as a child I even thought that I would have loved only one man forever. A man, not a husband. The idea of a husband bothered and frightened me. Maybe because the image of my weeping mother putting a rough blouse on me had left a wound in my subconscious.[4]

Although Fallaci has never been engaged to be married, she has loved several men freely and without obligation, remained faithful to each one, and refused the concept of monogamy. As in the novel, love has an important place in her world. However, she has persistently refused to abandon her profession, except in the case of one of her lovers, Alekos Panagoulis. "Aside from Alekos, I have never betrayed the silent promise that I made to my mother."[5]

Fallaci seems to be an extrovert but claims to relish privacy and considers herself reserved. She has made such a point of keeping her ties of affection private that critics have wondered whether she was capable of love or dedicated exclusively to a career. "Those who did not consider me a monster considered me a lesbian," Fallaci stated. She relates the story of a long interview by a journalist from *Life* who did not have the courage to ask the question. She asked for him. "For sometime now, haven't you been trying to ask me if I am a lesbian?" After receiving an affirmative answer, she burst into laughter. "Listen. Do not be offended; I don't like you. Therefore, I cannot prove to you that I am not a lesbian. But if you have a brother who is more handsome, send him to me. And then he'll tell you about it."[6]

Just as Fallaci had gone to New York, Giò also goes to the busy metropolis at her employer's request to obtain information for a movie that deals with a love affair between an American and an Italian woman. The protago-

nist willingly undertakes the voyage in spite of the objections of her boyfriend, Francesco, who wants her to stay at home, marry him, have a family,
and act more like Penelope than Ulysses. "It's your job to weave, not to go
to war. Can't you understand that a woman isn't a man?"[7] After a disappointing romance in America and Francesco's rejection, Giò resolves to face
the world with unflinching determination. "I'll show those fools who criticize
me because I am a woman. I'm better than a man and there's no room for
Penelope today. I go to war and follow the law of men: either me or you."[8]
She will show her talent and fearlessly prove her worth despite the observation of a famous British author. "Jane Austen said that an intelligent woman
should never show that she is."[9]

The thrust of Fallaci's feminism lies mainly in the personality of the
heroine, who effectively assumes the psychological disposition of a man. The
character Giovanna uses the shortened form, *Giò*, symbolic and suggestive
of its male counterpart *Joe*. "Not only because it was short and sharp and
sounded American, but because it could be taken for a man's name."[10] As a
child at the time of her first menstrual cycle, Giò had exhibited such stoicism
that her father wondered about her gender. "Other girls always cried when
it happened, but not her—she must have turned into a little man and not a
woman at all."[11] As an adult, Giò resolutely pursues career goals and demonstrates more masculinity than the leading male protagonists, Richard and
Bill, who display womanly attributes. Giò is in no way a repulsive individual.
On the contrary, as an attractive woman, she yearns to offer her affection to
a man and cultivate a warm, meaningful relationship. However, encountering nothing but frustration, she aggressively meets challenges, refuses to collapse before adversity, and courageously rises to face the future alone. Giò
stands as the champion that later feminist writers would struggle to create
in an attempt to assert their vision.

The secondary figure, Martine, reinforces this basic feminist stance when
she maintains that women are human beings, but they nevertheless learn
from childhood that they must respect and obey males. This situation contradicts all logic because both sexes have similar desires and men alone have
traditionally received society's approval to satisfy their sexual appetites.
"They can do as they want as soon as they're born, but until we're sixty they
go on telling us that virginity is the most precious dowry a woman can bring
a man. Why?"[12] Martine's first love resembles Giò's idealistic infatuation for
Richard, an American soldier she had loved as a child, but soon dissolves
into the brute reality of an unplanned pregnancy, an abortion on Easter Sun-

day, the sight of her fetus in a jar, and the medical diagnosis that she would never again have a child. After recovering from her physical and emotional debilitation, Martine takes a strong stand against innocent relationships and makes a reasoned existentialist choice for carefully selected liaisons that produce for her an abundance of material advantages.

In spite of her book's pronounced personal feminism, Fallaci bristles when classified as a woman writer and resists all attempts to categorize her separately from her male counterparts. After the publication of the novel, Bruno Fallaci called her to express his satisfaction and to offer encouragement for the future. "You can do better but you have one thing already: you write like a man."[13] The novelist's epic, cold, and detached style has always set her apart from such feminist writers as Dacia Maraini, Anna Banti, or Armanda Guiducci. Despite her uncle's comment, Fallaci thinks it ridiculous to catalogue artists according to their gender. She has her own style and refuses categories, whether for men, women, or gays.

In an interview, journalist Robert Scheer asked Fallaci how she got along with feminists. She answered that she was sick and tired of them, even though she used to say that feminism was the biggest revolution of modern times. "I said it for a couple of years. Until they started breaking my balls and became really unbearable. It is their victimization that disturbs me. I think it's like a dictatorship." Scheer fired right back. "How did they start breaking your balls?" Fallaci then explained to Scheer that they ignored and punished her. When *Ms.* received the manuscript of *A Man*, its editors were not interested. "So now I'm exiled, which is good, because I don't want anything to do with that fanaticism again."[14]

Over and above feminism, the generating force of *Penelope at War* springs from Fallaci's personal life and highlights a pattern that surfaces with the composition of each subsequent novel. Personal episodes from her past life provide the book its content. When Giò freely chooses to surrender her virginity, she reproduces one of the writer's early private experiences. In her late twenties, Fallaci chose to relinquish her innocence in a liaison that occurred in New York City. When Richard discovers that Giò is a virgin, he weeps, as did the man whom Fallaci had met. In fact, Giò's attempt to console her disconsolate partner parallels the author's effort to downplay her loss of personal virtue.[15]

Other incidents also reveal the writer's background. Giò's trip to New York to discover firsthand material for a movie alludes to Fallaci's participatory style as a journalist. "Before they always used to write films at home, now they send someone to the country where the film is to be set. Apparently it makes for greater reality."[16] The protagonist's hatred of metaphysics reproduces the writer's attitude towards ontological discussions and her refusal to accept the existence of a Supreme Being. Giò simply cannot determine whether God exists.

> I don't want to ask myself metaphysical questions. I asked them when I was sixteen, naturally I didn't find the answers, and ever since then I've steered clear of giving myself such a headache. Let's say . . . that I believe only in myself. It's simpler and more expeditious.[17]

Later in the novel, Giò and Richard take advantage of a magnificent autumn day to visit a friend in Connecticut and on the way stop to admire a beautiful landscape of colored leaves. Their walk through the woods not only illustrates the power of sensory stimuli to reawaken childhood memories but also permits a glance at intimate moments from the author's earlier life. Identifying the natural scene with similar outings that she and her father took to the Tuscan countryside, Giò essentially acts as the writer's alter ego. She visualizes the eel-filled gully where a swift river flows. Giò and her father, just like Oriana and Edoardo, attach their bait to a bulky thread of twine, which then becomes like a bead of slippery quivers. The rushing course rolls little stones over their feet and also vibrates the tender wood in its swift current. Giò/Oriana remembers too how the attached worms change color in the water to a lighter red. After everything is in place, Giò and her father do exactly what Oriana and Edoardo would do. They return home, determined to go back on the next day. Her dad walks first, and she follows. They always reach a grove of apple trees with much fruit on the ground and then take a shortcut where goat excrement appears scattered like berries. "Then they were home again and her mother was frying golden crispy pumpkin flowers."[18]

For a large portion of her life, Fallaci has preferred living in the United States and has chosen to establish her principal residence in New York rather than in Italy. In the letter to her Italian boyfriend, Francesco, Giò also reveals her affection for the metropolis and actually voices the author's opinion. "Home is not the place where you happened to be born but the place you choose when you are an adult, and you can decide what you want and what you don't want for the rest of your life."[19] She develops this predilection by poetically comparing the architectural beauty of the United Nations

Building, the Empire State Building, and skyscrapers in general against the ancient beauty of European cathedrals and monuments. "New York is a miracle that amazes me more each day."[20] Despite the preponderance of rectangular steel and cement buildings, everything looks magical to her, even when she is confronted by huge buildings that resemble "petrified giants."[21] The patch of blue sky at the end of each street heightens her pleasure while reflections of the sun on masses of glass dazzle her more than precious diamonds. Her unbridled enthusiasm for the city's size, power, and indestructibility knows no bounds. "In America everything expresses strength—from the skyscrapers to the waterfalls. Everything expresses security—from the money to the boastfulness."[22] Even Richard's metaphoric depiction of New York as a city of fairy tales reinforces her outlook.

> There are houses there that touch the sky. At night if you stretch out your hand you can tickle the tummy of the stars, and if you aren't careful you might burn your fingers. People fly like the swallows past the window sills, trains hurtle beneath the roads and tickle the devil's horns, and the rivers are so wide that they seem like lakes; over these lakes arch bridges as fine as silver needles.[23]

After Bill accuses Europeans of always criticizing America, Giò responds: "I love America. I love its friendliness, its efficiency, its supercivilization. I feel that I belong more to this country than to the one where I was born."[24]

Penelope at War contains a well-constructed plot but also conveys a mental truth that vitalizes the story. Just like Fallaci, Giò loves America and goes there for its opportunities. Her infatuation provides the main thrust of the novel. The young character experiences majestic awe as she views Niagara Falls and Manhattan skyscrapers. Richard and Bill live and work in New York City. Fallaci could have picked two Italians and placed them in Rome or Milan, but her choice of an alternate setting accentuates Giò's love for America, as well as her own affection. As a child, Fallaci neither knew the fictional character Richard personally nor had strong emotional attachments to anyone as Giò did. However, the episodes reflect the reality of the writer's preference for her adopted country and reflect the transforming power of imagination as she introduces new characters, formulates dialogue, and lyrically describes tender feelings about the United States.

Fallaci's attachment derives principally from her hatred of fascism during World War II. Her father, a hero of the Resistance, viewed the land across

the Atlantic as a source of salvation, as the origin of his own country's liberators, and not as a moneymaking factory for emigrants. When American
pilots unleashed their bombs on her beloved Florence, Fallaci hated them
for annihilating friends, relatives, and admired monuments. However, both
parents explained that they had to bomb the city before freeing it. In her
child's mind, she must have been confused, wondering why liberators would
kill if they were coming to rescue. Nevertheless, her parents' explanation was
reinforced when American soldiers actually entered the city as delivering
angels, throwing chocolate to the flower-bearing crowds around their tanks.
She never saw the "ugly American," just the beautiful young men wearing
helmets and uniforms who came to release them from chains of bondage.
Everybody welcomed them; the entire populace received them with open
arms.[25]

An additional event that fostered an appreciation of America occurred
when Tosca Fallaci gave her daughter *Gone with the Wind* as a gift. The
historical past of the Civil War, the Old South, Rhett Butler, and Scarlett
O'Hara, hypnotized her. The *Saturday Evening Post* and the cover illustrations by Norman Rockwell also captivated her imagination. The scene of the
little boy in a doctor's office, the mother saying grace with her child in a
restaurant, and all of his other paintings told about those interesting people
living their lives across the sea. In *Collier's* magazine, she discovered beautiful Connecticut homes, New York brownstones, and the lovely mansions of
New Orleans. The influence penetrated so deeply that at a certain point in
her life Fallaci acquired as her Manhattan residence a white brownstone with
black doors and windows. This same influence received the transforming
touch of the writer's imagination and surfaced as Giò's enthusiastic admiration for New York City.

Despite autobiographical resonances in *Penelope at War*, the writer succeeds in altering the facts in such a way that they appear to be spontaneous
creations. Verifying whether certain episodes in her books really happened
is an interesting and valid approach. However, Fallaci claims that a writer's
truth often has nothing to do with the documentation of lawyers, courts, or
journalism. Her novels, she maintains, especially the later ones, produce universal, reinvented truth that moves beyond whether or not something actually happened to the author. She believes that every artist on earth, from
Manzoni to Tolstoy, from Dostoyevsky to Flaubert, moves beyond life experience to a new reality. Using Charles Baudelaire's *Fleurs du mal*, she emphasizes that the French poet certainly must have stayed with prostitutes.

This certitude should not, however, be taken to mean that all questions about his poems absolutely deal with the whores he chose, the color of their hair, or whether he loved any of them.[26] Biographical details are important for tracing the artistic movement from raw material to literary creation; but, if they receive primary focus, they detract from the mysterious, varied processes of creativity that occur in each writer's mind. In Fallaci's case, she blends a medley of reality and fantasy that emerges as a fresher, more inventive story.

According to Fallaci, the essence of fiction encompasses the reinvention of what has already taken place. "In a novel, even reality becomes fantasy, fantasy becomes reality, and from a character who perhaps exists in reality . . . a new one is born who lives independently and dies independently."[27] Richard, with whom Giò has a brief affair, is an invention and, although she depicts him as an escaped prisoner of war who earlier had taken refuge in the protagonist's household, was never an actual person in Fallaci's life. The later encounter with Giò in America and brief romance lead to his eventual flight, attempted suicide, and final effort to establish a valid association with someone of the opposite sex. Giò's obsession with Richard further complicates the scenario, since, as a rule, novelists rarely invent women characters who fall in love with homosexuals. The character Bill is a thoroughly modern individual whose entanglement with Martine camouflages his affair with Richard. The growth of his affection for Giò further accentuates his bisexuality. The heroine finally decides to leave New York, fully understanding the impossible nature of her situation. "We couldn't sleep in a bed for three."[28] She returns to Italy and reveals her whole story to Francesco, who finds himself unaccepting of her experiences and finally leaves her. Despite any disillusionment, Giò now possesses the subject for a screenplay and is determined to write about Martine, her voyage to America, and her encounter with Richard.

Penelope at War sometimes remains at the level of the superficial. Bill's background, as well as his rapport with Richard, is insufficiently developed. The author's presence asserts itself too obviously in Giò's profession, independence, and love for America. However, even though it was written when Fallaci was young, it has a coherent structure and a strong narrative thread. The writer has successfully constructed a plausible and unified theme through Giò's trip to the United States in search of material for a movie script; her various personal experiences, which then become the actual subject; and finally her return to Italy after accomplishing her mission.

Fallaci sustains the organizational design through atmosphere, dialogue, voice, flashbacks, and character development. Many of these early techniques will reappear in later novels but in a more refined and developed manner.

One of Fallaci's literary mainstays is the realistic evocation of the sights and sounds of her setting. The plot unfolds in a New York that readers find credible and that supports the novel's content. After Giò and Richard accidentally meet, they go out together and start enjoying the city. They take the ferry to Staten Island, to the Statue of Liberty, and then back to Manhattan before visiting Wall Street, the Empire State Building, and Times Square. They eat chestnuts purchased from a street vendor, play games in amusement centers, and have funny newspaper photographs taken with the headline "Giò arrived in New York! Dick very happy."[29] They dine in a restaurant, see a John Wayne movie at the Radio City Music Hall, dance at the Palladium, take a cab to Washington Square, and finally go to Richard's apartment in Greenwich Village. The sketch of America's cultural capital becomes as important as the characters and sustains the reader's interest in the story.

Dialogue is her primary method of revealing personality. Rather than describe temperament in the third person, she uses direct discourse, which immediately discloses disposition and hidden emotional facets. In the case of Martine, her superficiality becomes obvious as soon as she speaks. "Mon petit chou! I am so happy. Why didn't you call me sooner, you wretch?" Insensitivity surfaces when she refers to her earlier affair with Francesco, despite Giò's present affection for him. "Dear, dear boy! Quite acceptable too, if he wasn't such a bore. But maybe you don't find him boring. Incidentally, I was so pleased when I heard he'd fallen in love with you. You know, he was really in love with you when he was running after me." Her attachment to jewelry and her cursory treatment of love and marriage emerge as she brandishes the diamond her former husband gave to her. "My ex. is a treasure, he still likes to give me presents. Say, I should never have divorced him. . . . Don't you think it's chic to remarry your ex-husband? It looks so faithful!"[30] Martine's newest lover, Bill, a writer of comedies, became an easy conquest at a cocktail party. "I go up to him and say I've seen his plays, and that very same evening things started to go with a bang."[31] Giò's final comment seals the verdict. "The rest of the meal was a non-stop monologue by Martine, who talked about clothes, lovers, shoes, Bill."[32]

The author's use of interior monologue facilitates the realistic and immediate portrayal of personal feeling. As Giò waits for a cab to take her to Gomez's office on Park Avenue, she remembers Martine's question about whether she had ever been in love and answers in her own mind: "Yes, when she stopped to think about it she really had been in love, and still was. But not with Francesco. With Richard."[33] After she receives lucrative employment from Gomez, she leaves her appointment overwhelmed with pride and allows her feelings to run wild. "With two thousand dollars a month, what would she care about Richard, about her remorse for having in a certain sense been the cause of his death, about her absurd childish romance?"[34] She possesses the financial freedom to enter the crowds of the metropolis without fear and to realize that anything is possible in a great city and land of promise.

Proustian association also communicates a frame of mind. Its appearance, although minimal, is significant because its usage matures to full fruit in her later novels. It occurs first during Giò's conversation with the Italian movie producer who sends her on the American assignment. She notices a big clock with a pendulum on the office wall and recalls the one at which she would gaze in the hallway of her home. This mental connection releases a flood of childhood memories—sleeping in the corridor while the escaped American prisoner slept on her bed in the living room, seeing a procession of monstrous spirits flow from the timepiece, observing them dissolve into the oil lamp near her bed, and then watching them assume such foreboding shapes as dragons and the mouths of weeping mothers. In her imagination, she would then flee to Richard's room only to encounter photographs of deceased relatives menacingly staring at her from their enclosed frames and then releasing an additional barrage of terrorizing phantoms. These nightmarish memories not only function as distractions during Giò's verbal exchange with her employer but also excite the seemingly impossible desire to visit New York to find the American soldier; she believes he might be dead. During the plane trip, the same method produces remembrances of the serviceman. Reflecting on Francesco's warning that she may become disillusioned, Giò fears that his caution might prove correct and consequently denies the importance of Richard's memory in her eyes. The word *eyes* acts as a Proustian madeleine cake and triggers a reminder of his red curls and bony shoulders.

Fallaci avoids descriptions of characters but instead exposes them through seemingly insignificant details. Richard once caressed Giò and told the twelve-year-old that she was beautiful. On another occasion, she saw him unhappy and tried to console him by promising to become his wife after the war. When he then embraced her more ardently, his soldier buddy, Joe, enters the room and angrily protests. The incident emerges in a significant light later in the novel when Richard's homosexuality is revealed. It represents sensual experimentation, an exploration of personal virility, and an analysis of the extended nature of his libidinous tendencies. Kissing an innocent and welcoming girl protects him from humiliating rejection and embarrassment. Joe's strong denouncement also leads to speculation about the nature of the relationship between the two men. Finally, Richard's difficulty in consummating a sexual union with Giò, as well as his tearful regret upon learning of the loss of her virginity, emerges as a plausible and logical outcome that is consistent with the earlier episode.

The method appears again right before Giò and Richard sleep together for the first and last time. He drinks a shot of whiskey in a quick gulp, as though he wants to build up his courage. This clue really represents his fear of the approaching heterosexual liaison rather than the simple timidity or shyness that might happen to anyone. The approach also functions efficiently when Bill's homosexual relationship with Richard clarifies in retrospect a presumably negligible item. At the Monacle in Greenwich Village, Richard is on the verge of revealing himself to Giò when Martine and Bill enter the bar. He then freezes and stares fixedly at his male partner, whose malignant smile further inhibits any possible disclosure. The smile itself underscores the fact that the two men have been lovers and further suggests that Bill dominates his partner. In addition, the sneering grin predicts failure by Richard in any attempt to establish normal sexual relations with a woman. It paralyzes Richard; he thinks that he may never break his imprisoning emotional tendencies.

The appearance of *Penelope at War* early in Fallaci's career represents an important indication that literary writing occupies a primary position in her professional ventures and that, despite activity as a reporter, it remained a great love and motivating force. Michele Prisco observes that narrative tendencies continuously drive Fallaci's journalistic inclinations. According to this critic, Fallaci's attempt to penetrate to the core of external values and to discover the essence or hidden elements of a human situation illustrate her approach to novel writing and are entwined with her journalism.[35] This filtering influence explains a major aspect of her reporting techniques. She possessed a literary spirit as a young person, fostered it as an adult, and promoted it as a reporter. More important, she allowed full expression of a temperament that could not resist putting her life's story on display, even in a novel.

After the publication of *Penelope at War*, Fallaci had the perfect opportunity to abandon her position with *Europeo* and to write fiction but instead remained faithful to her obligations. One certain impediment surfaced in the unwillingness of employers to release their talented, young employee. They energetically discouraged any thoughts of resignation and commanded her to continue gathering great stories. After *Penelope*, she might have written other good books and become a later version of Françoise Sagan. But the Sagan style of sentimental literature simply did not suit her as much as adventure, travel, investigative reports, war, and historical reality.

Prior to and after the publication of *Penelope at War*, Fallaci continued to interview and compose commentaries about international celebrities. From 1961 to 1963, she wrote sixty-seven articles on actors, producers, and film festivals; eight on high society and aristocratic figures; and four on fashion designers. From December 1962 to June 1963 alone, she interviewed eighteen celebrities in cities throughout the world. All of these interviews first appeared in *Europeo* and continued Fallaci's practice of giving full rein to her personality. Rizzoli Editore published some of them as a collection in 1963 with the Italian title *Gli antipatici*.[36]

In the preface, Fallaci indicates that she actually records conversations—not interviews—on a tape recorder and then transcribes them into written dialogues. She provokes reactions through her questions and expressions of personal opinion. "I have always thought that letting people talk and faithfully reporting what they say would contribute considerably to written profiles."[37] In the book itself, she introduces each interview by explaining how she obtained the meeting, how it proceeded, and how it concluded. In these preliminary comments, she also expresses personal judgments, biases, and conclusions on the person interviewed. Refusing to accept the existence of impartiality, she views so-called objectivity as hypocrisy or presumption because it supposes that an individual's report represents truth with a capital *T*. "When one writes a profile, there exists, there can only exist, the honesty of the person who furnishes the piece of news or the profile."[38] Realizing that she had not said everything about each subject, Fallaci consequently felt dissatisfied with the publication of the actual interviews in magazines. She therefore resolved to reveal everything in the book, including what originally may have been held back. This commitment to veracity exerted a wholesome, cleansing effect. "I feel as if a weight has been lifted from my heart."[39]

The interviews bear testimony to the perfection of a form that Fallaci has used successfully from the start and that she has continued to refine throughout her career. They provide an instrument through which she expresses personal views on such topics as friendship, politics, and aesthetics. At the same time, Fallaci becomes one of the most watchable journalists in the profession. What matters is not so much the completed interview as the performance that goes into its making—the pacing, refutations, revelations, aggregations of tone, and Fallaci's shaping presence. She emerges as a journalist without peer who uses her interviews as a stage, just as she does in *Penelope at War*, for a stunning dramatization of self.

During the meeting with Nilde Iotti, this longtime mistress of Palmiro Togliatti, head of Italy's Communist Party, states that, during the war, Communists were the first and almost the only Resistance casualties. Fallaci quickly argues against her position and refers to personal background as proof.

> It is not true. You Communists often commit this error and this injustice. There were not only Communists in confinement. There were not only Communists who fought. There were not only Communists killed. I could recite an unending list of my friends, and not yours, killed by Fascists, and nevertheless not Communists.[40]

She also chides Iotti by labeling wealthy Communists hypocrites and frauds. "It is easy to preach renunciation when renunciation is improbable. Rich Communists are liars."[41]

Following the interview, Fallaci uses an account of a bad dream to reveal negative feelings toward Communists. In the nightmare, she sees herself against a wall with both hands tied behind her back, facing a firing squad. The honorable Iotti then approaches dressed as a priest, wearing an expensive scarf and proclaiming that the execution would satisfy justice. Fallaci then recites her prayers: "The synthesis that derives from the thesis and antithesis of Hegelian dialectics according to the laws of historical materialism leads us to conclude that the theory of surplus value. . . . "[42] As she states the words *surplus value*, executioners fire and send Fallaci flying into hell where she burns. On Earth, the honorable Iotti falsely states that she thinks highly of Catholics and gives the impression that the Pope's death has filled her with sorrow.

Fallaci is much in evidence in the interview with Nilde Iotti and does not allow Iotti to occupy center stage. This same pattern reoccurs when she refuses to be intimidated by H. Rap Brown. "It would be hard to find a racist who is more racist than you are, a man more filled with hate."[43] She allows people to talk but stays in command from the first word to the last. After Anna Magnani complains that she can never find a man strong enough to dominate her, the actress finally asks: "Tell me, what do you really think of me?" Fallaci's reply concludes the interview. "I think . . . I think you're a great man, Signora Magnani."[44] When she catches Hugh Hefner in flagrant hypocrisy, she cleverly utters a familiar saying.

Fallaci: Here the donkey falls.
Hefner: What did you say?
Fallaci: Nothing. It's an Italian way of speaking.
Hefner: What does it mean?
Fallaci: It means that while I'll go to hell, you'll go to paradise, Mr.
Hefner. There, among the saints and martyrs, together with your
Bunnies, you'll go to discuss the sex of the angels.
Hefner: Do they have sex?
Fallaci: They don't.[45]

Fallaci's victims often react with predictable outrage when confronted with her aggressive style. She uses irony on Federico Fellini. "Not even about Giuseppe Verdi has so much been written. But then you are the Giuseppe Verdi of today. You even look alike, especially the hat. No, please, why are you hiding your hat? Giuseppe Verdi used to wear one just like it: black, broad-brimmed." He retaliates by labeling her a nasty liar and "rude little bitch."[46] The famous Italian director repeatedly broke appointments, made her wait, and then finally insisted on reading over the interview to make various corrections to his answers. Her low opinion of him is consequently revealed:

I used to be truly fond of Federico Fellini. Since our tragic encounter I'm a
lot less fond. To be exact, I am no longer fond of him. That is, I don't like
him at all. Glory is a heavy burden, a murdering poison, and to bear it is
an art. And to have that art is rare.[47]

The Spanish matador El Cordobés admits that she frightens him as much as an angry bull. "Why?" she asks. "Because you use words like the horns of a bull—I am not stupid."[48]

Fallaci also prods political leaders into saying more than they should. Despite U.S. financial and military aid to South Vietnam, she exposes Nguyen Cao Ky's latent anti-Americanism.

> I've never thought that the white race is a superior race, on the contrary. . . . You have to realize that the future is here among us, not among you whites. Europe is old, tired, dusty, and America should not be called "The New World" anymore; it should be called "The Old World." It's time is over.[49]

Fallaci's provoking questions also cause emotional and humorous reactions. Geraldine Chaplin speaks of her father and admits that she is afraid of him.

> I feel this constant reproof, this constant comparison, because I feel I'm in his shadow all the time, all the time, like all of us. . . . I feel that only when I'm no longer in his shadow, when I'm no longer afraid of him, that only then will I finally be able to do something myself.[50]

Alfred Hitchcock gives an unorthodox reason for filming so many thrillers over the years. "I spent three years studying with the Jesuits. They used to terrify me to death, with everything, and now I'm getting my own back by terrifying other people."[51]

Fallaci often rouses a subject to introspective eloquence, as in the case of the French actress Jeanne Moreau.

> Women, today, tend so much to minimize the gift of giving themselves and to belittle the woman who gives herself. In French novels of the last century one often reads this phrase, which I find so right. "I gave myself." Today it's no longer a gift, it's more like abandonment prompted by outside factors such as a pleasant evening, a momentary closeness, holidays, sunshine, whisky, a movie.[52]

The interview with the writer Natalia Ginzburg offers insight into Fallaci's autobiography. The story in the first paragraph of the introduction to the interview stands as a case in point. When Fallaci was a poor high school student, she often deprived herself of food to buy books. One day she bought Ginzburg's *È stato così* instead of a required table of logarithms, which contributed to her failing math that year. "I loved that little book because I liked her, that is, what I knew of her and because I liked her dry, virile style." She also underscores her desire to become a writer. "As an adult, I wanted to write novels and I dreamt of meeting her and asking her for advice."[53] Fallaci states that she read all of Ginzburg's books and specifically mentions *Le piccole virtù* and *Lessico famigliare*. Years later, her admiration turns to dislike. According to Fallaci, Ginzburg belongs to the leftist-oriented literary establishment in Italy that she detests.

During the actual interview, Ginzburg talks about her Jewish husband, who died after being tortured by the Nazis. Her story causes Fallaci to recall the frightening days of the Second World War. "It seemed to me that I returned to my childhood when we too, even though we weren't Jewish, lived with the terror of the doorbell ringing, the uncertainty of a friend coming to help you, or a Fascist coming to arrest you." When Ginzburg states that one never forgets the experience of suffering, Fallaci connects the comment to her participation in the Resistance movement against the German army. "Her modest, meager sentences brought back the torment of that time, the agony of those days, the fear of those notes that I had to carry and be ready to eat if a Fascist stopped me, my father telling me to warn everyone that someone had been arrested, the bicycle runs." She remembers the morning on which her father and three others were arrested in the middle of a square. "We were waiting for him and he didn't return. We waited all afternoon, evening, night, and the following morning, afternoon, night, and he didn't return."[54] The family initially had no knowledge of a formal arrest until they were informed and were able to visit him in prison. "A little man without a belt, tie, or laces on his shoes; a yellow face swollen from the beatings; a gentle voice that kept telling us not to worry; 'at the most, they'll send me to Germany; if they send me, I'll try to jump from the train.'"[55] The obvious difference between her story and Ginzburg's is that Edoardo Fallaci returned home, whereas Leone Ginzburg died in prison.

After meeting so many dignitaries, Fallaci no longer felt intimidation and began to accept these meetings as second nature. "The habit of being near the most diverse people canceled in me every complex or embarrassment."[56] Indeed, repeated encounters with intellectuals throughout the world actually resulted in disenchantment and lowered esteem. "Seen from up close, writers often create the same effect as actors: they disillusion you. They are often vain, incapable of humility, and less intelligent than they are or appear to be when they write books."[57] She views Italian literary society in a negative light and considers Italian writers prone to inbreeding and to the establishment of intellectual strangleholds. Years later, she was present at the awarding of the Strega Prize to Natalia Ginzburg and noted that many photographers, reporters, and writers in attendance had compromised their integrity through silence or cooperation with Italian Fascists.

When Fallaci's subjects read the interviews, they often complain that she has fabricated the quotations. She denies it but nevertheless does take a few liberties. "I transcribe the whole interview; then I make it into what I print in the same way that a movie director makes a film—eliminating and cutting and splicing." This procedure makes her a kind of impresario of interviews. "Of course, I'm an actress, an egotist. The story is good when I put myself in."[58] Although *The Egotists* reflects much that has remained part of the writer's thinking throughout her career, it testifies to a rising star's fervor but lacks the maturity and seriousness of *Interview with History*. Nevertheless, it combines a seductive journalistic style with linguistic clarity. More important, it provides a point of comparison to observe how the author's compositions evolve as she grows older and acquires more experience.

The writer maintains that, with the exception of *Penelope*, she has forgotten her early books. "It was some publisher who said to me: 'Let's get together; we'll make some money.' And I needed money and we did it. They do not belong to my work as a writer."[59] At the same time, it would be unfair to discard them as insignificant, as youthful errors of enthusiasm. They are early examples of Fallaci—the determined, conquering, and memorializing interviewer—taking her bows on center stage, overshadowing her subjects, and drawing most of the attention to herself.

Reaching for the Moon

5.

BY 1965, ORIANA FALLACI HAD ALREADY achieved a degree of fame in the world. Translators had worked her books into English, French, Spanish, and other languages. In addition, Fallaci claims that journalists from various countries began to copy her articles and declare them their own. Commentaries on her professional accomplishments began to appear in foreign newspapers and attested to the widespread popularity of the woman journalist from Italy. Through it all, she held tenaciously to the dream of becoming a literary writer, intellectually and emotionally recognized her capacity to produce the equivalent of Shakespeare in journalism, revolted against the splendid prison into which editors had placed her, and longingly eyed the vast and new horizons offered by space exploration as an escape. The big break came when her editor requested that she write about lunar conquest and astronauts. The fruit of the trip to the United States was a series of articles and a fifth book, *Se il sole muore*, the most important and mature publication of her career to that point.[1]

Many journalists would have proudly remained within the boundaries of a successful career that facilitated contact with the world's rich and fa-

mous and perhaps would have feared taking steps into new and unexplored
regions. Fallaci was different. She now had the opportunity to embark on a
new adventure and act as Italy's dynamic ambassador to America's space
community. It was as though she vicariously catapulted herself into the cosmos along with the astronauts. Fallaci's fame as an interviewer of famous
stars in show business had eclipsed other aspects of her talent and created
a mythical personality within the profession of journalism. The mystique
intensified further when she went to America to report on the moon.

The reportage not only consists of an investigative report on the National
Aeronautics and Space Administration (NASA), the sights and sounds of
America's space industry, and interviews of scientists and astronauts but also
projects Oriana Fallaci constructing her own stardom. It is the story of a
young woman from Florence reveling in scientific adventures, proclaiming
her views on everything from religion and love to politics and literature, and
pronouncing judgments with oracular authority. One critic says, "Throughout her chronicle Oriana is something of a Model 1966 Alice" wandering in
Wonderland.[2]

Fallaci's autobiography emerges prominently when she makes cross-ref-
erences to her father's opposition to space exploration and any benefits
that might accrue to humankind. As one critic notes, her dialectic arouses
an atmosphere of debate. "A dialogue between two generations, one earth-
oriented, the other space-oriented, is addressed to the author's father with
whom she argues about the past and the future. This unusual approach
makes for a polemical book."[3] According to Edoardo Fallaci, human beings
would always have the same problems, no matter where they might live, and
would do better to remain on Earth, where they can fish and hunt rather
than become victims of scientific research. He not only refuses to accept the
importance of *Sputnik* but even declines his daughter's invitation to take an
airplane to visit London's Botanical Gardens. "I love the Earth . . . I love the
leaves and the birds, the fish and the sea, the snow and the wind! And I love
green and blue and all the colors and the smells, and that's all there is . . .
and I don't want to lose it on account of your rockets."[4]

Despite paternal resistance, Fallaci remains determined to go to America
as planned, but instead of simply communicating her resolution, she places
what might have been a cold, logical decision against an intimate, lyrical
description of Tuscany as seen from her country home.

Through the windows came the fragrance of mushrooms and resin, the
woods were aflame with red and violet heather, the bunches of grapes hung

heavy with juice on the vines. It would soon be time for the grape harvest,
the grapes would boil in the vats, and in the intoxicating tranquillity the
chestnuts would start to fall with little round thuds.[5]

In the kitchen, her mother prepares blackberry marmalade; and, outside,
Cypresses offer seductive invitations to caress their soft, velvety branches.
On that beautiful autumn day, Fallaci fully understands her father's affection
for the earth but still resolves to visit the men in America who would soon
fly into outer space.

Although Edoardo fails to deter her mission, he reinforces affection for
the land of Tuscany and provides a source of consolation during uncomfortable moments. After flying to Houston, she finds the city and the dirty, spar-
tan motel ugly and depressing. During the night, intense loneliness motivates
her to call Edoardo and Tosca in Florence. Her mother can only talk about
Texas, imagining that it abounds with beautiful woods, vast prairies covered
with cattle, herds of horses, and cowboys wearing boots with spurs and ten-
gallon hats—the exact opposite of what Fallaci encounters. The exchange
with her father about his recent hunting expedition touches a nostalgic
chord, and she remembers the blind where she and her father would conceal
themselves from their unknown prey in the early hours of morning. They
would plan their strategy and nervously wait. The decoys in their cages
would begin to flap their wings and sing out a warning for the unsuspecting
prey. Then father and daughter would shoulder their rifles, aim, and as the
fluttering creatures whizzed onto the high branches of the cherry tree, they
would bring them down to the ground like ripe pinecones. Then with guilty,
uselessly repentant hearts, they would reload. "The waiting for the next flock
would be a tender cool shuddering, a serene boredom, a woodland whispering." In comparison to the beautiful dawn and landscape of Tuscany, she
finds the city of Houston even more repulsive than her lodging. "It was a
tomb of concrete and an asphalt road that led to NASA's Manned Spacecraft
Center."[6]

The tendency to place the subject matter in a personal framework ensures that readers continuously focus on Fallaci herself. They never lose sight
of her. She expresses her views on such subjects as technology, writing, death,
and religion. After arriving in Los Angeles, her visit with the space-age writer
Ray Bradbury produced an interesting exchange on technological processes.
She accepts Bradbury's view that earthlings must prepare to escape from
their planet because the earth could possibly explode or the sun cease to provide heat. When he admits his admiration for everything that aids humans

in becoming better, including plastic products and rockets, she counters by stating that a writer should exalt the small amount of beauty in existence, search for evil, and then denounce it. In her view, man should never be content but should seek truth only through rebellion. Her spirit of revolt again surfaces when addressing the question of dying. She can never understand those who say that death is normal and logical and that everything comes to an end. She refuses the concept of life as a transition to grass, air, water and then to fish, birds, or other humans. "For me, to live means to move with this body and this mind."[7]

During her second visit with Bradbury, the topic of religion arose, clearing the way for her revelation that the creed of her childhood had held her in a stranglehold. It had impeded the freedom of her spirit. As a young person, she was obsessed with statues of the saints and Christ crucified, reinforcing the image of a God creating heaven and earth in seven days. With the onset of incredulity and skepticism, she began to fear punishment and the fires of hell. The conversation with Bradbury freed her from spiritual captivity, placed old religious strictures far from the reality of the Space Age, and relegated biblical accounts like the Fall of Adam and Eve to the status of outdated fables. The Old Testament dogma that God created man in His image loses credibility as soon as an astronaut discovers intelligent creatures in other solar systems who possess nonhuman appearances. She concludes that man's great adventure into the universe breaks the chains of religion, as well as the force of gravity, and that humans have historically made up the idea of a divinity. "We can't do without God, and when he isn't there, we invent Him."[8] Bradbury upholds the thesis by affirming that the concept of a supreme being playing with material toys has become obsolete and that man has made himself God through his desire to ensure his continued existence everywhere in the cosmos.

This association between past and present continues in a meeting with Herb Rosen and again permits Fallaci's personal revelations. This specialist in electronic brain technology regards great cultural achievements as useless impediments to real progress and advocates destroying what has preceded the age of technology, including Florence, to facilitate a meaningful, rational rebirth.[9] His deprecatory comments shock Fallaci and trigger recollections of the destruction of Florence during World War II. To prevent the advance of American and British forces, German soldiers mined four of the five bridges spanning the Arno. The Fallaci family heard the consecutive blasts from their home and witnessed the red skies over the river. One of the demolished structures, the Bridge of the Holy Trinity, dated from the Italian Renaissance. The statues of the *Four Seasons* fell into the water below, and, even after reconstruction of the bridge, architects never recovered the head of *Springtime*. Fallaci's souvenir of cultural demolition not only solidifies her opposition to Rosen's point of view but also impregnates the exchange with regret, sorrow, and anguish.

During her visit to Downey, California, Fallaci entered the Apollo craft, experienced firsthand the physical limitations of the enclosure, viewed the movie demonstrating a simulation of the moon landing and, once again, introduced more personal memories into the narrative. That only darkness envelops a speeding capsule arouses the vision of astronauts lying on their cots in claustrophobic conditions, resurrecting the memory of her father's incarceration and his makeshift bed in an obscure cell.

> Yes, the prison bed was terrible, the night spent waiting for a dawn that might not come, I know. You lay there on the bed and watched the door: if the door opened there would be no dawn for you. For many there was no dawn: they had barely lain down to sleep when the door opened, and when they stood them against the wall the guns fired like meteorites in the cosmos.[10]

Fallaci also compares her father's loneliness during periods of captivity to the astronauts' solitude as they land on the moon. Edoardo experienced solitude and fear when confronted with the possibility of execution. What the space explorers feel surpasses his anguish. "Their fear, their loneliness is something beyond our knowledge. They have nothing with them, you understand me? Nothing except food and instruments and hope." In his confinement, Edoardo at least had the comfort of proximity to his beloved Tuscany. "You were without food and instruments and hope when you were in that prison. I know. But you had the Earth! Even if they killed you, you still had the Earth."[11] The two visitors to the moon would not have the comfort of dark, fertile soil; they would have only each other and a voice from NASA headquarters.

A moving moment occurs in Houston during the interview with Donald "Deke" Slayton, one of the most skilled and prepared of the astronauts. Their reserved exchange becomes much more emotional when he mentions that he flew over Italy during World War II. His statement awakens sensitive memories. "Like a blow, like a slap, it all came back to me—the wail of the sirens, the buzzing of those cicadas which weren't cicadas but airplanes, ten planes, twenty, a hundred, one after another, the whole sky filled with planes."[12] They sometimes flew so close to the ground that she clearly distinguished words on each fuselage and even observed pilots wearing helmets within glass compartments. Somehow these aviators managed to escape without harm like fleeing ants. Slayton's admission that in October 1943 he had bombed railroads in Florence provokes a stressful conversation and almost moves Fallaci to tears. "My eyes grew wet. It may be stupid, but my eyes always grow wet when I think of that day."[13]

Riding a bicycle, she was on the way to visit her imprisoned father. Tosca had prepared some warm soup in a pot, which she had strapped to the handlebars and delicately balanced. During the short trip, the air raid began; she could not untie the saucepan; she continued pedaling; the saucepan knocked against the handlebars like a pendulum. With every little bang, soup would squirt out, soiling the young girl's legs, dress, and shoulders. People wept and cried out to each other as bombs crashed into the ground. On that day, she headed for the shelter of a nearby bridge while praying with all her heart that God would let her make it. A bomb fell close by before she got there, spattering pieces of stone everywhere and creating a choking cloud of smoke. Then another exploded with a volcanic force that knocked her onto a pile of smoking debris. Lying there under the bicycle, she fortunately suffered only a foot injury. After hearing the story, a distraught and defensive Slayton profusely expressed his sorrow. "No! Oh, no! We missed . . . we missed a lot of targets, I remember. . . . I'm sorry. I'm very sorry. It was my job."[14]

Staring straight at Deke Slayton, however, she cannot help wondering about the face of her attacker and concludes that he must have had the face of a fine person as he dropped bombs on Florence at the age of nineteen. Her mind returns to the past and envisions Americans entering Florence after the German evacuation. She remembers how she hopped up and down, even with a sore foot, to see the infamous bomber but received instead pieces of chocolate from soldiers who pulled on her braids. While Slayton tells her that an astronaut's occupation will become as commonplace as any other, Fallaci is trying unsuccessfully to forget the shame she experienced as she accepted candy. Her mother had taught her that good girls never welcomed presents but also stressed politeness toward the bearers of gifts. A blushing and confused child, therefore, stood on a street in Florence with chocolate in her hand and looked with wide eyes at the marching conquerors. When the Slayton interview ends, Fallaci's final thoughts are of the irony in finally meeting the person who destroyed much of her city. "This man who will go to the Moon is the same one who twenty years ago nearly made me die of fright. At that time I hated him, I hoped he would crash with his bombs. Now I liked him and felt I was his friend."[15] They shake hands; she wishes him well; then he affectionately smacks her on the shoulder and leaves.

After inspecting space centers in California and Texas, Fallaci arrived in Orlando, Florida, to tour other NASA complexes and maintained her intense juxtaposition of personal recollections and events from the report. During her visit to Cape Kennedy in Florida, Fallaci met with Gotha Cotee, a NASA public relations escort, and read a copy of the survey "Courageous Women," which comments on the inner strength exhibited by astronauts' wives. An association with Tosca Fallaci's courage during the war immediately occurs: Edoardo, secretly fighting for the Italian underground, risked arrest every time he left his home. The day after Fascist agents arrested him at a munitions depot and took him directly to the dreaded torture center in Florence at Villa Triste, Tosca wept bitterly but mustered her determination to help him, put on her best dress, rode her bike to the infamous location, and nervously begged the murderous official, Mario Carità, for clemency. After receiving a scornful rejection—"You can go into mourning, Signora"—she began a search for possible witnesses against Carità or any of his men and discovered by chance that one of the torturers had shown disrespect toward Mussolini. She quickly returned to Villa Triste and threatened to publicize the information. "If you don't do something to help my husband, I'll tell them that you tore up the photograph of Mussolini." When Tosca received the good news that Edoardo had been released from Villa Triste and placed in a rat-infested prison, she was so happy, as Fallaci explains in her book, that she spontaneously aborted her unborn child in a miscarriage and then began a slow process of physical deterioration. "She began to suffer heart trouble during those months and since then her heart has never been the same."[16] Fallaci has always believed in her mother's courage, even though Tosca experienced fear in her actions, and expresses discomfort with the dignified composure of the astronauts' wives.

Extending the reflections on courage to her father, she remembers how he endured Carità's continuous beatings and constant questioning. She recalls memories of execution threats, his bound wrists, his face covered with blood, his teeth knocked out, and, through it all, Edoardo's scornful laughter. Despite his courage, he was afraid and looked like a white blur when she saw him in prison.

> Your whiteness was of fear, your eyes of fear, your voice of fear when you said don't cry, real girls don't cry, maybe they won't shoot me . . . maybe they'll just send me to Germany and I'll come back . . . but in the meantime you must swear you'll never give away the addresses, you'll never give up fighting them.[17]

Fallaci found it difficult to understand the absence of fear, the most human of all emotions, in the astronauts' wives. "Courage itself is born of fear . . . so then Christ, why weren't these people afraid? . . . What kind of blood did they have?"[18]

During her tour of NASA sights in Orlando, Fallaci had to return home after receiving a telegram stating that her mother had fallen ill. This emergency put the question of space exploration in a more personal context. Scientists wanted to create new races on distant planets but still could not prevent cardiac arrest or find a cure for cancer. Her thoughts must have been transparent to her mother.

> "I know what you're thinking."
> "What, Mother?"
> "You're thinking about the men who can go to the Sun and can't cure my heart."[19]

Tosca Fallaci never fully accepted her daughter's leaving medical school and on her sickbed remembered walking in the family garden and finding a dying pigeon that she wished to save. "Then I thought about you when you used to study medicine. Pity you gave it up. Perhaps you would have known how to cure him."[20] It was one way of telling Oriana that she had no right to denigrate anyone because she contributed nothing in the struggle against mortality.

During Tosca's convalescence, Fallaci did not forget her American experience and dreamt often of returning. After a few months, with her mother out of immediate danger, she decided to resume her work and headed to Huntsville, Alabama, to meet with Wernher von Braun, father of the *Saturn V* rocket and of the V-2 missile that rained terror on London during World

War II.[21] Throughout most of their exchange, Fallaci experiences an uneasiness that began the moment Braun entered the meeting room. His presence arouses in her the remembrance of a light odor of lemon, which strikes a perplexing chord until she recalls the lemon smell that permeated German soldiers—all of whom washed with a particular disinfectant soap. Whenever one of them came near, the sharp, pungent sensation entered her nostrils and even seemed to reach her brain and heart. "We all loathed that scent of lemon."[22] Fallaci's father used to say that collaborators reeked of it, and anyone having the smell spent time with Germans.

The lemon smell brings back from Fallaci's past a powerful memory. On a hot day in July, the child, her parents, and two Yugoslavian soldiers took refuge in an abandoned convent. The family had planted beans and wheat in the enclosed garden but had also hidden clandestine newspapers. When the sound of screeching brakes announced the arrival of Germans, Edoardo had to flee while his daughter hid the two Yugoslavs in the well, and, as enemy footsteps grew closer, his wife hurriedly burned all of the newspapers. "God they're coming, God let's hope they burn soon."[23] Storming into the room, they reeked of the sharp lemon smell, which overwhelmed the young girl. When Braun states that scientists must look into the real nature of things to get closer to an understanding of God, Fallaci remembers the Germans looking into the well and ordering the two Yugoslavs to get out. They climbed out and begged God to save them. "But God didn't hear them and the Germans took them away, together with their scent of lemon."[24] After Braun's final comment about the future being more interesting than the past, he departs, leaving the meeting room like an empty well.

As she stands before Braun, Fallaci experiences no disappointment in his mental capacity but uses the "odor of lemon" to refer to youthful remembrances of the German occupation and their atrocities. Hearing a German accent, she instantly associates Braun with the destruction of Coventry, Great Britain, and then mentally categorizes the creator of the *Saturn V* rocket as the scientist who rained terror on a civilian population. The entire encounter in Huntsville emerges as an allegory of her resentment toward Germans who arrested, shot, and tortured Italians during the occupation.

> The odor of lemon is not a physical scent. It is not that I was disappointed because von Braun carried the scent of lemon. No, it is an allegory. Far from being a disappointment, it was like a resurrection of my inability to forgive the Germans. And it is still not cured. I have been to Germany and I feel

uneasy there. I have never forgotten that they arrested us. When I have to deal with them, like with von Braun, I feel uneasy. Wernher von Braun was an intelligent man; he said interesting things. He had only one problem with me. He was German.[25]

The distaste that she felt for Italy's former occupiers would only disappear years later. In October 1986, she went to Cologne and spoke at a meeting of editors, booksellers, and publishers. Her talk dealt with her family's suffering during World War II, Edoardo Fallaci's arrest, and his subsequent torture. She reviewed for her audience how, shortly before his appointed date of execution, the entire family received permission to visit and to say goodbye. The heroic head of their household turned his daughter's fear to joy when he said that his captors would probably send him to Germany instead of shooting him. She believed that the Nazis had planned to send him to a lovely resort village for a cure from the torture inflicted on him by Fascists. After her mother explained that Dachau and Mathausen were death chambers, she grew angry. "Not knowing that it was one thing to be a Nazi and another to be a German, I nurtured a hatred toward Germany."[26]

In fact, Fallaci, even as an adult, has found it difficult to overcome her animosity. Before delivering her speech in 1986, she had gone there once or twice on business, left quickly, and persistently refused to do any book promotions. However, when invited to the meeting in Cologne, she finally came to emotional terms with the nightmare and attempted to establish peace with Italy's neighbor to the north. "I said to myself: this is a good occasion to say *enough*, to meet good Germans, fine Germans, who are not responsible for Dachau and Mathausen. Indeed they feel shame like good Italians, fine Italians, feel ashamed of Mussolini."[27]

An abundance of memories and sudden flashbacks in the midst of conversation remains a trademark of Fallaci's artistry and ensures her presence as the book's main character. In addition, she further personalizes her account through detailed descriptions. She wants her readers to experience what she sees and feels and thus reconstructs sights. She resorts as little as possible to pure historical narrative and invariably includes a personal reaction. During her visit to Downey, California, Fallaci traveled by helicopter to keep an appointment with Garrett Industries, the firm that was manufacturing such vital controls for capsules as heating, cooling, and oxygen systems. From her vantage point, she observes the sprawling, monotonous city, which seems to have no beginning or end and constructs a classic scenery description. Rows of small homes resemble the cells of a beehive; swimming pools in backyards reflect the brightness of light blue water; long streets stretch out like rifle barrels; artificial mountains stand like flat geometric cubes; columns of automobiles move steadily toward the space center, where huge parking lots await their arrival; junkyards filled with rust-covered cars dot the landscape. Arriving at her destination and entering the industrial hangers, she captures the depressing picture of workers on the assembly line and views their unchanging activities as absurd and senseless. The robotlike atmosphere of the workplace fills Fallaci with a sense of despair. "In front of each one of them, you would have wanted to scream out—move, wake up, work hard, do not allow yourselves to become addicted in this manner."[28] She ultimately accepts the necessity of their automated labor and gradually assumes an attitude of resigned pessimism.

During a stopover in San Antonio, Texas, Fallaci accidentally discovered the School of Space Medicine, learned that its directors select qualified candidates for the space program, and expressed a desire to take astronaut examinations. After passing prerequisite tests, she agreed to enter the simulator and participate in an acceleration procedure. Despite an inability even to look at a merry-go-round, to dance a waltz, or to take an elevator to a high level without experiencing nausea, she describes the main features of the centrifuge as though it represents an ominous kind of spinning wheel. "Seeing it from the control room was worse than receiving a blow on the head."[29] In the middle of the compartment below, an arm about ten meters long horizontally rests on a motor. The capsule itself at the very end of the bar resembles the sidecar of a motorcycle and contains just enough space for a person to lie down. Scientists behind a glass door electronically control the vehicle's movement from above. A calculator connected to sensors would monitor her body and immediately indicate any change that would require stopping the experiment. A television screen permits direct observation of every minute detail during movement. A motor initially accelerates, exerting only three or four g's, and then increases to higher rates of speed.

The detailed description allows readers to understand why Fallaci panics at the last moment and cannot enter the simulator. A Sergeant Jackson, a babyish twenty-two-year-old with blond hair and blue eyes, takes her place. The steel bar begins to rotate and quickly exerts on Jackson five then seven then ten and finally thirteen g's. As Fallaci narrates, she can no longer see the spinning arm, only a blue circle, and observes on the screen that the young sergeant's face resembles a formless mask on which she can distinguish only teeth on the verge of flying away. Fallaci then emphasizes her panic. She begs control authorities to shut down the power. However, the subject's capacity to endure the force motivates an increase of speed to exert a force of fifteen g's. She prays that he will raise his hand to signal a desire to stop; one scientist exclaims that the soldier is holding on; authorities finally give the order to conclude. The minutely detailed report illustrates the writer's skillful descriptive technique, brings to life one aspect of testing strategies at the center in San Antonio, but also keeps readers focused on the journalist's involvement.

When Fallaci met with astronauts in Houston, she paid close attention to their manners, trappings, and physical appearances. More important than verbal sketches are her accompanying commentaries. She assumes a position of moral authority and passes strong judgment on each of them. Her first interview is with Deke Slayton. "He was tall and strong, attractive; the tweed jacket was enough to show he hated ties." She perceives the harsh, hard, and virile face of a soldier who fearlessly braves the elements. His sharp blue eyes reflect irony and sadness. When he slowly raises his hand and introduces himself, he reminds Fallaci of her father. "I knew that voice: it was a voice from home. Just like yours, Father—low, vibrant, very beautiful."[30] She underscores his disappointment after learning that a heart murmur disqualified him from the honor of being the first to orbit Earth and finally highlights what she considers his existential core. His eyes indicate bitterness, indifference to fame, passion for flying, and the stubborn Lutheran faith of his ancestors who emigrated from the peaceful fjords of Norway to Wisconsin.

The interview with Alan Shepard, the first American to fly into space, stresses the proud, pretentious nature of his character. "If he isn't the first, he gets irascible, jealous, unhappy: when they chose Glenn for the first orbital flight, he was unmanageable."[31] She concludes that fame has gone to his head, aggravating the already existing passion for women, money, race cars, and applause. Despite his friendly reception, he also exhibited a certain reserve. "He was holding out his right hand invitingly and smiling at me with so much warmth that I could have fried an egg in it; and he, however, would have eaten it together with my hand, my arm and all the rest of me."[32] She ultimately loses all respect for him when he reveals his desire to become rich, discusses a contract with *Life* magazine, and goes so far as to regard his voyage into space more as a lucrative commercial enterprise than as a patriotic adventure. "What a joke, Commander, to think that one day the grandchildren of our grandchildren will speak of you as a romantic hero and that maybe your name will be given to a mountain, plain, a desert on the moon or on Mars."[33]

When she meets John Glenn, the first American to orbit the earth three times in outer space, Fallaci portrays him as a flurry of carrot-colored freckles and emphasizes the white teeth that line the most contagious smile ever seen. Fidelity to his wife, Anna Castor, and a disciplined code of conduct, which excludes alcohol, smoking, cursing, hunting, and all forms of arrogance, motivate the writer to attack his morally secure attitude. She proclaims that space travel invites doubt and loss of faith rather than confirmation of a personal creed. Glenn maintains that science has never demonstrated the existence of life on other planets. His belief that the Bible nowhere denies the possibility of alternate forms of God's creation in the cosmos causes Fallaci to wonder whether he would ever kill any of them. Although Glenn acknowledges the possibility of conflict, he remains optimistic that visitors from Earth would encounter friendship.

The second round of interviews took place a few weeks later and started with Walter "Wally" Schirra, whom she describes as rather short and thickset with heavy cheeks, plump lips, thick eyebrows, black eyes, and a dark complexion. He immediately wins her favor by his personal manner and questions. "Are you Italian? I've been to Italy several times: Rome, Naples, Genoa, Venice. Never to Sicily, however. . . . You could say that I am Italian too: my father immigrated from Sicily." He teasingly claims that Florentines are misers and not generous like Sicilians, quoting Stendhal to support his statement. Even though she yells back a rebuttal and calls the French writer a liar, Fallaci admits her affection for Schirra. "I liked this land monger whose father went to America in search of fortune and who brought a son into the world who would fly into space."[34]

Her favorite astronaut, Theodore Freeman, immediately won her highest favor when she discovered that he wrote poetry about Mars.

Soft silver hills, how I recall the sight
The woods were blue, and quivering in the night
A sky of green did put its emeralds pale
Upon the hilltops, and the air was light
The bright air lighter than a bridal veil.

According to Fallaci, NASA must have hired Freeman as a joke or just did not realize what a jewel they had. "Nobody to me was worth more than

Theodore, not even the ones I liked best. . . . Theodore was what I'd have liked to be and am not: purity, simplicity, faith." After their meeting, she vows always to remember his spirit. "I shall never sufficiently lament having found him and then immediately lost him, like a mirage."[35] She ends her account on the sad note of his unexpected death. "Suddenly, in the darkness, you find a Theodore and then immediately you lose him. Five months later Theodore died. His plane blew up, he was flying, and he died."[36]

In succeeding interviews, an eleven-minute time constraint prevented doing much more than breaking the ice. The quickness of these encounters explains why Fallaci communicates sparse information about the astronauts except for their baldness and elderly appearance. She feels that in a land where youth is a pagan and cruel cult they seem old. She receives this impression first from the youngest in the group, Roger Chaffee, who views traveling to the moon only in terms of serving his country and demonstrating the technological capacity of NASA. "Anything else is just fantasy. Adults don't live by fantasy."[37] As he leaves the room, Fallaci overhears him mumble that the meeting with her was a bore and a waste of time. The next candidate, Richard Gordon, immediately complains about his profession and regrets his lack of time to read, travel, or go to the theater. His expertise as a technical specialist requires that he make these sacrifices and that he remain faithful to it.

Her interpretation of Neil Armstrong is that his position as an astronaut represents a simple transfer from one office to another and that he has no personal ambition other than the success of the space program. He denies possessing a romantic temperament or any taste for adventure. "I loathe danger, especially if it's useless; danger is the most irritating aspect of our job."[38] When she first met him in 1964, she felt an aversion to his cold, calculating character and had the same reaction when she met him again in 1969 before his trip to the moon. "Of the fifty-two American astronauts, he is the one who most possesses the virtues of a robot."[39] According to her, nothing interests him except flying machines and the technical knowledge to accomplish his mission. Fallaci admits her failure to establish any type of sympathetic human contact with him unless she pronounced the words *Mercury*, *Gemini*, *Apollo*, or *LM*. Despite her opinion of Armstrong, she acknowledges that his temperament is suited for space voyages. "One goes to the moon in fact with computers and mathematics and numbers, not on the wings of sweetness and imagination. One survives there on a life support system, not with music and literature."[40]

When Fallaci wonders why Alan Bean is so very bald at the age of thirty-two, he attributes it to the boredom of his humdrum routine and considers himself too old to have dreams or to live dangerously. The fifth exchange takes place with Edward White, whom she considers extremely handsome. He volunteers information on his friendship with Deke Slayton while working with him on the Gravity Zero Project. He later joined Slayton in preparation for the moon landing and looked forward to that momentous occurrence. During her final interview, Fallaci challenges heaven and earth, the living and the dead, to prove that "the sixth old man," "that creature," Eugene Cernan, is only thirty years old. She describes him as overcome by melancholy, colorless, and exhausted. "It seemed that he could never have been young." Although he politely tells her about his difficult but dignified life, as well as a courageous and upright past, she finds it impossible to develop any real interest in him. "I couldn't care less about what he had to tell me."[41]

Fallaci finally concludes that the astronauts—elderly and somber in appearance—do not enjoy their youth and holds herself up as a point of comparison. Despite her rich and varied experience, the tremendous demands of journalism, and an age as advanced as theirs, she feels like their daughter. Offering Cernan, White, Bean, Armstrong, Gordon, and Chaffee her advice, she affirms how wonderful and free from constraint the age of thirty is and celebrates the lucidity of these years. "If we're religious, we're convinced of our religion. If we're atheists, we're convinced atheists. If we have doubts, we have doubts without shame." Much in the manner of a wise elder, she insists that no trip to the moon is worth losing an inner dynamism and urges them to reverse their early old age. "So wake up, stop being so rational, obedient, wrinkled! Stop losing hair, growing sad in your sameness! Tear up the carbon paper. Laugh, cry, make mistakes."[42]

In a later work, she writes that those who went to the moon "were stupid men" and similarly formulated less than flattering opinions about them.

> They had stupid faces of stone and they didn't know how to laugh, they didn't know how to cry. For them going to the moon was a scientific feat and nothing else, an achievement of technology. During the trip, they never said anything poetic, only numbers and formulas and boring information; when they showed a bit of humanity it was only to ask for the latest football scores.[43]

Fallaci alters her belief that the space program resembles a cancer capable of destroying the healthiest of astronauts when she meets Charles Con-

rad, commonly known as "Pete." After he declines to welcome her, stating that he does not give a damn about men or women who write, she automatically likes his rebellious spirit and would prefer to see Theodore Freeman go to the moon with him. Although thirty-four years of age, Pete looks
twenty-four and would seem younger with more hair. His contradictory personality fascinates her. He hates conferences but holds them anyway, likes
to drink but does not, and enjoys women, although while walking he covers
his eyes to avoid looking at them. "He is so funny, Father. He restores our
faith. . . . He proves that one can survive space contamination, that there's
still hope, that they aren't all automatons in this kind of society."[44] His idea
of a hero is someone who goes out in his underwear because he wants to
prove something he believes in. In her summary statements, she and Pete
joke about founding a chain of drive-in restaurants on the moon, Mars, and
other planets.[45]

In her interviews with the astronauts, Fallaci's unremitting interjection
of opinions and autobiographical details do not lower the quality of her reportage but simply play her world off against theirs. Her projection of *self*—
through personal reactions and judgments—is everywhere present in the
book. She relates the pleasure she found in conversation with her parents
about her trip to America and their spontaneous reactions. Her mother
quickly becomes a Slayton fan, especially after hearing about his heart condition, and also loves Glenn because he goes to church, says beautiful things
about God, and remains faithful to his wife. Edoardo remains bitterly opposed to the whole concept of space exploration and even finds little ways
to frustrate his daughter's keen interest. When she speaks about the Apollo
capsule, he turns away from her in boredom. He particularly criticizes the
space food that she brought back from Downey and places on her bookshelves for everyone to admire. When the toast disappears, Tosca breaks the
news. "Keep calm and I'll tell you. Your father was looking for some dry
bread to crumble for the fish. And there wasn't any. So he went over there
and took your toast. He even needed a hammer to break it up." The package
of dehydrated lobster soon suffers a similar fate.

> "Who took it this time?"
> "Who do you expect took it? I did."
> "You promised me you wouldn't take any more."
> "I promised you nothing of the kind and you know I can't stand having
> rubbish like that among the books."

"What did you do with it, Pa?"
"I put it in the pig food."[46]

He justifies his sabotage by stating that hogs need phosphorous, a substance contained in lobsters.

Fallaci's caustic humor surfaces during her encounter with Paul Smith of the United States Information Service (USIS). After she received a Ford Foundation scholarship, which would have subsidized her travels, he sent her a questionnaire about her belief in God, church affiliation, dietary needs, and health records. She answered all questions except those pertaining to religion. Mr. Smith in turn sent back a cold letter in which he ordered her to list people and places she intended to visit, as well as a timetable for the accompanying interpreter. Her description of her reply leaves no doubt about her true feelings. She refuses the interpreter and explains that she would escape if forced to have one. In addition, she provides no schedule of her travels.

> Besides I never know myself when I am coming and when I am going. It may happen, for example, that I'm in Saint Louis and suddenly get the idea of going straight to Mexico City to buy a sombrero. . . . You may find this odd, my father says it's crazy: but people who write are always a bit crazy.

She further chides that the Federal Bureau of Investigation (FBI) would inform him of her whereabouts and adds that she would never go to Russia for material on her book. "In Russia, I should finish up being shot in front of the Kremlin for Great Indiscretion and Gross Lack of discipline."[47]

A period of dead silence followed. In mid-April, Fallaci inquired about Paul Smith at the Foreign Correspondence Center, discovered that he was fine, and learned that the Governmental Affairs Institute still hoped to receive her along with other dignitaries. She therefore began preparations for departure and assumed that her American contact had simply refrained from continuing an unpleasant exchange. However, twelve hours before leaving, the American embassy called to reveal that the USIS had revoked the scholarship. She discovered then that Paul Smith had made the decision and also left a message with the liaison officer at the Information Center. "He says that if you're going to America to see the cherry blossoms, you're late: spring is over. If you're going to America to see the launchings, you're early: no launchings are scheduled till next year."[48] Undaunted, Fallaci went to an

Italian bank that very same morning to borrow the money and departed once again for the United States feeling quite content. Arriving in New York, she called "Say It with Flowers" and sent Smith a big bouquet of cherry branches in bloom. The writer's relentless insistence on having the final word illustrates a sense of humor that asserts itself even in her serious writing but also indicates a refusal to be upstaged by anyone.

By the time of her space reportage, Fallaci had absolutely no hesitation about asserting her own personal voice in her articles. She continued her commentaries about herself and her family and pronounced moral judgment on American astronauts. She did not avoid ambitious descriptions of herself in the midst of scientific achievements and placed emphasis on her own centrality. She describes how Pete Conrad, Theodore Freeman, and she ate together and took leisurely walks on the beach right before the launch of the Saturn rocket at Cape Kennedy. In Fallaci's account, Theodore speaks of the Saturn rocket as a prayer shooting into space. According to Pete Conrad, however, Fallaci's story differs from what actually happened. Before the launch of the Saturn rocket, it was only he, Conrad, who walked with Oriana along the beach and had dinner with her. The astronaut's version also differs from Fallaci's version of events in another way: he states that he—not Freeman—referred to the rocket as a prayer surging into the cosmos.[49]

According to Conrad, Theodore Freeman emerges in several instances as his alter ego. For a long time, he and Fallaci had a great attachment for one another. While writing *If the Sun Dies*, she kept in touch with him and corresponded about the book, asking for his opinions. He would answer but on condition that she not reveal his real name. She consequently divulged many of his views but, to avoid repercussions to Conrad from NASA for spending too much time with a foreign journalist, ascribed them to Theodore Freeman—in spite of her assertion of documentary accuracy. A significant detail. The sad part of the artifice is that Conrad does have a deep, thoughtful side to his temperament. But he did not always want to have fun at the time. Fallaci's description of him emphasizes the opposite and makes him look like the producer of comic situations.[50] In contrast, the composite portrait of Theodore Freeman as sensitive and artistic projects the image of poet and philosopher.[51]

After the Saturn launch, Fallaci returned to New York and then heard about Freeman's death in the crash. According to her report, the accident happened when his plane developed problems and his parachute failed to open. However, Conrad explained the incident differently and emphasized that Freeman ejected too late from the aircraft. It had nothing to do with the parachute not opening because of a deficiency.[52]

Despite Conrad's and Fallaci's conflicting versions of events, she, as author, enjoys a definite advantage in her attempt to rewrite the reality of America's space program because she combines her talent as a reporter with an intensely personal style and proven ability as a literary journalist. The end result is not "fictional" literature. Such a label would suggest that Fallaci has made up her story. *If the Sun Dies* reflects an active imagination, literary techniques, and an epidemic use of *self*. The book presents information in a fully developed manner instead of the cold, clipped, factual style of newspaper documentaries. It develops a detailed portrait of America's space industry and connects it to Fallaci's own life to give greater depth and dimension to her account.

At the end of August 1965, Fallaci left New York for Texas to investigate the private lives of astronauts but, time and time again, made herself more central than the space heroes. In Houston, she encountered James McDivitt in a grocery store wearing shorts and a Hawaiian sport shirt. He offered her a lift on his tandem. Italian readers consequently see Fallaci pedaling through the Nassau Bay suburb on the backseat of a bicycle behind an American astronaut. In the same article, they witness her dining at the home of Richard Gordon, a member of the final group chosen to land on the moon. They read about her arrival for the appointment and how she strolls across his lawn while he plays with his children. They smile with admiration as his wife, Barbara, prepares a spaghetti dinner. ("What else does an Italian eat but spaghetti?") Setting the table, McDivitt refuses all offers to help. "No, no, this is a job that I always do. This and washing the dishes and cleaning the floor."[53]

The article then shifts attention to Fallaci's polite, witty, and dominating presence. On the dining room table along with fine china and silverware, *Se il sole muore*, the book in which she writes of Gordon, catches Fallaci's eye. (Its English translation had not yet been published.) Gordon expresses his concern. "You know, I'm a little worried about this. We're all a little worried. None of us reads Italian and seeing our names, we wonder what she has written. That wicked person, what has she written?" Opening the volume and pointing to a page on which his name appears, he hands it to his guest. "What does it say? Translate." His children sit on the living room sofa clumped together like a bunch of grapes and listen with wide eyes as an embarrassed Fallaci obeys orders. "The second oldest was thirty-five years old and had six children. He was short and sturdy, had black eyes and hair and a forehead wrinkled into a thousand repressed curses. I liked him and felt that I had already seen him because he was like someone familiar from my youth, the all-purpose type of Resistance fighter." "Curses? I don't curse!" he interrupts, as though offended. All of his children jump up and run to the kitchen, crowing to their mother, "That one says that Papa curses." Barbara sticks her head out with a ladle in her hand. "Excuse me, Dick does not curse. We have been married for twelve years and I can swear to you that Dick does not curse."[54]

Fallaci tries to explain that the word *curse* is a metaphoric expression and injects light humor into the account.

> "But you said it. What will Italians think of me?"
> "Daddy, what are Italians?"
> "Those who live in Italy."
> "Daddy, is Italy a place?"
> "Yes, it's a place, far, far away."
> "On this planet?"
> "Children, that's enough now; go to bed."

After sitting down for the meal, a hurried swallow of food almost causes Fallaci to choke as Barbara catches her eye before signaling her husband to pray. Husband and wife bow their heads, close both eyes, and reverently utter words of thanksgiving while their guest, taken by surprise, says nothing, clears her throat, and blushes a little. Barbara exclaims:

> "There is something I would like to ask you. May I?"
> "Yes, Barbara, certainly."
> "Did you have a fight with the Pope?"[55]

Impressed by their simplicity, Fallaci enjoys the rest of the meal and the lemon dessert. When the doorbell rings, Barbara answers it and silently guides a string of guests into the parlor. Gordon explains to Fallaci that she is the main attraction and has to make an appearance before all of her old friends: astronauts Frank Borman, Eugene Cernan, Roger Chaffee, R. Walter Cunningham, Russell Schweickart, Edwin "Buzz" Aldrin, Edward White, Jim McDivitt, and all of their spouses. According to Fallaci, her exoticism consists not so much in her Italian origins—Italy was too far away on another planet—but rather in her New York residence. Many of the wives have never been there and ask about the big city. "Do you find New York beautiful?" "Aren't you afraid of living in New York?" The men express more interest in her negative commentaries on Braun, Nazi Germany, Mussolini, and fascism. According to the space walker Edward White, his colleagues and he learned everything they know about those subjects from books or films and, therefore, do not understand her hatred, especially in view of democratic conditions in contemporary Germany. Gordon refuses to judge or condemn her rancor and the animosity of other survivors. "We live in a kind of limbo; we don't know what hunger, arrests, and bombardments mean."[56] The lively conversation shifts to the savagery of America's Civil War, the enmity it caused between the North and South, and the analogous resentment that still divides Europe after the atrocities committed in Poland, Yugoslavia, France, Italy, Dachau, and Mathausen from 1940 to 1945.

Dinner at James and Marilyn Lovell's home, located next to Pete Conrad's in the Seabrook suburb of Houston, again provides her with center stage. Fallaci eagerly converses with her hosts, their neighbors, and their guests, Dr. and Mrs. Joseph Kerwin. Learning that the physician would fly into space as the first medical specialist, she attempts to pose a technical question but cannot complete her sentence. "Italian?! Do you know Sophia Loren?" he interrupts vivaciously. The conversation immediately centers on the famous actress, whom Conrad and Lovell also worship. Their wives are more interested in knowing about Alain Delon, why he left Romy Schneider, and Peter O'Toole. Fallaci excites their imaginations with the fairy tale of her country's celebrated heroine: "Once upon a time, there was a beautiful girl whose name was Sophia Scicolone."[57] Conrad uncorks two of the four bottles of Chianti that Fallaci sent him the year before, keeps two in reserve to celebrate a safe return from the next mission, and listens spellbound to the fable of Sophia Scicolone (Loren).

One moving moment in Houston demonstrates for her readers the NASA community's icy discipline regarding the hazards of space travel. A telephone call awakens Fallaci early one morning. "Hello. I am Faith Freeman, Theodore's wife. I heard you were in Houston. May I come to visit you?" One hour later, she knocks at the motel door along with her twelve-year-old daughter. Both the tall widow and her daughter look beautiful in their pink dresses.

"I brought you a copy of the *Houston Daily*. It talks about the letter you sent me together with a copy of the book. Thanks for dedicating your book to my husband. What a shame that you are leaving. Otherwise I'll have a party for you. I'll give it when you return."

"So you remained in Houston, Mrs. Freeman."

"Oh yes, Houston is a nice place; the climate is pleasant; my friends are sweet. My Faith goes to school here. And I even have a job—nurse for cancer victims. Why should I leave Houston? Right, Faith? Faith, honey, say something, smile."[58]

According to Fallaci, the child rarely favors anyone with a happy face and still seems to harbor the grief of her father's loss ten months earlier. "My Faith will be a model when she gets big. Her body is perfectly suited; don't you think so?" Fallaci wonders about her inner strength. From the moment of her husband's death, she refuses to shed a tear, dress in mourning, or afflict friends with her sorrow.

"Mrs. Freeman, don't you ever cry?"

"I don't believe in tears."

She rises, embraces Fallaci, and comments on her beautiful clothes and how they accentuate the French perfume. "I believe in life. Life is so beautiful. Life is a sublime gift, a miracle. Every morning, I smile and I say to myself that I am happy to be alive."[59]

The articles from Houston not only reinforced the basic message that astronauts were good, simple Americans but again placed Fallaci in the limelight surrounded by respectful, hospitable, and historical figures. In reality, they were not just investigations of the private lives of astronauts. They were journalistic mosaics about Oriana Fallaci's performances in their private lives.[60] The same performance journalism occurred during the summer of 1969 when she reported on the first moon landing.[61]

Before the first moon launch, Fallaci attended a press conference with a group of American journalists who were interviewing the astronauts via television. Walter Cronkite sent her a note asking whether she wanted to ask them anything. She wrote down her three-word question and sent it to him.

Cronkite: "I have a question here from Oriana Fallaci. . . . The question is: are you afraid?"

Neil Armstrong: "Well," he hesitated, "You know, the adrenalin goes up."

Fallaci: "Ah, bullshit. Say you're scared!"

Fallaci yelled out loudly to everybody in the press room. "Who cares about the adrenalin! Tell me, tell me, fear, fear! Walter, ask them about fear!"

Later, in another interview, Fallaci stated that she asked Armstrong the question as a child would. "That's the secret." However, her behavior also illustrates a Fallaci first-person performance designed to force a celebrity—in this case the first man who would walk on the moon—to respond to her question on her terms.[62]

Her article on Wednesday, 16 July 1969, from Cape Kennedy emphasizes herself with a telephone in her hand excitedly reporting to Italy an on-the-spot oral account of time clicking away to the final dramatic moment of zero hour. She stands there awestruck, spontaneously and repetitively describing the *Saturn V* rocket as it slowly leaves the ground and launches into space. The account then keeps the spotlight on her, along with a squadron of journalists, as she rushes to an airplane to fly to Houston where she follows Apollo's lunar voyage. The image of Fallaci wearing headphones at NASA headquarters then emerges. She recounts how, on 16 July, Armstrong describes the view of North America from the little window and how, on the next day, Houston informs the travelers of the day's news on Earth. More important, she focuses on the message indicating their landing. "From Tranquility Base. The Eagle has landed."[63] At that moment, readers see Fallaci's incredible outpouring of emotion, as well as the entire NASA assembly's shift to loud applause and jubilation. "Not only in the auditorium but also in hallways, radio stations, telegraph rooms, offices, and in the Control Center where they tell me that Braun cried like a baby. And Wally Schirra cried and so did many of the astronauts and project directors."[64]

Her public sees her wide-eyed before the huge TV screen when Armstrong turns on the open circuit. "At that precise moment, the screens lit up and we saw what the whole world saw. We saw the LM's legs, the lower part of the LM, and the moon's horizon. And then we saw that foot, that big foot that descended looking for the rung of the little ladder." She describes his final leap from the last step, his first words on the lunar surface—"I am at the foot of the ladder"—his slow and measured movements, Aldrin's exit with a camera, both men's experiments with walking, and the rushed completion of all operations before ending their mission.[65] Fallaci marvels at their success and wonders whether human destiny will always be as simple from this moment forward.

Fallaci introduces the group of astronauts designated for the next lunar journey, with a special emphasis on Pete Conrad. "For me he's not another astronaut going to the moon; he's my brother."[66] From the day of their first meeting in 1965 in his NASA office, she says, they had never lost contact and had grown to appreciate each other. Fallaci had come to esteem his wife and four children and, returning from long trips, would invariably call them. Failing to do so, they would telephone to discover where she had been. She enjoys telling anecdotes about how he, as a student at Princeton, had seen Albert Einstein eating strawberry ice cream and walking with one foot on the sidewalk and the other in the street. On the eve of his flight to the moon, she states that his biggest worry is whether he will curse if something goes wrong with the landing because everyone—from NASA directors to television producers—has forbidden him to use foul language. She also claims to have found the solution. "Pete, I'll explain what to do. I'll teach you two or three [curses] in Italian and you can say them. In America, nobody understands them and everybody will be happy in Italy."[67] According to Fallaci, she wrote his favorite Italian curse (*accidenti*) on the sleeve of his space suit and knew that he would say it as he stepped down from the LM ladder. She also chose him as the subject of a novel in which she would write about his life, his ancestors, and how he met his wife, Jane.

Conrad's testimony suggests that Fallaci exaggerated and embellished some information, as though her imagination magnified her own presence and importance.[68] Conrad states that the anecdote about giving him the Italian curse word is purely fictional. He maintains that she neither suggested the word *accidenti* or another curse to him nor did he ever agree to say what she suggested. In addition, writing such a word on the sleeve of his space suit never occurred.[69] In Fallaci's account, she herself, Conrad's wife, four children, mother, sisters, in-laws, cousins, and friends all gather at the Melbourne Motel on the night before his lunar journey. Conrad arrives, speaks to his family members, and then turns his attention to Fallaci. Seeing Fallaci's tears, he embraces her and growls, "If you cry, I'll not say that phrase that you like so much, understood?"[70] In her article, she states that Conrad said the word *accidenti* (damn it!) a second before putting his foot on the lunar surface.

Here too, the astronaut repeatedly denied every bit of the curse story. "I never remember talking to her about it or swearing in Italian."[71] The party at the Melbourne Motel actually took place two nights before, not one night before as Fallaci has it. A party on the eve of a launch was traditional, but Conrad was not there. Instead, he spoke to his family and friends from crew quarters. He freely visited them two nights before (at the time, astronauts were not quarantined before space flights). He did not stay long—approximately 6:30 to 7:00 P.M. Many of these same people had gone out to Cape Kennedy to visit on that second day before the momentous occasion; in fact, Conrad took his ninety-year-old aunt into a lunar simulator.

In *Se il sole muore*, Fallaci describes a car wreck in Las Cruces, New Mexico, that involved several of the astronauts and claims that the automobile driven by Pete Conrad was demolished and found overturned in a ditch. Actually, as Conrad explains, he was not driving the car; he was sitting in the right front seat; a NASA chauffeur was at the wheel; and the vehicle was not as damaged as she suggests.[72]

Conrad also disagrees with Fallaci about his speech on the moon. She places herself and him at a French restaurant in New York City on Fifty-fourth Street. According to her article, he hopes the president will not deliver an address while he is on the moon because he hates ceremonious, historical oration. She immediately reacts:

"Pete, I would not want to be in your place if only for the sentence that you would have to state the moment you leave the ladder. What the devil does one say who gets there second?"

"I know! I'll say what I thought hearing Neil's words—'That's one small step for man, one giant leap for mankind'—I thought: it's probably a little step for him, but for me it's a damn big step. Understand, I have short legs and the last step of the ladder is so high!"[73]

Conrad's side of the story completely contradicts Fallaci's report. In August 1969, at the time Armstrong made his speech about that one small step, Fallaci sat with him at his home in Houston. She immediately assumed that the American government had prepared it for him for propaganda purposes. He countered by assuring her that the United States government had not written it and that Neil Armstrong had figured it out on his own. When she refused to believe him, he composed his moon speech on the spot to prove his freedom to deliver an original declaration. "Look, Oriana, I'm the shortest guy in my office; I'll say it was a small step for Neil but it's a big one for me."[74] He then bet her five hundred dollars that he would say those words to demonstrate the lack of government control over speeches made by astronauts. They shook hands to seal the wager. Conrad did say what he promised; Fallaci accurately recorded it in an article.[75] However, she mentions nothing about how Conrad composed his moon speech or that she made a bet with him and never paid it. The astronaut has needled her over the years, continually reminding her that she owes him a certain sum of money.[76]

Despite her proclivity for amplifying her own centrality, Fallaci's articles on space proved immensely popular. Readers enjoyed them and accepted her statements as gospel truth. Average Italian readers vicariously lived her experiences and took note of their prima donna who did what no one else in the country could do. Rizzoli Editore collected several of her articles on the moon and published them as a book. The 1970 *Quel giorno sulla luna* (*That Day on the Moon*) was immediately adapted for children by Alberto Pozzolini and made available for use in Italian classrooms. The editorial division of *Europeo* created an international copyright office to sell her work and to protect its ownership. Fallaci acquired the reputation of a moneymaker for her magazine and earned the nickname *"la gallina delle uova d'oro"* (chicken with golden eggs).

Movie Screen in Southeast Asia

6.

IN 1967, FALLACI ENTHUSIASTICALLY requested to go to Vietnam, initiating an eight-year adventure as a war correspondent. In every sense of the term, the bloody debacle in Southeast Asia was a turning point.[1] She dove headfirst into the inferno of war and produced a series of articles for *Europeo*, as well as the prizewinning book *Niente e così sia*. Fallaci was one of the very few women reporting the conflict, but more important than her gender was the active brand of reporting that she accomplished. In her entire reportage from Vietnam, the desire to understand what a soldier thought and felt as he killed the enemy motivated her personal involvement in conflicts, patrols, and even a bombing mission against Vietcong positions. At the same time, her talent as a writer so permeated every line that it drew her readers into a vicarious reliving of events. Into her participatory journalism, Fallaci injected literary trappings of social realism. Utilizing powerful techniques of immediate and concrete portrayal, she brought the Vietnam War to life and captivated an audience, attentive to every detail of her adventure. Above all, Fallaci the war correspondent maintained her propensity to write personally, and she emerged as the main character both in the book and in her articles.

Beginning with her arrival in Saigon on 18 November 1967, she constructs the first formal scene by describing the sights that catch her attention en route from the airport to her hotel. At Than Son Nhut terminal, she makes her readers aware of the dangerous situation. "Jet fighters, helicopters with heavy machine guns, trailers loaded with napalm bombs, stood in line with unhappy-looking American soldiers."[2] Once in the city, she shares her surprise at not immediately seeing the full impact of the war. "There was a chaos almost gay in this Saigon in November of 1967. . . . It seemed more like a postwar period: the markets filled with food, the jewelry shops stocked with gold, the restaurants open and all that sunshine."[3] Much to her amazement, she finds herself in the tranquil atmosphere of a hotel that creates the impression of a city oblivious to the country's agony. "Even the elevator, the telephone, the fan on the ceiling were working, and the Vietnamese waiter was ready to respond to any gesture you might make, and on the table there was always a bowl of fresh pineapple and mangoes." Her concluding observation projects the image of an author forced into existentialist considerations. "Dying didn't occur to you."[4]

Fallaci—heroine, adventurer, correspondent, writer—places herself in the bloodiest battle of the war at Dak To and, through her writing, arouses admiration for her courage and boldness. Readers see her on the way to the battle site. In the helicopter, there is room for only four passengers in addition to two pilots and machine gunners. Combining description with commentary, she relates the fear of one of her fellow passengers—a television commentator—and uses his convulsive shaking to facilitate a transfer to her on-top-of-the-situation first personism.

> I felt so ashamed that I suddenly became another person—calm, lucid, alert. While he was groaning I leaned out of the helicopter and coldly watched the hills on the left, the black smoke coming from the napalm dropped by the Americans on the North Vietnamese. . . . I wasn't the least bit worried by our flying down the middle.[5]

During the description of her first night at Dak To, Fallaci accentuates her presence in a mortar attack that forces her to seek safety in one of the bunkers on Hill 1383. Although it is a light bombardment that lasts an hour, she still has time to develop the image of a woman journalist crouched in a shelter yet doing her job as a war correspondent. She listens to a group of soldiers conversing about draft dodging and takes on the role of expositor of ignoble motives. Their conversation casts new light on the character of many combatants, as well as their real attitudes toward the conflict.

> "You see, he told me he had to take care of his mother and so he managed to stay in Los Angeles and built himself a swimming pool."
> "Well, Jack was even smarter."
> "What did he do?"
> "He started drinking and drank himself into an ulcer, so they turned him down because of the ulcer."
> "Roll on the ulcers!"

According to one of the men, his friend Howard was the most skillful at obtaining a deferment:

> "When they asked him if he liked girls he said: 'Goodness no, everyone knows I go for boys.'"
> "Is he a queer?"
> "Of course not. You crazy? But if you say you're queer, they turn you down flat, didn't you know?"
> "No, dammit. Suppose I said it now?"
> "Too late, buster. You should have thought of it sooner. I should've, too."[6]

Once back in Saigon, Fallaci has the opportunity to expose her sympathetic attitude toward the Vietcong. She interrogates two enemy prisoners, develops their personalities in free colloquial exchanges, and projects her frame of mind in the forefront. Her obvious pro-Vietcong attitude also surfaces at other moments in the book. Nguyen Van Sam, the terrorist who had blown up the My Canh restaurant, reminds her of Edoardo Fallaci twenty years earlier, when he sat in a Fascist prison cell. Her description of their discussion, which lasts from midnight until two in the morning, stresses his humaneness and heroism as he suffers brutal torture at the hands of the South Vietnamese police. When she finally addresses his killing of so many people, he shifts the guilt to the American side. "I felt, well, I think I felt the way an American soldier must feel after he's dropped his bombs on a defenseless village. The difference is that he flies away and doesn't see what he's done. I did see it."[7] The second captive, the young girl Huyn Thi-an, proudly refuses to answer any questions, remains totally committed to the revolutionary cause, and projects a resigned dignity, reminiscent of a Madonna.[8]

Her tendency to romanticize opposition to the American presence also emerges when she publishes excerpts from the diary of an unknown Vietcong fighter. The selections emphasize the pain of separation from a beloved, the many tears shed in sadness, references to the American devil, and sufferings caused by American imperialists. In publishing the intimate thoughts of Le Vanh Minh, she openly expresses her preference for the adversary and chooses to cry much less for the Larry and Johnny types who arrive in Vietnam with their vitamins, rations, and modern equipment. The publication of Le Vanh Minh's love poetry further ennobles his cause, thereby lessening the positive image of American soldiers.[9] Although many of Fallaci's Vietnam articles displeased the U.S. military, she still had complete freedom to publish as she desired. The writer came fully to appreciate her autonomy during a later visit to Hanoi, where North Vietnamese authorities attempted to control everything she did and wrote.

In February 1968, Fallaci visited the city of Hué, where a savage battle took a terrible toll on human life and described the evolution of her pro-Vietcong attitude. Her reflections tend to become more universal than particular, and she expresses her shame as a member of the human race. "Suddenly I've been seized by a fear that isn't the fear of dying. It's the fear of living."[10] After an American lieutenant saves her from a sniper, a conversation ensues in which the soldier labels her a liberal journalist who unfairly and conveniently disparages Americans in favor of enemy forces. He points out that he, an American, has killed to protect her life, whether or not she likes it, and that she is free to leave with a clear conscience. He, however, lives with the knowledge that he has killed someone and must remain to do more of the same. Fallaci appreciates his point and questions her own objectivity in analyzing good and evil. "God, how hard it is to judge, how hard to see where good and evil lie. Was I wrong, then, when I chose to weep only for Le Van Minh and Tuyet Lan? I seem to have gotten into a blind alley."[11] This unique conversation indicates that Fallaci begins to doubt her views on what is right and wrong.

Covering the Battle of Hué, Fallaci becomes overwhelmed by the extraordinarily high number of civilian casualties. In her opinion, both Americans and Vietcong bear the responsibility for causing so many deaths. However, the salient feature of her commentary is the strong condemnation of enemy forces. For the first time, her comments toward them contain directly critical and negative overtones. "We can thank the Americans and the Vietcong and the South Vietnamese. For instance, it would be hard to decide if the Americans killed more with their artillery and machine guns and napalm or the Vietcong with their mass executions." The Vietcong had summarily executed throngs of people, killing anyone who refused to shoot at an American helicopter or who had refused cooperation in any manner. Writing of the massacres, she expresses her dismay. "We seem to be looking at Mathausen, Dachau, and the Ardeatine ditches. The world hasn't changed . . . and neither have men. Whatever the color of their skin or their flag."[12]

In May 1968 during the Second Battle of Saigon, the Vietcong executed captured journalists and contributed to further strengthening her disenchantment. She saw photographs and visited the execution site to reconstruct the tragedy. Her outrage at the guerrilla group stifles the positive feelings she had expressed earlier. This evolution of her attitude emerges as one of the most important aspects of her reportage of the war, as well as of the book *Nothing and Amen*. News correspondents had labored under the impression that they were immune from enemy killings. "The Vietcong had never shot journalists before. Never, since the war started in Vietnam. Anyone who was captured got away unhurt."[13] However, the brutal murders of Bruce Pigott, Ronald Laramy, Michael Birch, and John Cantwell were acts of pure barbarism. The subsequent execution of Ignacio Ezcurra, the young Argentinean reporter from *La Nacion* whom Fallaci had befriended, completed the deromanticization process and shattered any earlier idealistic visions she had of the Vietcong as freedom fighters. Her realization that even they behaved like animals is summarized in her response to the situation.

> It is hard, and it grows even harder, to accept the fact that the Vietcong do such things. In other words, that they aren't knights dedicated to justice and freedom, as we've painted them until now. It's sad, and it grows ever sadder, to admit that they are like the others—beasts like their enemies.[14]

Fallaci's having viewed the casualties in Hué and the photographs of slain colleagues was part of her technique to construct the scene realistically. She herself saw the mass graves filled with Vietcong victims and the pictures of slain reporters. The realization that not all Vietcong atrocities had been photographed, whereas pictures of brutalities committed by Americans or South Vietnamese always seemed to surface, provided her with a more objective perspective.[15] She might have viewed the death of Ezcurra and the other journalists in the same context as the brutal slayings of so many other innocent people. However, the vision of Ezcurra with his hands bound, with a bullet wound in the back of his head, shattered any abstract philosophical notions she might have had. "In my heart those five corpses had upset me as much as the corpse of Martin Luther King had upset the blacks of Washington, and instead of burning the shops on Fourteenth Street, I'd simply burned my sympathy and my admiration for the Vietcong."[16]

Shortly after the discovery of her own personal truth, Fallaci received a copy of Blaise Pascal's *Pensées*. The writings of the French philosopher offer some insights into the realization that truth is not always clear-cut and perhaps communicate the most satisfactory explanation for the chaotic state of affairs in the world, as well as for man's inhumanity to man. According to Pascal, heroes may frequently delude us, while objects of scorn may suddenly become attractive. The knowledge and understanding that the ideals of truth and falseness blend in real situations change Fallaci's absolutist views on right and wrong. "Everything is partly true and partly false, and right and wrong are mingled and those you respect may disappoint you, and those you despise may move you."[17] Pascal's belief that each person contains both the angel and the beast goes right to the heart of the matter and succeeds in easing Fallaci's mind. "Pascal had deeply modified my absolutism, my blindness."[18]

During her days and weeks in Saigon, Fallaci, following the pattern of other literary writers who also worked as journalists, gleans material for her articles on the fabric of life in the capital. True to her pattern of active involvement, she enters the closed world of Buddhist monks, writes the intricate history of their protest movement, and tells the story of the young schoolteacher Huynh Thi Mai, who burned herself to death on the terrace of the Tu Nghien pagoda. She interviews the venerable mother, Thich Nhu Hué, who commanded six thousand priestesses and alone gave them official permission for self-immolation.[19]

Fallaci weaves her observations together and composes a tapestry that remains scrupulously documented while simultaneously placing herself in the midst of daily existence. The collection of anecdotes for *Europeo* resembles short stories, with Fallaci as the main character. "The Execution" focuses on diplomatic efforts to save Americans whom the Vietcong threaten to kill in retaliation for placing three of their men before a firing squad. "The Children of Saigon" portrays Fallaci's encounter with three children sleeping on the sidewalk as she takes a walk late one evening. "The Stranger" depicts the impenetrable personality of an impassive physician, Dr. Khan, who tells Fallaci that he no longer understands the words *peace* and *liberty*, as used by Sartre and Pascal. "The Prostitute" consists of a conversation with a hooker in a bar, her views on the infections brought by Americans, advances made toward the interviewer herself, and Fallaci's rapid retreat. "The American Official" summarizes the anger of a foreign service officer after having invited two North Vietnamese to the American embassy as a prelude to negotiations and then seeing South Vietnamese officials arrest them, knowing that the action will automatically eliminate all future negotiations.[20]

After forty days in Saigon, Fallaci prepared for her first departure in February 1968, and although she would be back in time for the Second Battle of Saigon, at the time she felt as guilty as a deserter. The country and city had worked magic on her: the surrounding death and destruction made life so vibrant. In existentialist sentences, she writes enthusiastically about her newly formed friendships and her enjoyment of such ordinary things in life as food, city noises, and crowds of people. She loves and admires the miracle of birth and appreciates her own life.

After arriving in New York, she received a telegram from her editor to prepare an article on American reactions to news and television reports from Vietnam. A few intellectuals like Dr. Benjamin Spock protested and went to jail but, by and large, Fallaci discovered a tremendous lack of understanding of the Vietnam War, as well as scandalous indifference, and records many of these observations in her book. Dining in an Italian restaurant on Fifty-sixth Street, she speaks with the owner, who feels terror listening to the news about the war. His son works at the Defense Department studying Vietnamese and awaiting orders to leave for Vietnam. Sitting at Fallaci's table, he compares the British loss of empire to America's inability to obtain victory and gets into a violent argument with someone sitting next to him. The next day, her manicurist wants President Lyndon Johnson to declare an armistice and bring all the troops home. A taxicab driver insists that the military drop an atomic bomb on all of those "yellow faces" but changes the subject after she points out that even Americans would die. When her pharmacist hears where she has been for the preceding two months, he asks whether she had enjoyed herself.[21] A long-awaited attack on Saigon had begun at this point and arouses a quick reaction.

Once Fallaci learned that the Tet offensive had begun, she wanted it clearly understood that no power on earth could keep her from going back to Saigon. On Wednesday, 7 February 1968, she returned to the beleaguered

city via Bangkok on a military plane. The aircraft had to circle Tan Son
Nhut Airport until a lull in the battle at the southeast gate. Once on the
ground, she quickly ran to shelter and had to await armed escorts to enter
the capital; VC snipers lined the route to the downtown area, which had
become unrecognizable. A curfew began at two o'clock in the afternoon; store
owners had barred their windows; only armored cars circulated in the streets;
fighter planes and helicopters hovered above. The front line had suddenly
emerged right in the city itself. Even journalists had to submit to a seven
o'clock curfew. Fallaci was almost shot in a square surrounded by barbed
wire when she could not find the exit. She saved herself by shouting that she
was a journalist. The guards had already fired warning shots. Since the curfew also applied to restaurants, Fallaci ate military rations at the France
Presse office next to her little hotel, which had run out of food. Everyone in
the city felt the suffering of deprivation. "I had forgotten what it means to
be hungry."[22]

In her book, Fallaci reconstructs the First Battle of Saigon with great
detail and precision and explains how the Vietcong had successfully penetrated the city on 29 and 30 January. The battle itself lasted only twenty-four
hours. They had arrived from the country, had smuggled their weapons into
the city on pushcarts, and then during New Year's celebrations had begun
their attack. Wearing red ribbons on their left sleeves, they had moved slowly
toward their objectives: the American embassy, radio station, governmental
palace, police stations, explosives depots, and army barracks. No one had
realized an attack was in progress, and it had taken two hours to realize that
the assault on the embassy building was not an isolated event. In the heart
of the capital, the middle class had refused to help any of the invaders, who
had found themselves forced to retreat to the poor neighborhoods of Gia
Dinh, Cholon, and Phu Tho Hoa.[23] On Friday, 9 February, Fallaci visits these
areas and compares their destruction to Berlin's after World War II. In
Cholon, she finds the battle still raging and two American journalists, who
had been wounded ten minutes before her arrival. She sees government
troops execute six young VC soldiers between the ages of fourteen and eighteen. On Sunday, 11 February, she rides in a helicopter over Cholon and
reports that the neighborhood, along with one-fourth of Saigon, no longer
exists. General Nguyen Ngoc Loan, in charge of the city's defense, had chosen
to flatten large areas with incendiary bombs to destroy enemy soldiers. Despite an apparent victory, rumors had begun to circulate that a second attack
would occur within fifteen days.

In Saigon, Fallaci had begun to feel the effects of endless death and needed to leave for a period of time. However, she took advantage of her stay in the capital to obtain an appointment with Prime Minister of South Vietnam Nguyen Cao Ky. The six-hour interview took place in a villa in Rue Cong Ly. The interview covers his reputation as a playboy, his affection for his second wife, and his severe criticism of his own country's politicians. Nguyen dismisses America's altruistic motives as pure economic selfishness and responds to the rumor that someone in his own government has already planned his assassination. His coldness and impenetrability impress Fallaci. "He's a Vietnamese like plenty of others, neither tall nor short, neither strong nor frail, and physically distinguished from the others only by a black mustache that stands out on his dark amber face." She sees him as unattractive, sad, and arrogant; his glance is direct but at the same time somber and melancholic. What he says, however, greatly interests her and makes a profound impression. On his side of the barricade, Nguyen alone dares admit he belongs to a powerless, inefficient, corrupt regime. "I am the only one who says the Americans are here not to defend us but to defend their own interests and set up a new colonialism."[24]

Fallaci left the war-torn country for a new series of reports from Hong Kong. Her poetic description of the city's beauty, as well as its documented history, precedes an analysis of the Communist threat from neighboring China and its ever-present menace in the minds of the population.[25] On 4 April 1968, she flew to Memphis, Tennessee, when an assassin shot Martin Luther King Jr. to death. Thirty-six hours after the assassination, she stopped in Atlanta for King's funeral at the Ebenezer Baptist Church and then flew to Washington, D.C., which, with ten thousand soldiers on patrol, resembled a city under siege. Touring until two in the morning with a black photographer and an Armenian journalist, she compares the setting to Vietnam as guards stop them on streets that are as deserted as those in Cholon and Gia Dinh had been during the curfew of the Tet offensive. She also comments on how arrogant blacks were to whites who tried to help them.[26]

Fallaci left the United States; journeyed to India, traveling between New Delhi, Banaras, Punjab, and Kashmir; and investigated the Maharishi Mahesh Yogi and his teachings on Transcendental meditation, as well as Shanti Baba's alleged ability to produce objects from nothing through the power of thought. In both instances, she doubted their authenticity and concluded that they were greedy charlatans. Throughout the research, she is so attentive to rumors of an imminent Vietcong offensive that she fails to appreciate the landscape and humanity of a country that has always appealed to her: "At any other time of my life, I'd certainly have let myself be enchanted by the sight of an elephant decorated with rugs and flowers, or of a woman walking in her sari, balancing a fine copper jug on her head, or of a holy man praying beside the Ganges as the sky reddened in a fiery sunset."[27] She could certainly meditate on the desperate poverty and resignation of a people who do not rebel or struggle. However, the news of a new offensive against Saigon wakens her from a state of lethargy.

Fallaci unexpectedly learns about the events from the only radio in a Tibetan community at the foot of the Himalayas near Dharmshala in Kashmir. She had gone there to interview an ex-god, the Dalai Lama. His wisdom, as well as the serenity of his monks, so impresses her that she wonders whether retreating from the world, its battles, its violence and every responsibility, is the best path to follow. Everything seems to flow harmoniously and peacefully. The woods are calm; only a slight breeze rustles the leaves; the sharp summits of the Himalayas brightly loom like organ pipes. "Fear had no meaning anymore, and the word 'God' might have one."[28] Walking in the village square, where her car had been parked, she hears a school radio broadcasting news in English on the formation of a new Indian government, the possibility of Paris peace talks, and then the massive Vietcong attack throughout South Vietnam. "The guerrillas attacked with rockets and mortar at various points in the capital including the airport of Than Son Nhut, and more than a hundred and twenty-five other places including provincial capitals and American bases."[29] Despite a scheduled visit to Hardwar, sacred city of the Hindus, on 6 May 1968, Fallaci orders her chauffeur to return to New Delhi to catch the 3:00 A.M. plane to Saigon. She again arrives in the war-torn country, continues her bitter research as a correspondent, and realizes that it is impossible to substitute man for God.

Oriana Fallaci's approach to her role as a correspondent allows opinions, ideas, and commitments to permeate projects so intensely that her reporting merits comparison to the active zeal of missionaries. Her articles on the war in Vietnam, as well as *Nothing and Amen*, stand as classic examples of journalistic activism. The personal nature of her accounts runs counter to more conventional notions of objectivity and permits bias. Her general opposition to wars and the transformation of her pro-Vietcong feelings, along with the commitment with which she embraces her work, emerge as highly salient features of her book. She spent nearly a year on location in 1967 and 1968, interviewing fighting men in dangerous situations and almost losing her life in Hué, and would continue to visit the country at various intervals for the next seven years.

Fallaci is part of an active generation of the 1960s and 1970s and, much like the literary journalists John McPhee, Tom Wolfe, Joan Didion, Richard Rhodes, and Jane Kramer, she calls attention to her own voice. She consciously inserts character, motivation, and mood into her nonfiction. Norman Sims indicates that standard reporters and some writers of fiction criticize the new approach to journalism. They aim their disapproval at the category of literary journalists to which Fallaci belongs: "It was flashy, self-serving, and it violated the journalistic rules of objectivity."[30] In Fallaci's case, she understands the difference between fact and falsehood but does not accept traditional distinctions between literature and journalism. Tracy Kidder's commentary summarizes a defense of the approach taken by correspondents like Fallaci. "Some people have a very clinical notion of what journalism is. It's an antiseptic idea, the idea that you can't present a set of facts in an interesting way without tainting them. That's utter nonsense."[31] Fallaci's tendencies are far from machinelike. Her exposés exemplify nonfictional prose that uses the resources of fiction and that pushes writing into the realm of art. She elevates the war in Vietnam to imaginative truth writing—a genre as creative as fiction. At the same time, her articles and books cast herself on a Southeast Asian movie screen as a star immersed in spiritual and physical dangers, always ready to speak out against the war and be counted.

Fallaci's national and international success aroused in her an awareness of the power of her pen and her personal image. She had become *la Fallaci*, a journalist whose assertive aggressiveness demanded absolute control over situations and people. The eruption of this attitude occurred full blast in March 1969 when she journeyed to Hanoi to interview an American prisoner of war (POW) and to complete the first direct reportage on North Vietnam by an Italian journalist. Although she had never espoused communism, she still obtained a visa with no difficulty from the North Vietnamese, who knew that she had expressed anti-American feelings in her writings on the war in Vietnam and that she had, for a while, regarded the Vietcong as heroic resistance fighters. In the diary of her twelve-day sojourn, Fallaci not only explains that she has entered the country through Cambodia with a delegation of Italian Marxist women but also portrays herself as an astute journalist who would never allow Communists to use her as an instrument to further their political goals.[32] Immediately on arrival, she becomes aware of the reality of censorship. "I have already understood, in fact, that here I will not be able to work like in Saigon, with the freedom of movement that Americans give you even when you speak badly of them."[33]

Her interview of a young Vietcong heroine with one leg further reinforces her impression of a society indoctrinated by propaganda. Two guards listen to the exchange, scrupulously taking notes, as the girl explains how she killed her first Americans and how happy she felt as they blew up. She then claims that Americans cut off her leg three years later. "I am a victim of American atrocities."[34] All of Fallaci's monitors nod in a satisfied manner. However, they raise their eyebrows as Fallaci's questioning breaks through their game, and she gets the girl to admit that a small group of South Vietnamese soldiers had tortured her and then amputated her leg.

Fallaci's refusal to submit to the Communists' restrictions and remain within the officials' boundaries characterizes all of her interviews in North Vietnam. During her stay, Fallaci unexpectedly receives word that General Vo Nguyen Giap has decided to receive her, along with the three Marxist women of the Italian delegation. The famous military hero, who defeated the French at Dien Bien Phu in 1954, had already written a book entitled *People's War; People's Army*, which had earned money in the United States. Considered a shrewd strategist, he rarely meets with visitors but nevertheless welcomes the small group on a Saturday evening with the proviso that they not use tape recorders. During the presentation, Vo lets his guard down when he admits that the North Vietnamese have lost half a million men, distances himself from the Vietcong, admits that the Paris peace talks will never resolve anything, and indicates that only military maneuvers will settle the war. He iterates that Americans already know they will never win, that the Saigon government grows weaker by the day, and that the United States will soon encounter their own Dien Bien Phu.

After the conference with Vo, the four women quickly return to their hotel, assemble, and reconstruct the interview while it is still fresh in their minds. Fortunately, the four women follow their professional instincts: Vo soon withdraws some of his comments and gives Fallaci an official text, which he insists she use for publication and which contains few of his original statements. Fallaci obeys and submits it to her editor, but she also includes the original, authentic forty-five-minute interview. She herself states categorically in the article that they would only appreciate writings that suit their ideological goals. The North Vietnamese never forgave Fallaci for her independent judgment and for having dared to exercise the power of critical thinking. They had loved her earlier in 1968 when she exalted the Vietcong at the expense of Americans but easily forgot her praise of their guerrilla fighters when she criticized North Vietnamese wrongdoings and shortcomings. Insults and accusations of working for the CIA immediately followed the appearance of her articles on their country. The interview with Vo, which spread like wildfire around the world and even made it to the desk of Henry Kissinger, would provide the needed introduction for a future interview with the American statesman.[35]

Near the end of her stay, Fallaci interviews an American POW and credits herself with obtaining his release. She describes Navy Lieutenant Robert Franchot Frishman as young, very tall, thin, pale, and sweet looking. He enters the meeting room wearing oversized gray pants and a blue sweater over a checkered shirt. He walks bent like an old man and supports his injured right arm with his left hand. After fluttering his eyes as though the low light bothers him, he acts as though glad to see her. Not speaking to anyone for one and one-half years has begun to take its toll. Villagers had shot down his plane on 24 October 1967 and, after his capture, wanted to kill him. According to Fallaci's article, Frishman claims they were right because he had destroyed their homes. Uttering his last admission of personal guilt, he glances at the nearby official almost as though to verify that he understood. Eagerly accepting a cigarette, he again eyes the supervisor and adds that he does not want to be impolite. "I mean to say that Vietnamese cigarettes are very good, great, exceptional. I really like them a lot, really."[36] His daily schedule includes rising at five-thirty and two good meals a day. The moment he alludes to poor treatment, as proven by his emaciated appearance, the Vietnamese guard takes a giant step forward and immediately silences the prisoner.

According to Fallaci, Frishman agrees that war is horrible, that Americans do not understand its ugliness since the fighting occurs far away, that Americans are the aggressors against the North, and that no logic justifies this action. She reports that his future plans are to resign from the military, return to a university to study political science from a new perspective, and celebrate his return home with Fallaci at Mamma Leone's restaurant. He now believes in the necessity of a political solution to the war and the absolute legitimacy of the protest movement in the United States. When their time expires, he quickly gives Fallaci his wife's address with the message that she not consider him an invalid despite the injury to his arm. As he leaves the room, she is moved by his anxiety, fear, and obvious subjection to enemy brainwashing.

In August 1969, one month after the first moon launch, Robert F. Frishman was freed by the Hanoi government and arrived in the United States. Her interview echoed through the international press in numerous foreign newspapers, as well as in the American magazine *Look*, and even attracted the attention of the State Department, which issued a release stating that Frishman had spoken with an Italian journalist after a long period of isolation. This meeting could have been weighed in the decision to let him go. Fallaci had earlier criticized the way the Communist government treated prisoners and indicated Frishman's terrible lack of physical strength. She, therefore, expressed no surprise when hearing about his release, understanding how skillful Hanoi authorities had become at using events to create impressions favorable to their cause. According to Fallaci, they attempted to counteract her criticism of their propaganda machine and to create the impression of goodwill during the Paris peace talks.[37]

She claims that, when Frishman returned to New York on 7 August, the State Department did everything in its power to deny publicity favorable to Hanoi. Nevertheless, newspapers had released early stories on Frishman's arrival and dozens of journalists, correspondents, photographers, and TV crews were stationed all over Kennedy International Airport. Immediately after his arrival, the young pilot's superiors segregated him at Bethesda Naval Hospital for medical treatment and, on 2 September, allowed an impromptu press conference to which neither Fallaci nor anyone else from *Europeo* was invited. According to Fallaci, the navy command clearly intended to spare Frishman the questions that she would have raised and that he would have preferred not to answer. She did receive a copy of the text, objected strongly to its tone and content, and claimed that 95 percent of it came directly from the Pentagon's propaganda machine. After Frishman began a tour to support the United States war effort, Fallaci angrily claims that he contradicted himself. What he had not stated to her during the interview in Hanoi suddenly became the subject matter of his speeches. She wrote an open letter in which she protests what she considers his fraud.[38]

By ignoring her and refusing to laud her publicly as the principal reason for his liberation, Frishman had essentially hindered the full production of a Fallaci image—the liberator who, through the power of her pen, influences autocratic governments to free prisoners. She consequently has to teach Frishman a lesson and unleashes the full fury of her anger on him in the emotional first part of her open letter. She compares him to Huyn Thi-an, the young Vietcong girl she interviewed earlier in Saigon, and claims that her stoicism, pride, and even her scornful attitude far outshine his conduct in dignity, courage, and patriotism. "It does not seem to me that you acted the same way during the meeting we had." She next scolds him for saying that she had shown a sincere understanding of his situation yet failing to state that maybe the North Vietnamese had freed him precisely as a result of the publicity generated by her articles. "But gratitude is not one of your virtues." She further chides him for his change of attitude. In the Hanoi prison, he had agreed that war was terrible; after his return, he contradicts his statements. "I see that you again love war and joyfully describe the joy of hearing bombs fall on Hanoi and are pained that they no longer fall. Lieutenant, how quickly you have changed."[39] Her biggest surprise occurs not from Frishman's praise for his jailers, since anyone with a little intelligence would have seen that they forced him to speak that way, but from his statement at the press conference that he had resisted out of pride. "Lieutenant Sir, you did not resist anything and there was no pride in you." She even refutes his claim that he and others had recourse to American ingenuity, pointing out that he tried none of it with her even though she had given him many different opportunities to signal or to speak sincerely. "Instead I had to extricate news and impressions from you with forceps, insisting, sweating, and interrupting your constant returning to the generosity with which you were treated."[40]

During the original conversation, Frishman had made an engagement with Fallaci for dinner at Mamma Leone's restaurant, where they would have celebrated his return to freedom. When he breaks the appointment, she feels disillusioned but is then relieved, no longer desiring to eat or drink with him at the same table. "I'll tell you why. Heroes enchant me, but not everyone is born a hero. I ask you only to be a man. And being a man even means looking into the eyes of witnesses that you prefer to forget." Fully understanding that she has become a source of discomfort, she also censures herself.

> In reality, I am always embarrassing: for everyone and even for myself. What I narrated about the war in Vietnam was not comfortable for either one or the other: after my reports on Saigon, Americans considered me a Communist and, after my reports on Hanoi, communists called me a reactionary serving Washington. It is the destiny of whoever thinks according to his own conscience, and I accept it with pride.[41]

When Fallaci first sees Frishman at five o'clock in the afternoon, 7 August 1969 at Kennedy Airport upon his release, she is overjoyed at seeing him. After having written encouraging letters to his wife, cautiously telling her about his deformed arm, and communicating messages from the meeting in Hanoi, she had developed an attachment to the prisoner. When the airplane door opens in New York, she changes her attitude. The stairs are rolled over and a navy official descends in uniform. Standing on the other side of the barrier with journalists, Fallaci watches him walk toward the nearby podium with what she describes as an offensive look of determination but, ignoring it, she begins to cry out, "Frishman! Frishman!" However, he does not turn or acknowledge the call. His wife, standing next to him, whispers something in his ear as she points repeatedly at Fallaci. Yet he continues to look in the opposite direction. In her typically unyielding manner, Fallaci jumps over the divider and manages to pull at his arm and call his name before several policemen pull her away. Nevertheless, she does have time to say something as he turns in her direction. "Frishman! Don't you remember me?" "Yes, I do remember you. And how!"[42] Fallaci never saw him again.

The conclusion to the open letter dwells on the influence of Frishman's superiors. "They tell you what to do and what to say." In Fallaci's mind, they had immediately begun his indoctrination in Cambodia and had ample time to make suggestions, even insisting that he stay away from her, the only Western observer to see him in prison. In fact, Fallaci's name had been pronounced for the first time in Laos when journalists asked if what she had written was true and heard him give an affirmative answer. They then asked if Hanoi's treatment was as good as she had reported and received a less than enthusiastic response: "Adequate." Despite an attempt to justify what she considered the prisoner's unacceptable conduct, Fallaci returns to her reprimands, enlarges their scope to include the American military, and thanks God that someone always manages to defend the sacred rights of truth. "Is Mr. Frishman now a free man, or has he gone from the Hanoi prison to the one in Washington? It would probably be enjoyable to be forced to admit that to interview Mr. Frishman one has to go to Hanoi." Before concluding, she leaves the door open to receiving a refutation. "I am always happy to be wrong when it is a question of saving the dignity of a man."[43]

Although they provide unique testimony, Fallaci's two articles about Robert Frishman also point to the potential weaknesses of her personalized journalistic style. POWs in North Vietnam were allowed to be interviewed by pro-Communist journalists from Cuba, Albania, and other countries, but they had forced practice sessions to rehearse what and how they were supposed to communicate. With the slightest resistance, they were subject to

brutal forms of torture. Thus, measuring the statements Frishman made after his release against those pronounced while in prison hardly seems pro-
ductive or just. Indeed, Frishman himself admits that his tune changed after
his release but points out that there is only so much you can do with a gun
pointed at you. His view is that intelligent readers would see right through
Fallaci's accusations of inconsistency and would understand how much du-
ress military pilots were under when in Communist prisons.[44]

As to Fallaci's claim that her interview weighed heavily in winning his
freedom, the former POW could not say whether it helped or not. His picture
appeared in *Europeo* and revealed his weight loss. The North Vietnamese
might have released him to prove their benign treatment of prisoners. Maintaining that he could not read the minds of his captors, Frishman spoke of
Fallaci without bitterness. On the contrary, he praised her interview in Hanoi,
claimed that she assumed immediate control, and stated that she came across
as a warm individual as she did her job. Through the grapevine, he learned
that other interviews had taken place and how forceful authorities had been
as they persuaded detainees to give specific answers. He pointed out that
Fallaci was different. She had insisted on no preconditions or prepared questions, as would normally be the case. In fact, officials soon tried to end the
interview by saying that he was tired. They realized that, since Fallaci would
not allow them to push her in a specific direction, the conversation was not
going as they had intended.[45]

After his release, Frishman went to Laos for one day where he met with
the United States ambassador. Contrary to what Fallaci writes, Frishman
maintained that he was not immediately submitted to an intense debriefing
designed to counteract North Vietnamese propaganda. He insisted that his
first goal was to share information about other prisoners and to help the
American war effort. If the debriefing continued, it was because he wanted
it to go on and hoped that it would be valuable. In spite of what Fallaci
might like to believe, it had nothing to do with her. He was never instructed
to avoid the woman from Florence to save embarrassment. After his release,
officials did not brainwash him into speaking a certain way. He freely provided intelligence and caught up on current events by reading magazines
and newspaper articles, among which he discovered her interview with him
in Hanoi.[46]

Fallaci expressed anger when Frishman failed to acknowledge her in
New York. Her outburst of criticism began after his arrival at Kennedy Airport, when she described a uniformed official leaving the aircraft. "*Con aria*

soddisfatta, superba, arrogante. Sbattei gli occhi, tratenni il fiato: era Lei" (Looking satisfied, haughty, arrogant. I blinked. I held my breath: it was you).[47] In a traumatic reunion with family and friends, the "ungrateful" lieutenant had the audacity to allow no time for her. Despite scheduled meetings with the president, secretary of state, and other high officials, he sinned by failing to embrace Fallaci, set a time for dinner at Mamma Leone's, and hold her forever in his debt. Frishman stated that, at the impromptu press conference in Bethesda, the military division of public affairs put no limitations on him. He neither prevented her presence nor took the time to notice her absence. While Fallaci contends that navy officials refused to invite her to spare Frishman the questions she could have raised, he himself made it clear that he would not have objected to her presence.[48] Finally, it is common knowledge that the Hanoi government allowed Fallaci into the country for the same reasons that it received Jane Fonda. Most Americans with sons in Vietnam would have reacted with outrage if their government had granted the least bit of publicity to anyone who had expressed open sympathy for the Vietcong.

Frishman himself admitted another reason for his subsequent refusal to give an appointment to Fallaci. He spent much time with his family, underwent extensive medical testing, and voluntarily supported the American war effort. He was more concerned with these activities than with seeing her. At the same time, he had learned that she had a reputation as one of the world's foremost interviewers, that she was an aggressive *60 Minutes*–style journalist who normally got what she wanted no matter what, that she interviewed people and then censured them; and her encounters had begun to seem like tests of strength.[49] It was as though she had to force her subject—in this case a freed POW—into seeing life largely on her terms. Lieutenant Robert F. Frishman simply exercised a personal right and refused to bend his knee before her.

Fallaci's comment about being open to Frishman's refutation in order to save his dignity is offensive. The U.S. Navy lieutenant behaved with great decorum by ignoring her caustic remarks. Furthermore, he had no need to justify his courageous military record to the Italian journalist. For outstanding service as a pilot of Fighting Squadron 151, he received the Distinguished Flying Cross, nine air medals, two Navy Commendation Medals, and the Purple Heart. He flew 128 missions over North Vietnam in 1966–67. After his repatriation, he was attached to the naval hospital in San Diego, where he underwent operations and treatment for wounds suffered when his plane was shot down.[50] He subsequently became president of Concern for Prisoners of War, Inc., a nonprofit California corporation dedicated to obtaining humane treatment for POWs in Indochina. Fallaci's accusations of unmanly behavior cast a pall over otherwise brilliant episodes in this phase of her journalistic career.

Superstar on a Balcony

7.

IN LATE SEPTEMBER 1968, FALLACI FLEW TO Mexico City to report on student discontent with a government that continued to spend millions of dollars in preparation for the Olympics while a large segment of the population lived in dire poverty. She again immersed herself in the reportage and made her close call with death, as well as her emotional outrage with Mexican authorities, high points of her articles. Through her eyes, readers watched Mexican students in context and felt the inner dynamism of the crucial events. Fallaci allowed circumstances to speak for themselves but, once more, made sure that she was always at the center of the unfolding drama.

The entire episode, meticulously analyzed in articles for *Europeo* and in an addendum to *Nothing and Amen*, focuses on the image of a heroic, upright journalist who champions the underdogs against a totalitarian regime. The article written by Fallaci's editors, Tommaso Giglio and Renzo Trionfera, sets the pace. They emphasize the importance of Fallaci's style of reporting but also stress her degree of commitment, even though it resulted in personal injury during a demonstration. "It is the price paid when journalists believe in their work and write their articles not only for others but also for themselves."[1] Both editors herald her as a superstar who paid the bloody price for witnessing from within history in the making and reinforce the noble portrait of a champion dedicated to truth, no matter what the consequences.

Participating in a demonstration that the military had savagely quelled, Fallaci suffered injuries and underwent surgery in a hospital. The setting is ideal for her first-person style. The titles of her articles accentuate the journalist rather than the event: "Oriana Fallaci Relates: The Night of Bloodshed in Which I Was Wounded" and "Here Is the Article That I Had Lost."[2] The first article is in the form of a transcribed cassette recording. Fallaci, in her hospital bed, too injured to write, speaks into the microphone. "I feel sick; I am still confused. You see, there is something that hurts me more than physical pain, than this tremendous pain in my shoulder, lung, knee, leg . . . this recurring nightmare hurts me."[3] The Fallaci *I* punctuates the entire communiqué. Photographs in two articles strongly complement and magnify her personal voice. The first shows her in Vietnam wearing a GI's uniform and writing notes. The caption quotes Fallaci: "Mexico was worse than Vietnam." The second is her picture in the French hospital recovering from her wounds and dictating her story onto a tape recorder. The third, a dramatic series of photos taken by an Associated Press (AP) photographer, frames journalists wounded and killed on a balcony during the massacre—the same bloodbath in which Fallaci is shot. The fourth is one of Fallaci on her abdomen with her hand covering her face, as the operating surgeon medicates her back wounds. The fifth—a melodramatic photo of Fallaci dressed in black with a stylish haircut and holding dark sunglasses—depicts her inspecting the sight of the massacre on 2 October.[4]

Before the tragic event, Fallaci met with student leaders of the protest movement in a classroom at the Politecnico. She creates the impression that she has strong bonds of solidarity with the group. Thirty individuals anxious to reveal their innermost feelings to foreign journalists gather there and allow her to record their opinions, plans, and aspirations. The group had chosen three of their members—Ernesto, Graziano, and Socrates—to speak on everyone's behalf this day. Their anger, related to the three million pesos spent by the government on the Olympics, is also caused by their inability to communicate with the outside world about the popular discontent that had begun with the student uprisings in 1961. The thrust of the meeting, however, deals with their immediate survival needs since, unlike their American,

French, Italian, and German counterparts, they fight an establishment that brutally represses all opposition.[5]

On the day of the rally, Wednesday, 2 October, students had planned on celebrating troop withdrawal from the Politecnico, an apparent gesture of goodwill, and urging the evacuation of soldiers from their university campus and lecture halls. Student leaders had encouraged Fallaci to attend because they had predicted a huge, enthusiastic turnout. Fallaci arrives at 4:45, notices the square already half full, and walks up to the third-floor balcony of the Chihuahua Building, covered with banners and lined with loudspeakers. From the elevated position, readers see it all through Fallaci's eyes. She meets the four student leaders, Guevara, Manuel, Socrates, and Maribilla, who assure her that police will not interfere and that things will proceed peacefully as planned.

Fallaci stands above the thousands entering the plaza, where she mentally records her data. Angel, a strike organizer, hurriedly and nervously arrives with new information that armored cars and trucks have surrounded the square. Student leaders quickly meet and cancel plans to march after the general rally: they fear provoking the soldiers into using their weapons. Socrates takes the microphone to alert the ever-growing crowd. "My friends, . . . Let us not go on our march, because the army is waiting for us with armored cars, with bazookas. . . . I urge you to disband and return to your homes as soon as our meeting is over."[6]

After Socrates's announcement, the eighteen-year-old Maribilla begins the official event with a speech in which she insists that the struggle continue without violence until authorities seriously accept their program. "I want to ask that you remain peaceful."[7] Everybody below applauds. Socrates then follows by also stressing the movement's peaceful intentions and desire to celebrate the beginning of troop withdrawals. At the same time, he issues a call for the continuation of evacuations from secondary schools and urges the beginning of a hunger strike on the following Monday. "From now on, we are searching for peaceful methods. . . . Whoever wishes to participate in this hunger strike will get settled in the University City in front of the Olympic swimming pool and will do a hunger strike until the end of the Olympics."[8] As soon as Socrates finishes his speech, a green army helicopter begins to circle the plaza, gradually decreasing its altitude. Fallaci views the development with great alarm and tries to warn student leaders but to no avail. Then the launch of two green flares really concerns her—similar actions in Vietnam indicated an attempt to pinpoint a target. "Boys, something bad is going to happen. They've got flares." Again, they remain calm and attribute her anxiety to past experience. *"Eh, tù ves las cosas como en Vietnam"* (Come on, you are not in Vietnam).[9] No sooner do they finish their statement when thundering noise announces the arrival of trucks and armored carriers that literally surround the open, wide space on four sides. Soldiers pour out of their vehicles and immediately start spraying the crowd with bullets.

For two or three minutes, Fallaci, along with everyone on the third-floor balcony, stares in disbelief at the nightmarish scenario unfolding before their eyes. People begin to run, scream, and fall. Not yet realizing that the troops have every intention of killing them, Socrates runs to the microphone, appeals for calm, and calls the soldiers' action a provocation. "My friends, don't run! Don't be frightened; it's a provocation! They want to frighten us. Don't run!"[10] Socrates continues to cry out—"Don't run"—but guns drown out his voice as women begin to flee with children in their arms. On the roofs there are more soldiers with machine guns and automatic weapons. Fallaci freezes but understands exactly what is happening. "All of a sudden, I began to see them fall. You know, when you go hunting and hares start running, as hares do when you hit them, they do a kind of somersault and then lie there."[11]

The military have them in a trap and are beginning to focus their attention at the third floor, where loudspeakers signal the presence of leadership. Moving to the elevators, Fallaci finds them without power. At the same time, she writes, Maribilla approaches, screaming for Angel, who then goes down to the ground level, where he finds dozens of plainclothes policemen beating their victims. Fallaci, in the meantime, has her back to the wall to observe better the action below and suddenly sees around sixty middle-aged men arrive on the balcony. For identification purposes, they all wear white shirts and white gloves on the left hand and carry revolvers that they shoot at the floor or wall as they arrest everyone present.

One of them grabs Fallaci's hair and shoves her against the wall between Moses and Manuel, where she sags to the ground. Other journalists from Germany, Holland, France, and Japan suffer similar treatment. Fallaci identifies herself as Italian but receives in reply a revolver against her temple with the order to raise both hands. On the balcony, only the balustrade offers some protection against the gunfire from below. All of the police with white gloves quickly position themselves on the floor behind the balustrade while keeping pistols aimed at their prisoners flush against the wall. "Thus, we were a very beautiful target for those shooting from the square and from the helicopter. We were everybody's target."[12]

In Vietnam, bunkers and trenches had offered shelter against enemy fire. Nothing protects the prisoners on the third-floor balcony. Every time they try to move from the wall, their captors fire warning shots. At a certain point, Fallaci pleads with the police for help and for permission to move closer to the protective balcony. *"Por Favor, per favor quiero me hagar venir, me haga venir cerca, cerca!"*[13] Nevertheless, they surrender no ground to their captives until Fallaci makes believe that she has fainted, falls to the ground, and inspires the others to do the same. Moses, already wounded, begins to bleed from his hand; Manuel tries to protect Fallaci's face and hands. The sheltered officers object and force them to raise their arms. In such a vulnerable position, Fallaci manages to move about one-half meter along the base of the wall, saving her own life. With men firing from the helicopter, one bullet would surely have struck her head; instead it hit her shoulder. Among the several wounds she receives, a bullet fragment enters her back a few millimeters from the spinal cord, while another fragment enters from behind the knee, miraculously halting between the main artery, a vein, ligaments, and the major nerves without damaging any of them. A third fragment pierces her leg and leaves behind several splinters that radiologists will soon discover. Screaming for help in English and in Spanish, she then curses her impassive captors. Later she recalls that the sound of machine guns drowned her cries.

After one and one-half hours, two policemen approach and literally begin dragging her down the stairs. "Each time I hit a step, I started yelling like hell because it was like a knife moving inside me."[14] In addition to the physical pain, Fallaci suffers the indignity of being robbed: she remembers green shirtsleeves and a hairy hand with square fingernails taking her watch. They finally pull her into a first-floor room flooded by water pipes hit by machine-gun fire. During all this, Fallaci holds onto a student to prevent the police from hurting him. "He's my translator; he's my colleague." After forty-five minutes, she asks for an ambulance but is simply told that the colonel does not want any to come. She responds that her embassy knows of her location. "If I do not go back, you will be in trouble."[15] When she again attempts to identify herself as a journalist, they call her an agitator and place her on a stretcher. They then situate her face under dirty water pouring down from the broken pipes. One of the student prisoners then shows much courage by removing a sweater, placing it over her, and calling for her to be brave.

The Mexican Ministry of Defense's version of the incidents on 2 October differs from Fallaci's account. According to General Maximino Garcia Barragan, the police and army intervened at seven o'clock to prevent an uprising aimed at overthrowing the government. The official communiqué also confirms that there were dead and wounded on both sides, that the army initiated its mopping-up operation at nine o'clock, and that army casualties included a dead corporal and two wounded officials. The testimony of Ian Borg, a United Press International (UPI) cameraman, who also stood on the balcony, confirms Fallaci's accounts, not the government's. He explains that the student speaker suspended his speech when he noticed the green rockets that gave the signal for the shooting spree and the army's arrival. He observed around fifteen policemen (a number significantly different from Fallaci's sixty) bursting onto the balcony and ordering everyone to line up against the wall with their hands above their heads. He then specifically comments that the army began to shoot and that the police ordered them to lie down.

> We stayed that way for one hour, with bullets crossing above our heads. I heard people screaming. Amongst them Oriana Fallaci. She was hit twice: once in the shoulder and once in the arm. To my left a man was wounded and I saw blood pouring down his face. I could do nothing. The area was under the command of bullets. A projectile punctured a water pipe and water began to pour onto us. We quickly found ourselves immersed in water, colored with the blood of the wounded.[16]

Ian Borg's account also includes how police agents stripped him to check for weapons, marched him down to the plaza, and finally let him go. The photographer further relates that the demonstration had started peacefully, that leaders had asked everyone to leave quickly and with no agitation, and that they would have succeeded had the forces of repression not turned the day into a tragedy. Even the British Reuters and French AFP agreed that the signal to shoot had been given by rockets fired from helicopters and that only after the aggression did students disperse and try to defend themselves with stones, vases, and sticks against machine guns. Even bazookas inflicted heavy damage against the balconies at the higher levels where students launched their makeshift arms and pieces of furniture at troops below.

When an ambulance finally arrives for Fallaci, the nightmare is still far from over. She goes to two hospitals on that terrible night before receiving the required treatment, but first she enters a first-aid station filled with casualties from the massacre. In at least one instance, half of a victim's face has been shot off; in others, people have lost parts of legs or arms. She then receives transportation to one of the city's public hospitals, has to lie in an emergency room for well over an hour without any treatment, and then is surrounded by policemen in plainclothes. Speaking to her in a threatening manner, they ask if she is an agitator and again hear that she is a journalist for an Italian newsmagazine. Their main interest then turns to the question of her religion: "You aren't Catholic! You aren't Catholic!" She boldly responds, "No, why?" and insists on seeing her ambassador. When they even refuse this basic right protected by international law, she loses control. "First the Mexican police shoot me, then they even deny me the right, which is mine as a foreign citizen, to immediately call someone from my embassy." As they coldly and indifferently walk away, a kind nurse approaches and whispers in her ear, "Don't tell anyone. I'll call the embassy. What is your name?"[17]

Two hours later, after someone arrives from the embassy stating that a doctor is on his way, hospital authorities find time to X-ray her injuries. Then there is what Fallaci refers to as a miracle: Dr. Giovanni Viale arrives with his assistant, Gabriel Espinosa. They thoroughly and respectfully perform an examination and then escort her from hell into heaven. Covering her with a raincoat, they accompany her down the stairs toward the exit. The kind nurse who had called the embassy approaches and makes a request, as though Fallaci is her champion of truth. *"Le pregunto un favor: escriba todo lo que ha visto."* A young doctor from the staff also draws near and asks the same thing in English, "May I ask you a great favor? Will you please tell all you saw?" Arriving at their car, Viale and Espinosa carefully sit her down, drive across the city, and arrive at the French hospital, where she eventually undergoes surgery. During the night, authorities keep guards outside her room to keep strangers away. Her forwardness has offended governmental interrogators and could have repercussions. However, Fallaci shows no signs of fear or repentance and stands ready to challenge the authorities. "The Mexican police would have had to cut out my tongue to keep me quiet."[18]

Fallaci believes that Mexican police officials visited her often at the public hospital to make sure that she had not died, knowing that the killing of a journalist represented the worst form of publicity for any government. What

particularly incensed her was the position taken by some of her fellow journalists—the Mexican reporters—who could never have legitimately ignored
the manner in which she acquired her injuries. They claimed that she had
suffered only light scratches and had left the hospital walking. Worse yet,
Fallaci maintains that they told a story in which they attributed those light-
scratch wounds to sharpshooters.[19] When the same group of Mexican journalists arrive in her hospital room with a bouquet of roses, she writes, she
refuses their gift and tells them to send the flowers to the wounded students.
The head of the delegation asks where the injured are, provoking an angry
answer. "I responded that certainly I could not have known but they should
have taken the flowers to the tombs of the dead students."[20] It was to her
advantage to refute in her article the claims of the Mexican journalists.

Fallaci's image as heroic victim would have lost its power if her public
had seen her injuries as superficial, and her flair for the melodramatic could
have motivated her to overstate their seriousness. After she left the operating
room, astronaut Pete Conrad was the first to call her. According to Fallaci,
her nurse refused to awaken her, but Conrad yelled and screamed so loudly
that the attendant put the receiver to Fallaci's ear. "They got you good, huh?
It serves you right. Serves you right. This way you'll learn to stick your nose
into wars. Do you hear me? However, you're not going to die, huh? Because
if you die, I'll cry."[21] Conrad's side of this story too contradicted Fallaci's.
He maintained that she was not asleep and answered herself. A nurse was
never involved. The astronaut also maintained that she greatly exaggerated
her injuries, and he commented on the strength of her utterances. "Her voice
was so loud that it could have carried from Mexico City to Houston."[22]

An outpouring of sympathy and support emerged from the Mexican
population. An Italian journalist told of a taxi driver who wanted him to give
Fallaci his best wishes. Hundreds of telegrams arrived from Italy; bouquets
of flowers flooded her room; visitors surreptitiously left antigovernment
newspapers on her night table; students and waiters sent their greetings;
unknown callers confided tragic stories about their children.[23] Fallaci's personal tragedy and solidarity with the fifteen hundred students arrested and
one hundred fifty people killed received major coverage in the international
press and focused more attention on Mexico's protest movement than had
all of the student demonstrations of the preceding years.

Fallaci's reportage even develops the dimensions of a detective story, with
herself cast as the clever protagonist outwitting the Mexican government. On
Tuesday, 8 October, she recuperates in her room at the Isabel Hotel while

authorities continue to treat her as a spy. They maintain a twenty-four-hour surveillance of her movements and tap her telephone calls, including the one from her mother in Florence. When Tosca asks, "Is it true that they want to expel you?" someone cuts off their conversation and makes it impossible to reestablish contact. During her convalescence, she wonders often about the fate of her student friends. The eighteen-year-old Mirta from the Politecnico had disappeared right after the helicopter launched its two flares. She had followed Fallaci everywhere, even imitated her style of dressing, sat next to her during a press conference, and accepted an invitation to visit New York. Isaia, son of a railroad worker and student of electrical engineering, had stayed near Fallaci on the balcony and had covered her wounds with his filthy hands. On Wednesday morning, she calls his home and learns that the military had detained him at Camp No. 1. Gabriele, the most intelligent of the students (Fallaci invented his name to protect his identity), had discussed *If the Sun Dies* with Fallaci, labeled her an antiquated coward for fearing automation, and called her enjoyment of good clothes and jewels bourgeois.[24] Nevertheless, she likes this bespectacled young man who also had stood on the third-floor balcony.

Gabriele calls on Thursday, 10 October. "You are alive!" she exclaims. "More alive than you, and not even three blocks away. I'm coming right over." Fifteen minutes later, he knocks, and Fallaci's sister Neera answers the door. "I brought this bottle of wine to you to drink to our good fortune. You are alive. I am alive." Everyone becomes very emotional, especially after he reveals that Socrates, suspected of being a traitor, has given his name to the police. "They are looking for me."[25] He shows her the *Diario de la Tarde* and his name under a big headline on the front page. Realizing authorities are keeping watch on the hotel, Fallaci, her sister Neera, and two visiting colleagues surround the Mexican dissident and begin to act like tourists. They go down with him in the elevator, walk by the strategically located reception desk, speak only English, and call him George. Once outside, they hail a cab and go to a safer location. There, for three hours, the only interview with a student survivor of the Tlatelolco massacre takes place. After the meeting, Gabriele quickly disappears into the night but promises an appointment for the following evening in a crowded cafeteria.

The following day, Mirta's death becomes public. Neera had gone to the girl's home, where her mother weepingly told the story and then made a tearful request. "Signorina, please do not ask me any more. I have five other children. Mourning has invaded our household: I am interested in nothing else." Fallaci then sadly recounts her conversation with Mirta about the planned visit to her home in Manhattan. "Is it true that New York City is beautiful, above all at night when the lights are on?" "Yes, Mirta, it is true, you will see. You will see."[26]

Leaving her hotel that night to keep the appointment with Gabriele, she notices that someone reading a paper gets up and begins following her. She and a colleague walk down the Paseo de la Reforma but cannot shake the conspicuous spy. He makes a mistake by crossing first at a green light and allowing her the time to jump into a cab for a quick getaway. She then meets Gabriele at the cafeteria and completes the interview.

Walking slowly, they discuss whether or not Socrates has truly betrayed the student leaders. Many of them would not consider him a traitor, since he has supposedly furnished names of political leaders who have no connection with the protest movement. The real proof of his innocence would surface if his captors send him to prison. On the other hand, amnesty would be a true indication of guilt. Students would then find him, organize a trial, and, if found guilty, execute him. When Fallaci asks what she can do for him, he smilingly asks her to offer him dinner. That evening, all bad things in the world seem to disappear. They eat in an ordinary restaurant as though they are in New York or Rome and discuss life on other planets. He refuses to accept Earth's inferiority and defends the privilege of birth as a human being, even though men have killed Mirta.

> The struggle between good and evil is the essence of life: trees and fish do not know what is good or evil. Listen, I don't know whether we will ever see each other again, but deep in my heart, I feel that we will never see each other again. However, you must promise me this. You must swear it: you must never get angry with men and say that it would have been better to be born amongst trees or fish. Because I too am a man, and if you don't believe in men, everything becomes useless. Have you understood? Promise?[27]

Fallaci pledges to herself and to her readers to do as he wishes, experiences a great feeling of happiness, says a tearful good-bye, and watches him proudly walk away.

Gabriele's disappearance into the anonymity of a crowd brought the hellish nightmare of Mexico City to a close. This important period of the writer's life exposed with clarity the abuses of totalitarian regimes and solidified the image of a twentieth-century heroine shaking her fists at a dictatorship trying to undermine the power of free thought and expression.

Performances of a Lifetime

8.

FALLACI'S MOST IMPORTANT INTERVIEWS occurred with heads of state and significant political figures. They broke the limits of print journalism, sometimes resembled theatrical productions, and were often aggressive. During her encounters, she often argued, turned her direct questions into frontal assaults, and rarely suffered a defeat. She became known as the Italian woman from Florence who interviewed the big ones—Kissinger, Colby, Gandhi, Walesa. Her exchanges represent mythmaking in process, a ritual that kept her confronting one Goliath after another and subduing each of them. Fallaci emerged from her interviews as the idol of a mass audience that vicariously relived her experiences through her interviews.[1]

It is impossible to teach the Fallaci interview; each encounter finds its explanation in a woman who was born in Florence of certain parents, had specific experiences during World War II, wanted to become a writer, and worked as a correspondent. Students desiring to imitate her commit a grave error. A sociocultural orientation predisposed the journalist to a particular approach. In addition, she pours her own temperament into her work and profits from years of experience. She enters the mind of each subject and questions them about their thoughts, emotions, decisions. She then dramatizes their responses, leaves her own imprint on the exchange, and bares her soul in some of the greatest performances of her life.

Fallaci's techniques and originality as a political interviewer have fascinated critics and make most exchanges seen on American television look tame.[2] One salient feature of Fallaci's work is the recurring air of mystery and adventure. She portrays herself as a correspondent who seems to revel in dangerous situations. Her points of reference are hidden Palestinian bases; secret rendezvous with their leaders; the jungles of Cambodia, Vietnam, Bolivia, and Sri Lanka; and battle zones in India, Pakistan, Bangladesh, and even the Plaza of Three Cultures in Mexico City. Foreboding encounters, the pervasive presence of death, and an unflinching refusal to cower before an adversary call forth the high degree of her special talent and then invest the words with an almost magical seductiveness.

She begins the articles with the Palestinian resistance movement at a secret Al Fatah base, interviewing Abu Asham to discover why, as a guerrilla, he participates in nightly attacks against Israel, and reporting the moving story of his birth in a refugee camp in Lebanon. She meets the base commander, the handsome thirty-year-old Abu Mazim, who offers her a meal and asks if she has ever eaten with a terrorist. "Many years ago. . . . When we fought the Germans."[3] He likes her answer and then explains that he and his fighters have earlier destroyed an Israeli potassium plant and an electric power installation. During the conversation with Abu Mazim, one of the other fedayeen asks whether she thinks they are right in their struggle.

"Yes, Abu Mazim. I fear that you are right. However . . . "

"However?"

"However, I have to tell you a simple short story. When I was a child, I loved a schoolteacher very much; she was the best girl in the world. Her name was Laura Rubicek, and she lived with her elderly mother, very sweet and white haired. One night Germans came and took them away. Because they were Jewish. And they came back no more. Do you understand?"

"I understand."

"And I do not want this to happen again. Never again. Understand?"

"I understand, signora. Now, can I answer you?"

"Please."

"My answer is simple and brief, too. We do not hate Jews. Many of us are married to Jewish girls. Many of us are friends with Jews. We hate Zionists. Because being a Zionist is like being a Nazi: it means believing in a racist, expansionist, and imperialist state. You Westerners identify Israel with Jews. It is not the same thing."[4]

A fedayee asks to speak and removes his *kassiah*, revealing the face of a young boy. He too understands Fallaci's concerns; his parents had lived next to a Jewish family and detested the extermination camps. However, as an Arab Palestinian, he refuses to accept responsibility for the atrocities. Instead, he accuses Jews of acting toward Palestinians the way Germans had treated them. "Today we are the Jews."[5]

Returning to a hidden location in Amman, Fallaci somehow managed to meet with Yassir Arafat for the longest and most complete interview ever obtained by a journalist until 1970. At first glance, she writes, he conveys no impression of authority or charismatic leadership. "He was small. . . . Even his hands and feet were small: too small . . . to support two very fat legs and such a massive trunk with wide hips and a stomach that was obese. On all this, a head rose with a face framed in a *kassiah*."[6] (On the first page of the article, a large, flattering photograph of Fallaci in a fur coat and smoking a cigarette contrasts sharply with the negative description of the Arab leader.) The meeting takes place at ten o'clock at night in the presence of a tall, slim, elegant bodyguard whose appearance suggests to Fallaci the leader's sexual preference; a big man dressed in civilian clothes; an interpreter; and Abu George, who listens carefully to the exchange after inspecting Fallaci's prepared questions. She characterizes Arafat's cordiality as superficial, finds him ready to turn hostile for insignificant reasons, and accuses him of rhetorical evasiveness. "Among all the Palestinians I met for this report, Arafat is the one who impressed me least of all."[7]

Fallaci's denigration of Arafat's bodily appearance and sexual orientation brings into question the combative and unprofessional aspect of her style. Robert Scheer accuses Fallaci of character assassination, pointing out that she had been unable to come up with anything of substance with which to "get" Arafat; consequently, she had resorted to personal attacks on his physical features (e.g., "teeth of a wolf"). Scheer severely takes her to task when he himself interviews her. "What if the introduction to this interview said Oriana has crooked teeth?" He continues the offensive by quoting her description of Arafat's fat legs, massive trunk, huge lips, and swollen stomach. "I'm suggesting you didn't nail him in the interview, so you went a cheaper route. You wrote that it was an unsatisfactory interview because you couldn't get anything out of him." When she protests that Arafat had nothing to say, he catches her in an obvious inconsistency and indicates the Arab's contradictory statements, which she should have corrected. "He said at one point, 'We have to liquidate Israel!' Then, in another part of the interview, he said he has nothing against the Jews and he is for a democratic state. Why didn't you ask him how he could be for both?"[8]

The Arafat encounter has boomeranged and exposed Fallaci's intolerance of homosexuals and her hypocritical efforts to maintain tight control of what reporters write about her. During that famous *Playboy* interview, Scheer reminds her of what she had written earlier. "In the preface to your interview with Arafat, you implied that he is a homosexual." Her response reinforces the original impression.

> He had at that time the most gorgeous young man I have seen in my life. He was a German. So handsome and so gorgeous and he even behaved in a funny way with my photographer. He was a very handsome man and he never looked at me. He looked at my photographer. He was provoking him. He was doing things like that [licking her lips] and he was looking at him.[9]

Fallaci states that, maybe because she is more manly than homosexuals, she irritates them.

> I'm not crazy about them, the homosexuals. You see them here in New York, for instance, moving like this [makes a mincing gesture], exhibiting their homosexuality. It disturbs me. . . . Do you know the ones who have the high heels and put powder on and go to Bloomingdale's hand in hand, and they squeak? . . . I just can't stand them. . . . There is a form of fanaticism in them, of dogmatism, of exhibitionism, of Mafia sense, all of what I despise."[10]

In her view, their spirit of solidarity goes beyond comradeship. She compares them to a strong political party in the arts and never wants to be obliged to love them. The story of her trip to London with her mother further emphasizes her repugnance.

We were in front of Westminster Abbey and we saw these two workers, laborers, kiss each other on the lips. She almost fainted. . . . Those Bloomingdale types that I cannot stand, or the homosexuals in Arab countries—it makes me sick. I can't imagine a homosexual in any position. When they swagger and strut and wag their tails, I can't bear them.[11]

During the exchange, Fallaci takes additional jabs at homosexuals but, at the end of her meeting, refuses to accept responsibility for her comments and wants them erased. "I'm sorry I touched that subject. When you talk hours and hours like this, you always make mistakes. Wipe it out, please." Scheer does not comply, however. He knows well how ruthless and relentless some of her interviews have been and takes her to task on the spot.

"Hold it. Here we have Oriana Fallaci, who has published comments from the high and the powerful they wish they could retract, asking us to erase something she said. . . . We can't tailor the questions or the answers to what makes you sound liberal."
"If you insist on publishing it, you are making a tyrannical, fascist act."
"It wouldn't be tyrannical; it would just be poor journalism not to publish it, something you'd never allow yourself."[12]

Fallaci met her nemesis when she allowed Robert Scheer to interview her. He brings to the surface her inconsistencies, refutes the argument that her comments would cause intolerance, and points out the ironic nature of her attempt to disclaim or modify a sincere expression of belief. "Don't overreact. Confessing to a personal distaste, a chink in your armor, won't necessarily unleash the oppression you fear. You, of all people, shouldn't be involved in retracting statements."[13]

Interestingly, after meeting George Habash, founder of the notorious Popular Front for the Liberation of Palestine (PFLP), Fallaci adamantly refused to "wipe out" some of his statements. In the interview, his terrorist activities emerge as the main topic. He had organized the explosion at the headquarters of the Israeli airline in Athens and had orchestrated a series of such terrifying events as a shoot-out at the airport in Monaco, an inferno at a Hamburg synagogue, and the destruction of a Swiss Air carrier with forty-seven victims onboard. The exchange takes place next to a refugee camp

on the outskirts of the Jordanian capital in an apartment containing only a
desk, a few chairs, and anti-Zionist signs. In this atmosphere of secrecy,
Habash justifies his terrorism as acts of war against nations that support
Zionism at the expense of Palestinians and refutes her charges of indiscrimi-
nate killing.[14]

After the interview was republished in *Life*, Habash had an improvised
information office of the PFLP send a missive to Fallaci to argue against her
use of the word *terrorist*, claiming that he would never have allowed it; to
denounce her as anti-Semitic, in view of the fact that Arabs consider themselves Semites; and to deny that he had expressed indifference at the possibility of a third world war. Fallaci replied in an open letter, defending her
integrity by threatening to replay her tape to refresh his memory.

In it, she reviews their discussion and states how easy it had been to
transcribe the ninety-minute interview.

> I repeat, that which I wrote is recorded on the tape and only Dr. Habash's
> tears and convulsive shivers—human reactions that I liked—are missing.
> And here, I confess, I may have made a mistake. His so-called Information
> Department insinuates that I am a fascist. I only respond to this vulgarity
> that, when Dr. Habash was doing nothing to prove himself antifascist and
> his people got along so well with the Nazis, I was a little girl with braids
> combating Fascism in the Italian resistance. I remember that there were no
> Palestinian journalists present to interview us and to show sympathy by
> risking their hides.[15]

In Ceylon (Sri Lanka), Fallaci experienced a cloak-and-dagger–type es-
capade. She first discovered that the press in the capital city of Colombo had
written nothing about the bloody student uprising in the country. She then
journeyed three hours into the jungle to meet with leaders of the revolutionary movement. The conclave in an improvised shelter produced much valuable information on the history of the antigovernment movement.[16]

During the war between Bangladesh and Pakistan, Fallaci went to Dacca
to meet with Prime Minister Mujibur Rahman. After suffering the indignity
of his arrogance and one lie after another, she vented all of her accumu-
lated exasperation, calling him a contemptible, vulgar person and a hysterical crazy man who would end unhappily. The leader's Mukti Bahini guards
then followed her to her hotel, where one angry soldier confronted her for

having insulted the country's father. However, she landed him with a right and, during the turmoil, sneaked into an escaping car with five Australian businessmen headed for the safety of an awaiting airplane.[17]

For one series of reports on Latin America, Fallaci flew to Bolivia to interview the French prisoner Régis Debray. A war council, summarily organized in a village hidden in the Andes, had condemned the revolution theorist to thirty years' incarceration. She describes her arrival in La Paz in October 1970 to interview President Alfredo Ovando and her receiving his permission to journey to Camiri to visit Debray. For fifteen days, she writes, the press and radio had spoken of her presence in La Paz and of her desire to verify that Debray is still alive. General Rogelio Miranda, head of the armed forces and mortal enemy of President Ovando, reluctantly issues a safe-conduct pass to Fallaci but nevertheless makes things difficult for her. No seats are ever available on the little plane that travels to Camiri twice a week. Fallaci finally rents a single-motored Cessna and hires two adventurous pilots who have no familiarity with the terrain. They get lost over the Andes and land in a gorge right in the middle of a coca field; there, the pilot asks an Indian family where the town of Camiri is. The small group finally lands at their destination with no assistance from anyone. Only a woman nursing a child mans the control tower.

The town itself consists of a few huts and shops, a church, and a brothel. Once in town, Fallaci sees to the difficult task of getting permission to interview Debray from the head of the local garrison and then from Debray's jailer. She easily wins their cooperation by presenting them with several bottles of whiskey, assuming that the gift buys her the privilege of recording the interview. Afterwards and despite her gestures of goodwill, authorities unsuccessfully try to confiscate her cassette tapes. She flees with the two pilots and escapes while officials attend a cockfight. The interview and getaway arouse international interest. "You could say that Debray is more uncomfortable to his captors today than he was in 1967."[18]

Fallaci described to Scheer another narrow escape that occurred in 1980 when Fallaci tried to interview Iranian President Bani-Sadr during the hostage crisis. (He had acted as interpreter during her 1979 interview with Ayatollah Ruhollah Khomeini and knew her well.) She had received a visa, despite warnings not to go. Her confrontational conduct with Khomeini had earned her so much resentment that one of the country's newspapers had published her photo torn in half. In a country with a 50 percent illiteracy rate, only an enemy of the people would have a photo publicly torn in half. After flying into Teheran, she was detained on the airstrip.

"You have no visa."
"What is that? That is my fucking name."
"So what?"[19]

When they started pushing her into a police room, she started shouting, "You bastards," the kind of tactic she always tries when in such situations. Fallaci usually counts on her shouting to tire them out.

After a man from the Italian embassy finally conducted her to a hotel, she stayed hidden until she met with an official at the foreign ministry who ignored the fact that Bani-Sadr had promised her an interview. The official called her and the Italian government a nest of liars. A day later, she received a warning that her life was in danger; militant students were in control. Finally getting in touch with the right people, she managed to leave Iran. Two days after her escape, Bani-Sadr was in London for an economic meeting and sent a message to her through the Italian ambassador. "Psst. Tell Miss Fallaci that I ask to be forgiven, I really couldn't do it. There will be a next time." She responded, in typical Fallaci fashion, "Fuck Bani-Sadr. There will not be a next time. I will never grant him an interview."[20]

In addition to casting herself as an adventurer, Fallaci also places herself at the center of history in the making, as she does in writing about her audience with King Hussein. The Jordanian monarch seems uncomfortable and hesitates in responding to personal questions. The high point of interest relates to the Palestinian refugees he had accepted within his borders, as well as the military forces of Arafat and Habash, who act as though they are the country's ruling authority. The big question deals with the limits of the king's power. "Majesty, but who is in command in Jordan? At the check points, people are stopped by the fedayeen, at the borders the fedayeen attack, in the villages it's the fedayeen who decide. It's no longer paradoxical to say they've set up a state within your state." Hussein responds diplomatically, cautiously, and compassionately, making it clear that he would not halt their activities or order them to leave his kingdom. "Not because I can't but because I don't want to. . . . Because they have every right to fight, to resist. They've suffered for twenty years, and Israelis are occupying their land."[21]

In retrospect, Fallaci explains, Hussein's discomfort during their meeting may be due to his having told her an immense lie. From his throne, the king had expressed solidarity with the Palestinians and had preached both tolerance and peace. Nevertheless, five months later, he unleashed his Bedouin troops against the Palestinian fedayeen and decimated them in a nightmarish bloodbath known as Black September. Even in refugee camps, Hussein's legions put thousands of people to death without pity, decapitating or dismembering victims, old people and children alike. Fallaci concludes that Hussein knew that he would do an unexpected about-face and authorize the massacres to solve his Palestinian problem. He essentially had no choice but to lie during the interview. However, the efficiency with which he distorted his real feelings impressed Fallaci as indicative of a man who is both tragic and treacherous. "Tragic by destiny, treacherous by necessity."[22]

The encounter with Lech Walesa during Solidarity's struggles against Poland's Communist regime and the threat of Soviet intervention took place at his home in Gdańsk. He begins in an argumentative spirit. "I can leave a general in the lurch without saying goodbye, and as for you, I can do the same." Fallaci allows no one, not even Walesa, to set the pace and counters with her own startling gambit. "I look at you because you resemble Stalin. Has anybody ever told you that you resemble Stalin? I mean physically." When he expresses his discontent with how journalists insert their own interpretations in interviews, she has to set the ground rules. "If you don't mind, I am the one who asks. Now let's start."[23] The heart of the interview deals with his sudden rise to power and responsibility, the need for the country's evolution, his organization of political rallies, the worker strikes in Gdańsk, the possibility of a Soviet invasion, and the union leader's commentaries on himself.

Walesa is comfortable with the content of Fallaci's questions but experiences fatigue under her probing barrage. He claims several times that her difficult queries give him a headache. Yet she remains ruthless in her persistency. This refusal to give Walesa any respite characterizes most of her interviews. She maintains absolute control, even when other journalists question her. A noticeable exception occurred during the Robert Scheer interview. He utilizes to perfection her adversarial style and administers a dose of her own medicine. Scheer so mercilessly pounds her with difficult questions and evidence of her inconsistencies that she resembles Walesa seeking refuge behind the protection of a headache. She responds evasively when he asks her to defend her negative views of homosexuals.

"Tomorrow. . . . Tomorrow I'll tell you."

"You don't like being worn down in an interview?"

"I'm tired, I'm tired. Tomorrow I promise I'll do it."

"Have any of the people you've interviewed said to you, 'Oriana, I'm tired of talking to you, I don't want to talk anymore.'? Would you accept that?"[24]

Fallaci's meeting with Walesa led to personal discontent and disenchantment. "It is the only interview in my life that I am not proud of. This is the reason. It is the only time in my life that I have not been sincere."[25] She instinctively felt that Walesa was arrogant, ignorant, aggressive, and fascist and could not respect him. The source of annoyance lay not only in his unrefined, haughty, and overbearing temperament but also in his limitless audacity to claim that he would become president of Poland. The Catholic Church, specifically Cardinal Stefan Wyszynski, would assure him of his future rank. Her dilemma emerged as she transcribed her tapes.

> Do I write the truth about Walesa, saying that he is a bluff invented by the Church and that he is arrogant, fascist, etc.? I then do the Russians and Polish Communists a favor, since they want to crush him and Solidarity. I thus help to impede the attempt to establish democracy in Poland. Or else I write, like everyone else, that Walesa is a good person and offer my little contribution toward the birth of democracy in Poland.[26]

She tended to think, however, that although leadership of the revolution had been delegated to an unworthy person, democracy remained the main priority. Reasoning in this manner, she abjured the expression of her true opinion and included none of her negative convictions in the published interview. Perhaps Fallaci genuinely felt that her truthful statements published in an Italian magazine would have worked against the establishment of a free society in Poland. Be that as it may, she decided against declaring what she truly believed.

A similar hesitation to communicate her true convictions took place during her exchange with Polish Vice Prime Minister Mieczyslaw Rakowski. The historical high point of the interview occurs when he admits that Soviet forces would have invaded Poland had civil unrest grown. Despite a long series of disagreements and ideological differences, an emotional moment takes place at the end and facilitates an understanding of Rakowski as a human being. Bringing up the subject of his two sons who had defected to the West, she is surprised to see him weep. After discussing the divorce with his first wife and his entire family's disagreement with his political orientation, she actually expresses sympathy. "What a tragic man you are, Mr. Rakowski. See, not even those who love you and whom you love understand you. And yet you don't want to admit being wrong."[27] Her empathy for the isolated man reaches its peak after he explains that Germans executed his father in 1939 as a Polish sympathizer.

Fallaci experienced positive feelings about Rakowski. "He seemed like an intelligent man, an enlightened Communist, a democratic Communist like [Enrico] Berlinguer."[28] Her esteem, however, failed to emerge in the published interview. "I could have been more generous with him. And again political considerations motivated me. He was Communist Rakowski. I didn't trust him."[29] She simply refused to let what could have been a line of Communist propaganda trick her into becoming a political tool. Her attitude toward him changed for the better when he reprimanded her. "Look, you have been too generous with Walesa. Walesa is worth nothing. I know him well."[30] Then he revealed such things as Walesa's love for leadership, fascination with the popular myth that had developed about him, and belief in his personal grandeur. Rakowski disclosed the union leader's irrationality, slyness, naïveté, and trickery. Everything he said reinforced her negative opinions of Walesa. Her retrospective view on the meeting is that she treated Rakowski with respect but could have legitimately regarded him with more warmth and generosity.

In her interviews, Fallaci not only assumes the stance of a participant in history but sometimes functions as a catalyst for events. After Zulfikar Ali Bhutto had seen the interviews with Mujibur Rahman and his archenemy Indira Gandhi, he requested equal time. The results of the meeting caused diplomatic and international pandemonium. Finding offensive Gandhi's evaluation of him as a man lacking equilibrium, he calls her a "mediocre woman with a mediocre intelligence," "a woman devoid of initiative and imagination," a "drudge of a schoolgirl," and a politician without even one-half of her father's talent. Bhutto reacts with so much hatred that Fallaci tries to moderate his outburst. "Aren't you being a little excessive, a little unjust?" However, her exhortation falls on deaf ears: he utters other slanderous comments that would have serious consequences. "I'm ready to go to New Delhi. . . . The only idea that bothers me is that of being escorted by an honor guard from the Indian army and physical contact with the lady herself. It irritates me. God! Don't make me think of it."[31]

Discussion ranges from Bhutto's denial of responsibility for the massacres in Dacca and the imprisonment of Mujibur Rahman to honors bestowed on Tikka Khan, the Pakistani general who directed the actual slaughters in Bangladesh. Nevertheless, the heart of the dialogue remains his invective against the Indian prime minister.[32]

After the war between their countries, Bhutto and Gandhi had scheduled the signing of a peace treaty. However, after reading in New Delhi newspapers sections of Fallaci's interview with Bhutto, Gandhi suspiciously asked to see the entire text, which Fallaci then transmitted via telegraph from Rome. After studying the unaltered dialogue, Gandhi angrily canceled the upcoming peace conference—an action that so filled Bhutto with despair that he solicited Fallaci's assistance. His ambassador in Italy contacted her in Addis Ababa to make an extravagant request. Bhutto wanted her to write a second article to state that his interview with her had never taken place, that she had actually dreamed it, and that the statements about Gandhi had occurred in her imagination. Fallaci cannot believe her ears, she tells her readers, and asks for clarification.

"I said that you should write that you invented everything, and particularly the part about Mrs. Gandhi."
"Are you crazy, Mr. Ambassador? Has your Prime Minister gone crazy too?"
"Ms. Fallaci, you must understand, the lives of six hundred million people depend on you, they're in your hands."[33]

Although Fallaci literally cursed the ambassador and told him to go to hell, Bhutto remained obstinate and continued to use important diplomatic messengers to repeatedly request she repudiate the interview. Despite protests that her hands were too small to contain six hundred million people and that his insulting supplications bordered on absurdity, the nightmare ended only when Indira Gandhi magnanimously decided to act as though the interview with Bhutto had never happened. The two leaders then met to sign the peace treaty. Fallaci enjoyed seeing both of them on television as they shook hands and smiled at each other. Indira Gandhi's smile seemed triumphant; Bhutto's revealed such discomfort that, even on a black-and-white screen, his whole face seemed to turn red with shame.[34]

Fallaci's flair for the dramatic often emerged in her unwillingness to be intimidated or shouted down. Her ability to face each head of state without blinking sometimes turned encounters into confrontations. When meeting with the Ayatollah Ruhollah Khomeini in the holy city of Qom, she focuses the interview's attention on his government's intolerance of adulterers, prostitutes, and homosexuals and even contradicts him when he calls her accusations lies. She also questions him on why Iranian women must wear a chador and other uncomfortable garments. If they participated in the war against Iraq, even suffering imprisonment and torture, they should at least enjoy the privilege of comfortable dress. In response, the Iranian leader smugly composes a series of insulting remarks. "The women who contributed to the revolution were, and are, women in Islamic dress, not elegant women all made up like you, who go around all uncovered, dragging behind them a pack of men." He maintains that coquettish women who put on makeup and go into the street showing off their necks, hair, and shapes had not fought against the shah and do not now know how to do anything socially, politically, or professionally useful. Ignoring his insolent comments, she refuses to give ground. "That's not true, Imam. In any case, I am not only talking about a piece of clothing, but what it represents. That is, the segregation into which women have been cast once again after the revolution."[35]

Referring to women's inability to study at a university with men, work with them, go to their section of the beach, or even wear a bathing suit motivates Fallaci to ask, "By the way, how do you swim in a chador?" Khomeini's response is angry and rude: "This is none of your business. Our customs are none of your business. If you do not like Islamic dress, you are not obliged to wear it. Because Islamic dress is for good and proper young women." Fallaci's instantaneous reaction shows that he is dealing with someone who will not timidly submit to his sarcasm. "That's very kind of you, Imam. And since you said so, I am going to take off this stupid, medieval rag right now." She tears off the chador she had donned to be respectful and throws it at his feet.[36] He, in turn, storms out of the room, only to hear her insultingly call, "Where do you go? Do you go to make pee-pee?"[37] Fallaci's next tactic was a lengthy sit-in, despite the pleas of Bani-Sadr and the ayatollah's own son. She agreed to leave only after Khomeini swore on the Koran that he would again meet with her on the next day.[38]

Controversy also followed her interview with Prime Minister of Iran Mehdi Bazargan, only this time she had it with John Shepley (who translated the exchange into English). Her meeting with the head of state took place just five days after her encounter with the Ayatollah Khomeini. Shepley's rendition appeared in the *New York Times Magazine* on 28 October 1979. However, no credit is given to him as Fallaci's translator. Calling her, he asked politely, "Why was my name not mentioned in the article? Did you or the editors of the *New York Times* decide to leave my name off?" Shepley explained that Fallaci hit the ceiling and informed him that she had no need of a translator's name on her articles and that if he pushed the point, he would never work (for her) again.[39] This was the final break in an already strained relationship and a sign of her hostility toward translators.

The same confrontational style characterizes the interview with Colonel Muammar al-Qaddafi. When she defends America's refusal to deliver the shah to Khomeini, she compares it to the Libyan leader's reluctance to return Idi Amin to Uganda. Qaddafi replies on the spot. "If Amin were here, I would think about a reply to your question. But since he is not here, the comparison does not hold up."[40] One of Fallaci's most daring statements follows.

> Amin is here, Colonel. Indeed, we know very well that Amin is hidden here, that he is your guest. He lives in a villa with a park and a swimming pool near Tripoli. He is there with two of his many wives and ten of his innumerable children. He was even interviewed by that Philippine journalist whom you had arrested as a punishment.

After he insists that the deposed African leader is not in Libya and that he had simply been there on a visit, she has no qualms about correcting him. "Come on now! What visit? If we want to call it a visit, then even the shah is on a visit to New York."[41]

Fallaci audaciously explains why people everywhere despise him. "Where shall we begin? Perhaps with your friendship for that bloody criminal Idi Amin. People ask: 'How can Colonel Qaddafi be a friend of such people?'"[42] When he avoids a direct response, she frames her accusation in even bolder terms. "Why [*sic*] can you, a self-expressed champion of justice and freedom and revolution for oppressed peoples, give hospitality and protection to that pig Amin?" She easily traps him as he defends his policy of noninterference. Fallaci states, "It's time to remind you that, under the pretext of helping oppressed people, people who, by the way, are oppressed only when it's convenient to you, you interfere very much in the affairs of other countries. Even too much. In Chad for example."[43]

Defending his right to interfere in Uganda against Julus Kambarage

Nyerere of Tanzania and in Chad to help the people fight against French troops only results in charges of inconsistency and incoherence.

> Excuse me, Colonel. First you tell me that you didn't help Uganda to get rid of Amin because you don't have the right to interfere in the internal affairs of that country; then you tell me that you wanted to help the people of Chad because you had the right to intervene. First you say one thing, then you say the opposite. For the sake of coherence, may I remind you that you were already in Amin's Uganda before the war with Tanzania?[44]

His justification of support for Amin, which is based on Amin's anti-Israeli policies, draws a further attack from the interviewer. "If a tyrant who slaughters his people merits [your] friendship . . . just because he hates the Jews, then [you were] . . . born forty years too late. . . . Hitler would have been a very good friend for you."[45]

Fallaci duplicates her frontal assault against Qaddafi in her heated interview of William Colby, Director of the Central Intelligence Agency (CIA). She and Colby stand at opposite sides of the ideological spectrum and engage in an exasperating, agonizing, angry brawl. He represents power, the omnipresent, invisible octopus that dominates and strangles everything. She believes in the right to personal liberty. It is his prerogative to spy, interfere, corrupt, overthrow governments, intrigue, and kill—even to control Fallaci by tapping her telephone. The encounter with Colby consequently revolves around her deep hatred for him; but, although this motivates her first abrasive question, it does not lead to a long list of insults. She waits for his disclosures before designing her appropriate comebacks. In the exchange, neither finds any common ground or arrives at any feeling of respect. Rather, each tries to inflict a mortal blow on the other. In Fallaci's analysis, the ordeal fills her with poisonous anger, while her opponent remains stoic, controlled, and sure of himself. "He resembled a priest from the Inquisition or a Communist civil servant in the Soviet Union."[46]

She begins by demanding to know the names of corrupt Italian politicians who have accepted money from the CIA. "Italy is not a banana republic of the United Fruit Company, Mr. Colby, and it is not fair that an entire political class should be suspected. Do you not believe that [the] President of our Legislature has the right to know those names?"[47] Colby refuses to divulge that information to protect uninvolved individuals, and he challenges her to obtain the names of Italians on Soviet payrolls. Thinking fast, she has to reply to his challenge but not allow him to set the pace of the conversation. "We will talk about Russians later. For now, let's talk about the CIA." After next admitting that the FBI would arrest Fallaci if she were financing American politicians to protect her interests in the United States, Colby essentially provides the spark for her next rebuttal. "Fine. So I ought to report you, your ambassador, and your agents to the Italian police and have you arrested."[48] No holds are barred as she expresses her outrage. "There is only one type more disgusting than the corrupt: the corruptor." When he admits regarding influential Italians taking bribes from the CIA to be good clients rather than corrupt officials, Fallaci then seizes the opportunity and bitterly sums up his idea. "So you consider yourself the lawyer for Christian Democrats and Social Democrats in Italy."[49] Colby's praise of U.S. Ambassador Clare Boothe Luce as interesting and capable also ignites a quick refutation: "[capable] above all for interfering with my country's business as if it were her colony." She also seizes the opportunity for a follow-up comment on the CIA's relationship with Italy's secret service. "It is not only through your embassy that you operate in Italy: we all know that the CIA's real foothold in Italy is the SID. And I ask you, by what right do you allow yourself to spy on me in my own home using the secret service of my own country?"[50]

During the interview, Fallaci repeatedly alludes to Colby's readiness to overthrow any possible regime in Italy, just like the Salvador Allende government in Chile, and dramatizes her statements by challenging what she takes to be his notion that Italy is his personal property. "Mr. Colby, I am trying to get you to admit that Italy is an independent state . . . not your colony!"[51] Defending the CIA's record of opposing Soviet expansionism, Colby acknowledges the necessity of occasionally working with authoritarian leaders. Fallaci responds by listing names of rightist dictators whom he has bolstered to support democracy.

> From Franco to Caetano, from Diem to Thieu, from Papadopulos to Pinochet. Without counting all of the Fascist dictators in Latin America. Brazilian torturers, for example. And therefore, in the name of freedom, you have become the supporter of all those on the other side who kill freedom.[52]

Her acerbic instinct inspires her to use the standard trick of offering just enough information to provoke an incriminating response. "Tell me about the mafia and how the CIA uses the mafia." That short imperative draws Colby's admission of an attempted collaboration with the crime organization to assassinate Fidel Castro.[53] He then tries to cover his tracks by stating that former Director John A. McCone knew nothing of the endeavor. Nevertheless, Fallaci will not allow the matter to rest and relies on her familiarity with history. "Bobby Kennedy knew about it, however. Therefore, even John, the President, knew about it. Do you know what I think? Those who are the most discredited are not members of the CIA; they are Presidents of the United States."[54] This same bitterness impregnates every give-and-take right up to the last, when Fallaci asks to read her personal dossier in the CIA's files.

Publication of the Colby interview, as happened after an interview with Alvaro Cunhal, aroused a flurry of commentaries in newspapers throughout the world.[55] In fact, Colby used the media to declare that the written text proved his victory in the debate and challenged her to interview the head of the KGB, the Soviet secret police. Then, sending her brief letters to prove his liberal spirit, he gently scolded her for anarchist and leftist tendencies but also acknowledged her accurate and honest reporting. "We can disagree with each other, and in fact, we disagree with each other quite a bit, but I maintain that it is beneficial for a free society to be able to discuss and exchange ideas without fear of each other."[56] Fallaci never responded to his communiqués and refrained from asking what he meant by a free society and the exchange of ideas without fear. "I certainly was not and am not afraid of him or his CIA but I must confess that, seeing his signature, I would get the shivers every time."[57] Fallaci could not forget that for years the CIA monitored her movements. In addition, she had strong reasons to suspect the agency's involvement in the death of Alekos Panagoulis, with whom she had been involved, and could not shake these unsettling thoughts, especially— given events at the time—when Colby's Christmas greeting arrived in 1976— a card showing the Madonna wrapped in a blue veil, tenderly embracing the baby Jesus.[58]

In 1982, General Ariel Sharon, Israel's powerful defense minister, received Fallaci shortly after his forces had bombarded Palestinians in Beirut. The dialogue itself, which has several moments of tension, deals mainly with his success in forcing Arafat and his troops to leave Lebanon and his admission that the enemy has nevertheless scored a political victory. Fallaci accuses him of bombing civilians. "I can tell you because I have followed all of the wars of our times and for eight years the one in Vietnam. Not even in Hué, not even in Hanoi have I seen ferocious bombardments like the ones in Beirut." When he protests that his forces had bombed only sections where the Palestine Liberation Organization (PLO) had bases in the city, she counters again. "But you did not only bomb those areas, you also bombed downtown—houses, hospitals, newspaper offices, hotels, embassies. Ask those who were in them. Ask the journalists who were at the Hotel Commodore." When Sharon hesitates to admit that children had been harmed in the bombings, Fallaci opens her bag, pulls out a photograph, and points to the image of dead children from one to five years of age. The most frightful thing is not that they are dead but that they had been torn to pieces and crushed. "Here a little foot is missing from the body of the smallest; here a little arm is missing from the body of the oldest; there a little hand is open as if imploring pity."[59] At the end of their time together, Sharon praises Fallaci's professional style and defines an important aspect of her technique.

> I know all of your interviews and I know well that you wanted to add another scalp to your collection. You are hard, very hard. But I liked every moment of this tempestuous meeting because you are a courageous, faithful, and capable woman. No one has ever come to me as well documented as you. No one goes to war as you have done under bombs, only to prepare an interview.[60]

Fallaci can be more fierce in an interview than a prosecuting attorney. This antagonistic approach is dangerous; famous people might simply choose to avoid her. As her reputation for hard interviews grew, political figures in Washington, D.C., like Gerald Ford, refused to grant her access. In assuming a provocative stance, she can cause a subject to become belligerent, to distort truth, or simply to lie. She bullies and harvests disclosures of stupefying indiscretions from well-seasoned statesmen we would hardly expect to yield. She has even been known to lecture and intimidate reporters who displease her. On one occasion, she had asked a *New York Times* reporter to place off the record a personal detail of her life, but when it was published on the basis that it had already appeared elsewhere, Fallaci was outraged. When the *Yale Daily News* ran an unflattering picture of her, she refused an interview with the paper the next day, which prompted the college reporter, nineteen-year-old Neil De Crescenzo, to observe, "It's sad to see a person who writes about the use of power abuse it so blatantly."[61]

Fallaci met her match with Robert Scheer, the man who conducted famous *Playboy* interviews with Jimmy Carter, Jerry Brown, and John Anderson. Conservative journalist William F. Buckley Jr. says of Scheer's argumentative style, "He can catapult an exchange into the shouting stage quicker than anybody since Huey Long."[62] Scheer, a tough interviewer, applied to Fallaci the same pressure she applied to her own interview subjects. Making no secret of the fact that she considers interviews pieces of theater with a story inside, Fallaci yells, screams, and makes scenes to get at a larger truth. However, as Elizabeth Peer points out, Fallaci can bristle at any hint of criticism—"a touchiness that is downright hilarious in someone so quick to attack."[63]

Fallaci's interviews are not always disputatious; they can also be intimate and create the image of a warm, loving figure. Fallaci's 1972 exchange with Golda Meir in Jerusalem lasted fourteen hours. Strong questions, personal comparisons and inquiries, and affection characterize the discussion. It is love at first sight; the head of the Jewish state immediately reminds Fallaci of her mother. Golda, wearing a black dress, had powdered her nose just like Tosca did before receiving a guest at home.

> Though my mother was younger and had a much prettier nose, also much prettier legs, they resembled each other so; the same structure of the body grown heavy by fatigue and carelessness about looking attractive, the same grey curly hair that no comb could fix, the same deep wrinkles on the face shaped by courage and sorrow. Even the same manner of dressing in contempt for the superfluous: a plain skirt with a sweater and possibly a necklace of pearls, flat shoes with strings that squeezed feet deformed by arthritis. But, overall, the same disarming simplicity . . . and her motherly appearance.[64]

Prior to the interview, Fallaci had sent Meir a copy of *Nothing and Amen*, which provided a stimulus for their discussion of war, terrorism, Palestinians, the Occupied Territories, and the possibility of dialogue with Anwar al-Sadat or King Hussein. Three days after receiving the book, Meir greeted Fallaci in her office, and political problems took second place to childhood stories, family history, ideas on religion, personal disappointments, friendship for the Italian Socialist Pietro Nenni, and her experience as a woman in the world of diplomacy. When the subject of women's liberation is raised, Meir expresses the belief that the movement is full of crazy women who burn their brassieres and hate men. "[H]ow can one accept such crazy women who think it's a misfortune to get pregnant and a disaster to bring children into the world?"[65] Meir knows herself too well to become self-complacent and prefers to be like her daughter, Fallaci writes. "Sarah is so good, so intelligent, so intellectually honest. . . . I really can't say the same for myself. When you're doing the job I'm doing, you always have to stoop to compromises, you can never let yourself remain one hundred percent faithful to your ideas."[66] She has little patience for those who consider her the symbol of Israel. "Are you maybe pulling my leg? You didn't know the great men who were really the symbol of Israel, the men who founded Israel. . . . I can't say that if I hadn't done what I've done, Israel would have been any different."[67]

On the day after the interview, Fallaci returned to Rome around 8:30 P.M. with three full cassettes and arrived at her hotel room an hour later. She placed the tapes in an envelope, left them on a desk under a pile of objects, and, after leaving her room key with the porter, went out for fifteen minutes to eat a sandwich. When she returned, the key had disappeared. Someone had entered her room and taken the cassettes. Italian authorities investigated the crime as an act of political thievery but found no evidence. However, unexpected clues soon surfaced. Fallaci had simultaneously asked Meir and Qaddafi for interviews. A few days after the burglary, the Libyan dictator invited a journalist from a rival weekly of *Europeo* to meet for a dialogue. Qaddafi used sentences in that interview that sounded like responses Golda Meir had given earlier to Fallaci. She legitimately wondered how it was possible for Qaddafi to say something that had never been published and that no one, other than Meir and herself, knew. Logic—and Fallaci's discovery of an Arabic note in the garbage bin for that floor of the hotel—indicated that he had ordered the theft of the tapes.

Fallaci remains convinced of Qaddafi's guilt but prefers to focus on Golda Meir's reaction to the crisis. As the Israeli ambassador in Washington, Simcha Dinitz, explains, Meir had invited him to dinner and was speaking of the Italian writer in the most flattering terms when an aide handed her the cable: "EVERYTHING STOLEN REPEAT EVERYTHING STOP TRY TO SEE ME AGAIN PLEASE." She reads it, puts her hand to her breast, and for several minutes is silent. Then she raises her old sailor's voice and roars: "Obviously somebody doesn't want this interview to be published! So we'll have to do it over!"[68]

The women meet and redo the entire interview on 14 November—cigarette after cigarette, coffee after coffee. Old material is covered and new information surfaces. During the October interview, Meir had not succeeded in speaking about her husband and the great tribulation of her life. In November, she reveals this painful truth even though it breaks her heart. When

she is unable to continue, she promises to receive Fallaci again the next day
to conclude their exchange — the splendid hour in which she speaks of old
age, youth, death, and the fear of living too long.[69]

After the second meeting, Fallaci felt friendship for Meir and defended
her against political satirists. Although critics often caricatured what they
considered her ugliness, the writer regarded her as a beautiful elder and
considered her a lady through and through. The last time Fallaci saw Meir,
she wore a blouse of sky blue crepe and a necklace of pearls. Caressing them
with the tips of her fingers as she spoke, she seemed to inquire whether they
looked good hanging from her neck. Fallaci's thoughts as she left her underscored her personal regret. "A pity she's in power, a pity she's on the side of
those who command. In a woman like this, power is an error in taste."[70]

Robert Scheer severely censures Fallaci's kid-glove treatment of Golda
Meir and her failure to ask a single question about Zionism. In addition, he
chides her for her contradictory anger toward Jews and, in the interview,
traps her into making an unfounded and hasty generalization about why she
dislikes them.

> For many things. If you want to take the example of America, how they
> hold the power, the economical power in so many ways, and the press and
> the other kinds of stuff. . . . You see Jewish names as directors of TV and
> newspapers. The owners, the directors. I never realized how it happened
> and how they came to control the media to that point. Why? . . . At the
> *New York Times* they are all Jewish.

Scheer corrects her and counsels her to visit newspapers and networks to
discover that her information is wrong. "That's a European perception and
it's just not true."[71]

In 1980, Fallaci journeyed to Beijing and, continuing her long string of
historic encounters, met with the Chinese Vice-Premier Deng Xiaoping, one
of the few Western journalists granted that privilege. She owed her good
fortune to the same set of circumstances that had earned her access to the
Ayatollah Khomeini. Her articles and books enjoyed popularity in China
just as they did in Iran. Often smiling and sometimes laughing, the powerful statesman responded with frankness and candor to all her questions,
even the most insolent and unconventional. Conversation revolved around
changes in China's political life, criticism of China's Gang of Four and Mao

Zedong, the mistakes of the Great Leap Forward, the condemnation of the Cultural Revolution, and the possibility of scaled-down capitalism in China.

Throughout the interview, moments of fun periodically alleviate the weight of serious discussion. Her questions about why he has always been someone's second in command and his nickname in the west as the Chinese Nikita Khrushchev provoke outbursts of laughter. When Fallaci expresses her good wishes for his birthday, he acts surprised.

"My birthday? Is my birthday tomorrow?"

"Yes, Mr. Deng, I read it in your biography."

"Well, if you say so. I never know when my birthday is. If tomorrow is my birthday, though, you shouldn't congratulate me: it means I am 76, and 76 is a decadent age."

"Mr. Deng, my father is 76, and if I say to my father that 76 is a decadent age, he slaps me."

"And he does well! You wouldn't tell your father such a thing, would you?"[72]

At one point, they argued: Fallaci unfavorably comments on the gigantic portraits of Karl Marx, Friedrich Engels, Vladimir Ilich Lenin, and Joseph Stalin in Tiananmen Square. The next day, Saturday morning, driving through the spacious plaza a second time, things seemed different to Fallaci. The portraits had been taken down.

"Mr. Deng! Stalin isn't there any more! Nor Marx, nor Engels, nor Lenin! Mr. Deng, it isn't my fault is it? You didn't take them out because of me, did you?"

"No, no, not quite. We are simply returning to the old practice, as I told you before yesterday. When necessary we'll put them back."

"Pity! I was so happy. I liked so much the idea of boasting that I had been able to take Stalin off Tienanmen [sic] Square!"

"I know it, I know it. I understood it, I understood. But I shall not give you such satisfaction."[73]

Despite Deng's refusal to admit a desire to please her, he removed the four giant pictures from central display in the city and must have been influenced, at least in part, by her remarks. Fallaci would like on her tombstone that she was the woman responsible for having the huge pictures of Marx, Engels, Lenin, and Stalin removed from Tiananmen Square.

The adventurous, historical, confrontational, and personal aspects of the interviews account for much of their richness but fail to explain fully their worldwide appeal. The colloquies' success also derives from her methodology. Attempting to impose a literary imprint on the interview, she is confronted with the difficulty of journalistic requirements. She must rigorously duplicate everything said, right down to the commas. Extemporaneously creating questions during the interview of each subject resolves that dilemma. Because of her painstaking preparations, she is able to write the interview as it progresses; that is, she imagines the interview during the exchange to avoid accidentally and prematurely betraying the subject's response. This spontaneity—perfectly suited to Fallaci's sense of the dramatic—draws her readers in, allows her to adapt quickly to each situation, and indeed differentiates her queries from the banal.

When Fallaci traveled to Addis Ababa in June 1972, she understood that Haile Selassie, emperor of Ethiopia, ranked high among the despots of the world and, although fully aware of the need for politeness, knew in advance the inevitability of a dramatic showdown. As the conversation unfolded, she alone could decide on the *how* and *when*. The sight of intolerable poverty, especially the memory of the emperor's visit to Gonder, where he allowed his soldiers to distribute scraps of leftover food to hordes of starving people, enraged Fallaci even before she received permission to enter the royal palace.

In his cavernous, red receiving room, filled with stucco designs, curtains, rugs, and rococo armchairs, she bows before him three times, observes his magnificent throne lined with pink-and-blue-flowered light material, and, despite her awareness of the turbulence that it could cause, cannot resist asking about his nation's poverty.

> Your Majesty, there is a question that has bothered me ever since I saw those poor people run after you and crush themselves for a dollar, worth two hundred forty lire. Your Majesty, what do you feel giving alms to your people? What do you feel at the sight of their misery?

Haile Selassie then develops his thesis that individual merit determines who will eventually become rich. Fallaci's shocked rebuttal—"Your Majesty, do you mean to say that whoever is poor deserves to be poor?"—provokes an irritated justification. "Each person is responsible for his own tragedy, his own destiny. It is not right to await help from above, like a gift: one has to merit wealth! Work is one of our Lord Creator's commandments!"[74]

Sensing his frustration, Fallaci shifts direction and leads her subject through a series of irrelevant questions and then, without his expecting it, springs her trap. Haile has refused to discuss the coup that his two trusted advisors, the brothers Mengistu and Germane Neway, had initiated. Both men died before Haile could have the pleasure of seeing them executed. When an attempted escape failed, Germane shot his brother to prevent capture and then took his own life in prison. Haile vengefully ordered that their bodies hang from the gallows for eight days. To reach this untouchable topic, Fallaci poses an apparently unrelated question. "Your Majesty, if you don't wish to speak about certain things, speak to me still about yourself. It is said that you love animals and babies very much. May I ask you if you love men as much?" He responds that he only loves men who are courageous and dignified. Then, she seizes the opportunity and makes her key statement. "The two protagonists in the coup d'état had dignity, Your Majesty. They had courage." He realizes that he has been cornered and gives vent to his annoyance by angrily commanding her to refrain from that line of questioning. "That's enough, that's enough! Enough of it!"[75] During the course of the interview, he vehemently orders her to change the subject at least six different times.

Fallaci's final question maintains her reputation for provoking tyrants and for creating drama. She asks how he feels about death and his personal mortality. The query particularly inflames him because he abhors the word *death* and grows pale at the thought of dying. His anger and frustration hysterically burst forth, as he orders Fallaci to leave his presence at once. "Death? Death? Who is this woman? Where does she come from? What does she want from me?!? Away, enough, that's it! That's it!"[76]

The publication of Fallaci's interview infuriated Haile Selassie. To better explain his statements, she had inserted parenthetical observations that only served to further his displeasure, resulting in threats, official protests, and diplomatic problems between the Ethiopian and Italian ambassadors. Even Italians living in Ethiopia reproached her for possibly causing a vendetta. According to Fallaci, the majority of Italians living there still spoke of Mussolini with nostalgia and consequently had little patience for her approach to journalism. She received "affectionate" letters from these countrymen, advising her never to return to Ethiopia so long as Haile Selassie remained alive. "I beg of you, follow this advice."[77]

Fallaci's technique of extemporaneous composition was also put to use during her meeting with Henry Kissinger at the White House. She recognized the necessity of penetrating his mysterious persona to arrive at the source of his unparalleled success as the U.S. government's most influential envoy. His willingness to receive her surprised Fallaci; he reputedly spoke only at press conferences and never permitted private interviews with journalists. According to the statesman, her interview of the North Vietnamese General Vo Nguyen Giap in Hanoi in February 1969 favorably impressed him and proved the deciding factor. Nevertheless, he modified his assent by allowing first a preliminary meeting at which Fallaci had to do most of the talking so that he could decide whether to see her again. She entered his office for the first time on 2 November 1972. He entered out of breath, without smiling, and greeted her. "Good morning, Miss Fallaci."[78] In a study filled with books, telephones, papers, abstract paintings, and photographs of Richard Nixon, he seemingly forgot about her presence and, with his back turned, began to read a long typescript. Despite his rudeness, the interval allowed her to study him. According to Fallaci, he was not only short, thickset, and far from seductive but also tense, unsure of himself, and quick to establish an air of authority as a protective shield.

After deciphering the transcript, she writes, he invites her to sit down and starts his interrogation—just like a professor examining an untrustworthy student. His mannerisms remind Fallaci of her math and physics teacher at the Liceo Galileo Galilei, a man she had hated because he had enjoyed instilling fear by staring from behind his glasses. Kissinger even has the same baritone, the same guttural voice, and the same way of leaning back in his armchair, crossing his legs while his jacket buttons strain from the pressure of his belly. The nightmarish memories of school fill her with terror. "Oh God, will I know the answer? Because if I don't, he'll flunk me." His first question deals with General Giap: "As I've told you, I never give personal interviews. The reason why I'm about to consider the possibility of granting you one is that I read your interview with Giap. Very interesting. What is Giap like?"[79] She responds that he had been jovial, arrogant, and like a French snob but that his predictions about the Tet and the Easter offensives had come to pass exactly as he had indicated. In her opinion, Giap had correctly analyzed the weakening American position, since the United States had accepted a Paris agreement that displeased President Nguyen Van Thieu. Kissinger then asks for her opinions about the situation in Vietnam as though he sincerely wants to know and quizzes her about famous statesmen, the art of governing, and the consequences of a cease-fire. He finally concludes that she has passed the exam and merits a real interview.

On Saturday, 4 November, at ten thirty, she again enters his office at the White House for what she labels perhaps her most uncomfortable and worst interview. Every ten minutes Nixon calls Kissinger on the telephone like a child "who cannot stay away from its mother."[80] Then, at the high point of their talk, when he begins to discuss the elusive nature of his personality, Nixon again interrupts and requests his presence. Kissinger obediently jumps up and asks Fallaci to wait; he will try to give her a little more time. After waiting for two hours, his embarrassed assistant arrives to tell her that both leaders have left for California.

During their hurried time together, Kissinger remains evasive and reticent about himself while also trying to avoid highly sensitive issues related to Vietnam. As a result, Fallaci uses all of her wiles to discover his real thoughts. At one point in the conversation, she catches him off guard and places him at a disadvantage. Bringing out speeches and clippings in which President Nguyen of South Vietnam challenges the American secretary of state to tell the real reasons for their disagreeing on a peace treaty with North Vietnam, Kissinger's response reflects his awkwardness. "Let me see it. . . . Ah! No, I won't answer him. I won't pay any attention to this invitation."[81] She also uses dramatic questioning: "Dr. Kissinger, if I were to put a pistol to your head and ask you to choose between having dinner with [Nguyen Van] Thieu and having dinner with Le Duc Tho . . . whom would you choose?"[82] She continues to bombard him with questions about Vietnam and the impending peace agreement with the North to the point that he practically implores her to stop pursuing the topic: (1) "That's enough, I don't want to talk anymore about Vietnam. I can't allow myself to, at this time. Every word I say becomes news. At the end of November perhaps. . . . Listen, why don't we meet again at the end of November?"; (2) "I cannot answer that question"; (3) "I cannot, I cannot . . . I do not wish to answer that question"; (4) "And don't make me talk about Vietnam anymore, please"; (5) "But, really that's enough talk now about Vietnam"; (6) "But are we still talking about Vietnam?"[83]

Fallaci probes relentlessly for information. One of her tactics involves going from the general to the particular. First, she asks in broad terms what he will do when his term in office expires. Not receiving a satisfactory answer, she changes to a specific possibility. "Would you go back to teaching at Harvard?"[84] The high point of the interview occurs when she intuits Kissinger's vulnerabilities and poses her questions accordingly. Flattering queries reflect her belief that Kissinger's weakness is his massive ego. "Dr. Kissinger, how do you explain the incredible movie-star status you enjoy, how do you explain the fact that you're almost more famous and popular than a president? Have you a theory on this matter?"[85] At this point, Kissinger gives a psychological reason for his success as a diplomat and makes his disastrous cowboy statement, which becomes a hot topic in the American press for months afterwards.

> The main point arises from the fact that I've always acted alone. Americans like that immensely. Americans like the cowboy who leads the wagon train by riding ahead alone on his horse, the cowboy who rides all alone into the town, the village, with his horse and nothing else. Maybe even without a pistol, since he doesn't shoot. He acts, that's all, by being in the right place at the right time. In short, a Western.

Sensing a climax to the drama, Fallaci recapitulates the substance of his revelation, hitting the nail right on the head. "I see. You see yourself as a kind of Henry Fonda, unarmed and ready to fight with his fists for honest ideals. Alone, courageous."[86]

Much to Fallaci's surprise, his self-described status as a hero of the Wild West created a journalistic furor. Rumors began to circulate in Washington that he had lost favor with Nixon for attributing his diplomatic triumphs exclusively to his personal skills. Reporters condemned the presumption or the imprudence of his remarks. How dare Henry Kissinger claim all the rewards for what he had done as Nixon's envoy? How dare he relegate Nixon to the role of spectator? Where was the president of the United States when the professor entered town to take care of things? Cartoons of Kissinger dressed as a cowboy galloping toward a saloon or wearing spurs and a ten-gallon hat appeared in newspapers everywhere. Soon afterwards, Kissinger admitted that having received Fallaci was the stupidest thing he had ever done and subsequently declared that she had distorted his remarks.[87] His retraction forced her to threaten to publicize recordings of the interview. She strongly defended her account of their conversation in *Time* and *Newsweek*; on CBS and NBC television, she said that he was not a gentleman and that he lacked the courage to acknowledge the accuracy of his own statements. After two months of intensive publicity, Fallaci could no longer bear to hear Kissinger's name and so detested him that she failed to realize he had no choice but to shift the blame onto her. She admits candidly her incapacity to have wished him happiness during that time.[88]

Fallaci's most scathing attack is in a 1975 open letter in *Europeo* in which she labels Kissinger a little professor who is vain, pretentious, and reactionary. According to her, he is like a presumptuous and arrogant cowboy who believes that galloping to the distant villages of China, Moscow, Tel Aviv, and Cairo will settle things down. Shortly before the 1973 massacre at Rome's Fiumicino Airport by Palestinian terrorists, Kissinger's admirers from Italian television called to invite her to be interviewed about the statesman, stating,

"That son of a bitch did it again."

"He did what again?"

"Peace! Peace in the Middle East!"

"In what manner would that son of a bitch have made peace in the Middle East?"

"The agreement! The agreement between Golda Meir and Sadat!"

"What agreement?"

"Well . . . a real agreement not yet. The meeting! The meeting!"[89]

Fallaci responded that an agreement between Golda Meir and Anwar al-Sadat would not mean peace because it would never take place until the Palestinian question had been settled. She finally agreed to be interviewed only if she could express her honest thoughts about Kissinger. Two hours later the phone rang again and a cold voice asked what those thoughts were. Her scorn arose from his tricking people into believing that he promised peace just as he had done in the case of Vietnam. She was asked,

"Are you affirming that Kissinger is stupid?"

"Oh, no! . . . I can assure you that he is not stupid at all. The stupid ones are those who believe in him."

According to Fallaci, Kissinger lives in the past, fails to understand the present, and does not foresee the future. "For this reason," she writes, "you fail in every undertaking and your successes are always flashes in the pan: smoke in the eyes of imbeciles."[90]

Kissinger regards the interview as the most disastrous conversation he has ever allowed with any member of the press and, in contradiction to

Fallaci's claim that her interview occurred as a result of her published interview of General Giap, admits that he had talked to her out of vanity. "She had interviewed leading personalities all over the world. Fame was sufficiently novel for me to be flattered by the company I would be keeping in her journalistic pantheon." He had not bothered to read her interviews, had not afforded himself the opportunity to discover her evisceration of other victims, and so paid the price of his naïveté. The quotes ascribed to him, "statements of marginal taste gathered in what she presented as a conversation," were the most self-serving he had uttered in his entire public career.[91]

The publicity generated by his cowboy statements overshadowed his complimentary remarks about Nixon. In the published interview, Kissinger praises the president for his courage in selecting a chief advisor whom he did not know and for sending him to Beijing. He lauds Nixon's expertise in foreign affairs and for making his diplomatic successes possible. What had distressed Nixon was the quotation that Kissinger claims Fallaci put in his mouth: "Americans like the cowboy . . . who rides all alone into the town, the village, with his horse and nothing else. . . . This amazing, romantic character suits me precisely because to be alone has always been part of my style or, if you like, my technique." Kissinger denies that the context of the statement was presented accurately and that it was about himself. He remains convinced that he was the subject of some skillful editing and points out that Fallaci has consistently refused to make the tapes available to other journalists.[92]

Fallaci labels ridiculous any comparison with the toughened television interviewer Mike Wallace. "I'm a writer who does journalism. In no case can you compare me to a person who performs journalism for TV." She refuses to pronounce Wallace's name, claiming she would not do so even if threatened with death.[93] The two pages about the interview that Kissinger includes in his memoirs infuriate Fallaci. After *Time* published excerpts, she wrote the magazine a letter saying that someone had heard the tape—meaning Mike Wallace.[94] *Time* then received an answer from Mike Wallace in which he admitted hearing the tape but that it was fuzzy.[95] "What fuzzy? If he wanted to get Kissinger on *60 Minutes* and be the servant of Kissinger, he's going to say a lie like this? The tape was far from fuzzy. He heard it when he was interviewing me for *60 Minutes*." Fallaci also bitterly complains about the publicity photo that *60 Minutes* released. "It looked like a 123-year-old woman; I don't know where they got that ugly photo."[96] Today, Fallaci carefully controls the photographs released in Italian newspapers and those (flattering) that appear on her book jackets. She dislikes television appearances, possibly because they expose her wrinkles.

The same ability to adapt quickly to each situation and to choose an advantageous direction after an unexpected or indiscreet disclosure appears in her interview with the shah of Iran in October 1973. Revealing that he has visions of prophets and saints, the head of state discusses them with her. Fallaci later tells Scheer that she profited from this confession by a tongue-in-cheek reaction. "You mean you could shake hands with them?" After an affirmative response, she renews her sarcasm. "If I am there with you, can I see them?"[97] In the same exchange, she notices that the shah's face looks forlorn and thus composes an appropriate question. "Why are you so sad, Majesty? I may be wrong, but you always have such a sad and worried look."[98]

Fallaci vivifies the encounter with Qaddafi with sudden bursts of creativity. When he asserts that he is much loved by his people, her response is appropriately provocative. Gesturing toward his battalion of bodyguards, she asks why he needs so much protection. "Before getting here, I was stopped three times by soldiers with guns, then I was searched as if I were a criminal. And there is even a tank at the entrance, with a canon pointed at the street. . . . And why do you live inside a military camp?"[99] One query dealt with his religious belief, normally a topic of marginal interest. "Do you believe in God?" The Libyan dictator began to yell hysterically for ten minutes straight that he was the Gospel, naturally intimidating the entire entourage. At a certain point, Fallaci, who almost never interrupts, boldly cut him off and delivered an appropriate punch line: "Stop! Stop! Do you believe in God?" Qaddafi: "Of course, why do you ask?" Fallaci: "Because I thought you were God."[100]

The interview with the Ayatollah Khomeini takes an unexpected twist when the religious leader proves that he is an intelligent man not just a religious maniac. When she avers that his people's adulation comes not from love but from a dangerous type of Fascist fanaticism, she opens the door for his clever rebuttal. "Fascism and Islam are absolutely incompatible. Fascism arises in the West, not among people of Islamic culture." Fallaci then understands that he is no pushover and has to rephrase the question. "Perhaps we don't understand each other. . . . By Fascism I mean a popular phenomenon, the kind we had in Italy when the crowds cheered Mussolini, as here they cheer you, and they obeyed him as they obey you now." However, once again, he demonstrates his acute understanding of the incompatibility of the Italian movement with Islam and outlines the only conditions that would foster a rightist crusade in Iran. "Fascism would be possible here only if the Shah were to return or if Communism were to take over."[101]

Immediately after this intriguing introduction, anything could have happened. The Ayatollah could have ordered her to leave as Haile Selassie had done; he could have angrily refused to continue. However, he reacted improbably. He remained cold and polite but responded that he thought she was wrong, that he was not a tyrant, and that his country's culture could never tolerate the rightist military dictatorships of Western society. At that moment, to say the least, Fallaci was caught by surprise; she understood that she confronted someone different and changed the whole scenario. She had to deal with a learned man who reacted cleverly enough to sustain the conversation rather than banish her. She began to target specific contradictions in his style of leadership, thereby injecting drama into the structure of the interview.

Her interviews go beyond the tape recorder; it's the way she conducts them. She is on stage and performs with great gusto, doing everything in her power to make sure that no one steals the spotlight, which she surrenders only in a tightly controlled framework. "They are pieces of theater. I prepare the questions but I follow the ideas that come. I build the suspense, and then I have *coups de scéne*."[102] This creative orientation helps explain their universal popularity. In 1974, Rizzoli Editore took many of the famous interviews and published them in her eighth book, *Intervista con la storia*. Rather than simply reprinting what had already appeared in *Europeo*, the collection includes a long essay before each interview in which the journalist explains many details and circumstances omitted in the original. In addition, the interviews published in *Europeo* were often abbreviated because of the limitations of space; they were presented in their entirety in the book.

In the introduction to the English-language *Interview with History*, she explains why the interviews were done.[103] She wanted to understand the powerful and how they control lives. Each encounter is arranged "with the hope of understanding in what way, by being in power or opposing it, those people determine our destiny." After painstaking preparation, the writer then undertakes a grueling inquisition of each subject. "I went [into an interview] with a thousand feelings of rage, a thousand questions that before assailing them were assailing me." Fallaci believes that only a few individuals control human destiny and calls this condition "atrocious."[104] World leaders are capable of changing the course of events by means of an idea, a discovery, a revolution, an assassination, even a simple gesture. In view of this belief, she acts as the official representative of the cheated, the abused, the suspicious, the defiant, the insanely brave—all the people who say no to those who attempt to decide the fate of humanity.

After obtaining the appointment, Fallaci begins the game of getting at the truth, invariably changing her readers' perceptions. "Not even a selective criteria justified power. Those who determine our destiny are not really better than ourselves; they are neither more intelligent nor stronger nor more enlightened than ourselves."[105] To discover the intricacies that actually produce decisions, Fallaci uses every possible professional interview skill. What also makes her persuasive is her degree of conviction as she laboriously searches for each subject's inner life. "On every professional experience I leave some of my soul."[106] Her passionate involvement makes each interview more than a document for students of power and antipower. Fallaci refuses to become a mechanical repeater of what has been seen and said and refuses to define herself as a journalistic doctor of anatomy or an impassive recorder of events. Encounters become not only a study in power but also a portrait of herself as she tries to generate meaningful revelations. They are a strange mixture of her ideas, temperament, and patience—all of these elements driving the questions that enable her to conduct an inside-the-skin interview. This journalist certainly knows how to pose the right queries and adds something extra that provokes each subject to emotional disclosure. Fallaci the playwright composes her own drama and emerges as a star in each engaging production.

To Be or Not to Be

9.

● AFTER THE PUBLICATION OF *INTERVIEW WITH History*, Fallaci began a new phase in her career. She had succeeded at breaking the limits that journalism had, to her mind, imposed and once again pursued her desire to produce a purely literary work. Thus, she took a leave of absence to write a poetic novel, *Lettera a un bambino mai nato*. Much concerned that the metric quality of her Italian prose not lose its lyricism in English, she asked John Shepley to do the translation, completed as *Letter to a Child Never Born*. In 1975, she expressed her faith in the American translator. She wrote to him, concerned that her book had a particular rhythm she could not find in English, and concluded he was the only person she knew who could do something about it. She admitted that Shepley had a grasp of Italian and could capture the flavor of her novel. She expressed her esteem for him and her confidence in his capacity as a translator.[1]

Years later, Fallaci expressed a notably different opinion during a television interview, *Un soldato di nome Oriana*, conducted by Francesca Alliata Bronner.[2] Fallaci criticized the English translation and maintained that it was not good enough to be read commercially. It needed to be redone, she explained, but she had neither the emotional energy nor the time to do it. She had just prepared *Lettera a un bambino mai nato* as a trade cassette. The American actress Faye Dunaway had suggested reciting it in English as part of a theatrical rendition of the book. According to Fallaci, she had not carefully studied the language of the English translation when it first appeared but, after Dunaway's proposal, attentively looked at it and then criticized it. Fallaci's comments during the RAI Radiotelevisione Italiana (RAI) interview retract her earlier expression of faith in Shepley. They also emphasize her desire to present herself to the world not just as a novelist but also as a translator in possession of English linguistic expertise. Her reversal about Shepley's translation signaled the controversy she had developed with translators (who knew that the image of Fallaci the translator was weak). Most translators knew that she was not in a position to judge accurately the merit of Shepley's translation.

Fallaci draws upon the analogy of physical exercise to explain why she cannot simultaneously write novels and newspaper articles. "Literature and journalism are like two different sports. Playing tennis develops body muscles that are not the same as muscles developed by a soccer player or swimmer."[3] Likewise, the demands journalistic projects make upon the writer's time—traveling around the world doing interviews, gathering data for articles—make it virtually impossible to achieve the concentration needed to write novels.

Fallaci is very aware of the difference between an active, literary journalist and a novelist. Journalism prevents the full emergence of her creative energy. A character from one of her subsequent books expresses this point. "The writer is a sponge who absorbs life to spit it out again in the form of ideas." According to the character, a novelist not only perceives and imagines new insights but also anticipates and transmits them.[4] Fallaci possesses a type of imagination that exists in authors of fiction but passes many journalists by. Her dilemma never consists of an incapacity to create but the inability to break away from the journalistic requirement of gathering and communicating accurate information. "This literary impulse was restricted in the straitjacket of journalism, that is, the rigor that journalists must have in the observance of truth."[5] As a novelist, she has license to relocate events in time and place. "One of the precise differences between a journalist and a novelist derives from the fact that a writer's duty is to unleash and launch imagination."[6]

Letter to a Child Never Born emerges as an intense form of self-revelation and historical sensitivity. These features combine with novelistic elements of freedom and spontaneity and result in the creation of popular literature.[7] She has written what Dwight Macdonald calls a bastard form having it both ways, "exploiting the factual authority of journalism and the atmospheric license of fiction."[8] The end product, written in poetic prose, dramatizes an intensely personal situation from Fallaci's life and becomes a subtle form of journalistic, memorializing literature.

Fallaci conceived *Letter to a Child Never Born* long before actually writing it—"maybe five years, maybe six or seven"—and owes its inception to the deeply emotional experience of a spermatozoon uniting with "the egg of imagination." It was caused directly by the trauma, grief, and despair of losing a child. She admits to having lost several. One of these miscarriages inspired her to write the book. She immediately began to compose the story of her tragedy but could finish only three or four pages. Fallaci's German publisher, whom she had informed of her postponement, protested. "Why did you stop?" She recalls her response, "Because I am not ready."[9] In rich biological language, Fallaci maintains that, for years, the idea remained fixed in her mind like a frozen embryo in the womb of her imagination.

One day in 1975, Tommaso Giglio, the editor in chief of *Europeo*, asked her to do an assignment on abortion—an issue that everyone in Italy passionately debated during the 1970s and that the media exhaustively covered. Cultural feminists broadcast the issue in graphics and language that shocked people. Political feminists gathered the testimony of thirty thousand women on maternity, sexuality, and abortion and published the accounts. Small groups and assemblies of women discussed the issue. Neighborhood, workplace, and school collectives formed around the controversial topic. Parliamentary approval of a bill on abortion occurred in 1977, and abortion was legalized in 1978. In 1981, a referendum to appeal the abortion law was defeated. The most important feminist theme of the 1970s was that a woman's right to her own body was "the capstone of her liberation."[10]

Never expressing great interest in women's problems and even considering feminist studies a strange anomaly, she first reacted disapprovingly to Giglio's request. Oddly enough, though, she could not bring herself to say no and started writing about the most timely and controversial topic of the 1970s. She went home and began to type. "Last night I knew you existed: a drop of life escaped from nothingness."[11]

She continued to type for two or three days and, after realizing that a book was unfolding, called her editor. Fallaci refers to Tommaso Giglio as the only really intelligent editor she ever had—a man of culture and intelligence, similar to Bruno Fallaci, although much younger and more modern than her uncle. He encouraged her to finish the book and planned on publishing sections of it in *Europeo*. Thinking that she would work quickly, he gave her a one-month leave of absence. However, not even Fallaci could do the impossible; she requested six months. Giglio expressed his reservations: future events might overshadow the abortion debate and render her book outdated. His refusal to grant the request caused her to take a sabbatical without pay. Fallaci could no longer accept confinement by an employer. It was time to allow her own aspirations to determine her course of action. She rented an inexpensive studio in Florence on Viale dei Conti and wrote the entire book there in six months. She further asserted herself when she submitted the manuscript to Rizzoli Editore rather than to *Europeo*. She then revealed her decision to a justifiably upset Giglio.[12]

Despite her tangible presence in everything she writes, Fallaci still claims to speak of her personal life with reluctance and suffers whenever discussion of an intimate subject is approached. Aside from Alekos Panagoulis, she hesitates to talk about the men with whom she has had sexual relationships. She freely admits, however, that personal choice and professional ambition have had nothing to do with her never having had children. "This was a choice made by destiny. I have never had an abortion but have always lost them. Maybe I decided to have them too late in life. Or maybe I didn't take care of myself enough; indeed I didn't take care of myself at all." Her problem has always been finding the right pill to facilitate gestation and birth. "And the only pill to have children was the tranquility that I never had." The anguish of remaining childless haunts her to this day, arousing feelings of incompleteness. "One dies twice when one dies without leaving children. It's terrible to be a plant without flowers, a tree without fruit, to die without having sown the seeds of your own self. To die forever." Writing about that tragedy provided a book that would survive after her death. "When I die, I would like to leave a child. At least one made out of paper."[13]

Both sides of the abortion debate can claim Fallaci as their proponent and can find grounds for their respective positions. Those who favor choice readily find ammunition for their arguments. Before her scheduled business trip, the main character in the book, the mother, begins to hemorrhage, and her doctor orders total bed rest in the hospital. At that moment, she rebels against the idea of having a child, despises putting her job in jeopardy, and wonders about the necessity of enduring such agony. Rationalizing that the little bundle of flesh in her body does not think, speak, laugh, or cry, she concludes that the mother lives in the fetus and not that the fetus maintains a separate existence. She enunciates a familiar point of view. In the third month, no conscience directs human activities; dialogues do not occur. Human beings emerge at the moment of birth and develop as individuals through intercourse with others. Lying on the hospital bed, the protagonist has no intention of sacrificing her position and defends her right to fulfill her personal responsibility toward her employer. She refuses to help the unborn child by remaining in bed for the rest of her pregnancy and goes on her trip.

Despite the protagonist's reasoning, Fallaci herself hesitates to take a strong position on the issue: the book also establishes a strong pro-life point of view by poetically tracing the development of the fetus, referring to it as a mysterious flower and a transparent orchid. A photograph at the age of three weeks inspires her awe. The outline of a head with two swellings will become a human brain; a type of cavity will evolve into a mouth. Despite its minuteness—two and one-half millimeters—a sign of the eyes is already apparent, as well as something resembling a spinal cord, nervous system, stomach, liver, intestines, and lungs. A heart already has a shape, beats regularly, and pumps blood. The evidence of life overwhelms the mother and, before she changes her mind in the hospital, motivates her to have the child. "How could I throw you away?"[14]

As the mother lies in a hospital bed after finally losing the child, she looks at the fetus in a jar, imagining him growing to manhood and their future life together. She regrets not having done more to bring about a successful pregnancy. She envisions him as a strong, gentle person who supports his elderly mother as she walks down the stairs. She sees herself as having supported him as a child, recalling the day he refused to heed her advice, and sees how his independent spirit hurt her. Wanting to apologize for the attempt to dominate him, she imagines searching for him, remembering the little smile on his lips, knowing that he understood. Her final reflection places them at the foot of a magnolia tree from which he picks a flower, something that she could never do. "And now you're no more. There's only a jar of alcohol where something is floating that didn't want to become a man or a woman, that I didn't help to become a man or a woman."[15]

In Italy, the abortion debate divided the population, caused the fall of a government, and generated a national referendum. Fully realizing the political implications of her work, Fallaci decided against favoring one particular side. The book also suggests that she could not take an unequivocal, purely intellectual stance. It flirts with an absolute liberalism that provides justification for anyone who believes in the legitimacy of abortion and seems to oblige legislative bodies to legalize a woman's right to make a choice. At the same time, she shows evidence of instinctive repugnance at the idea of deliberately aborting a fetus while simultaneously refuting religious beliefs as the basis for this stance. The legacy of Catholicism furnishes no ammunition in her polemical outlook. Her belief in life actually derives from a more subtle source. A subconscious urge to preserve life is a more reasonable explanation than spiritual training received during childhood. "Therefore, it must be an animal reaction with maternal instincts."[16]

Fallaci expresses her own despair when she bemoans the tragedy of never having had a child, when she grows angry at the idea of aborting so easily the life for which she has always thirsted. As the mother begins to experience spasms that signal the beginning of the end, she does not want to let the fetus go. "I don't want them to tear you away with a spoon, to throw you in the garbage with the dirty cotton and gauze. I wouldn't want that."[17] The result of this reasoning is a conclusion that resembles the Catholic viewpoint, despite the book's obvious refusal to validate Italy's major religion. "I feel that if I do an abortion I am killing a person."[18] And yet, sympathetic understanding of the opposing viewpoint injects so much ambiguity into the story that opposing factions can easily claim Fallaci as their own. "You were wrong to say that I don't believe in life, Child. I do believe in it. I like it, even with all its infamies, and I mean to live it at all cost. I'm running, Child. And I bid you a firm good-bye."[19] This ambivalence with regard to Italy's ideological factions explains the unprecedented and instantaneous success of the book. Its fluidity permits individuals to decide whether the main character is for or against abortion, for or against allowing children to be born.

When Fallaci herself became pregnant, she was not married. While she had no concern for what people would say about her, she did fear for herself and for the child and expressed this anxiety in the heart of the novel. Just like Fallaci, the mother has a hard time deciding whether she has the right to bring a human being into the world and then whether she should risk losing her job. When the editor in the story hears about the pregnancy, he counsels her to think about her professional goals, to avoid destroying them by making a sentimental decision, and to remember that she could easily change the entire course of her life. He reminds her of the voyage that she must take to complete an important assignment and threatens to send a male reporter. "Certain-accidents-don't-happen-to-a-man."[20] She rebels at the idea of becoming a mother, decides not to sacrifice her professional fulfillment, and refuses to remain in the hospital, but then she freezes with indecision as the child moves within her for the first time. Despite her burning throat and tearful eyes, she rises from the bed, packs her bag, and undertakes the voyage that ostensibly precipitates the miscarriage.

A highly emotional moment occurs when the mother realizes the child will abort. She tells him the fairy tale of a woman who wanted some moondust. She knew the men who went to the moon and said they were stupid, "had stupid faces of stone," and did not know how to cry or laugh. "Going to the moon was a scientific feat and nothing else." During the trip, they never spoke of anything "poetic, only numbers and formulas" or questions about football scores. Even their moon statements had been prepared for them. When they came back, she begged for some moondust. They refused to share any and stated that they could not because it was forbidden. She again called them stupid and men without souls.[21]

One of them, an ugly man, seemed "a little better" than the others. He promised her "a little moon." Then, one night after the voyage, he showed her a hoe, a spade, and a tube. All of them were covered with moondust, and he allowed her to gather a light film of the silver powder on her hand by handling one of the objects. Having lost his soul to success, the little man wanted his possessions back immediately and became hard when she asked for the promised moondust. "You had it. I let you touch it."[22] According to the woman, he did exactly what wealthy people do to the poor when they allow them to admire a jewel in a store window. Quietly observing the moondust on her hands, she knew that it would soon disappear. Though she finally possessed it, she prepared to throw it away forever by washing her hands and watching the black liquid flow down the drain. In the fairy tale, the fetus is the moondust that the mother wants to have. "With the same certitude that paralyzed me on the night I knew you existed, I know now that you're dying."[23]

In the book, the pregnant mother's traumas, fears, sadness, and anger reflect Fallaci's personal life. The pregnant mother who works for an editor is, of course, the author herself. They share the same anxieties and the decision to pursue a career. Fallaci's reaction to the pregnancy is as described for the main character. As Fallaci herself states, she could never have so intimately portrayed the protagonist's anguish without having lost a child herself.

The obvious connection with autobiography even emerges in the fairy tale about moondust. The woman who dreamed of a little piece of the moon is also the Fallaci who reported on the NASA missions and ultimately felt disillusionment with the astronauts. At the time, she had considered the astronauts on the first moon trip middle-class Americans whose intelligence failed to measure up to the magnitude of their mission and whose vision of life remained curtailed by religious, social, and moral taboos. "On Saturday morning they cut their grass, and on Saturday evening they go to the movies to see Doris Day films. On Sunday morning, they attend mass or services at their Presbyterian, Methodist, or Episcopal church. On Monday morning they return to work, and on Monday evening they betray the wife." Fallaci had then described them as men who believed they should support the Vietnam War, regarded communism as a bad word, and avoided the company of Negroes. She had admitted that a small group of astronauts held alternate opinions but added that they remained silent out of fear of losing their opportunity to go to the moon.[24]

She had censured Al Shepard for his commercial interests and emphasized her disillusionment. "Heroes, said La Rochefoucauld, are like paintings: to appreciate them it is necessary to stay distant."[25] She had portrayed Buzz Aldrin in a negative light when he viewed moon travel as a technological accomplishment—nothing romantic. She had particularly disliked him for regretting not having bombed Hanoi during the Vietnam War.[26] In a comparison, Fallaci had referred to Neil Armstrong as boring and presumptuous.[27] When Armstrong made his famous statement—"That's one small step for man, one giant leap for mankind"—she had criticized the words. "It was a rhetorical sentence and sounded a bit false, a bit funny, in his technological pilot's jargon. As though realizing it, Armstrong said it very fast and in an embarrassed whisper."[28]

In addition, Fallaci's attachment to and fondness for Charles Conrad, "her brother Pete," is an important part of *If the Sun Dies* and also appears in the fairy tale.[29] The mother draws a favorable portrait of one of the space travelers—a direct reference to Conrad: "And yet there was one who seemed to me a little better. Because he knew how to laugh and cry. He was an ugly little man with gaps between his teeth."[30] In an article for *Europeo*, Fallaci includes a photograph of Conrad—one showing his teeth with a big gap and a funny hat on his head.[31] Her claim that she and Conrad talked about what he would say on the moon is given in the fairy tale as the ugly astronaut's conversation with the mother.[32] "Each time we met, he grumbled, 'What shall I say up there? I'm not a poet, I don't know how to say profound and beautiful things.' A few days before going to the moon, he came to say good-bye to me and ask me what to say on the moon."[33]

Similarly, the woman's enthusiasm then wanes toward the astronaut just as Fallaci's had toward Conrad. After openly expressing many disapproving comments about America's space heroes, Fallaci eventually liked Conrad, but then she disliked him. Rather than openly express her disaffection she cautiously describes it under the protective veil of a fairy tale. After the flight of *Apollo 12*, Fallaci, who had been in Vietnam, wanted Pete to meet a French journalist with whom she had worked in Saigon. They went to Pete's home for dinner and began to discuss politics. Never having liked Nixon, she began to criticize the president for daring to order the bombing of Laos. Pete then committed the unpardonable offense of opposing Oriana Fallaci in the presence of her friend. He told her in no uncertain terms that there was noth-ing wrong with bombing Laos. The Vietcong had chosen to use the country as a route for their supply lines—something they should not have done. The astronaut explained that Fallaci argued right back. However, she had mis-taken his even temperament for submissiveness. He promptly stated that if American politics were so displeasing to her she should pack her bags and go back to Italy. There, she could contemplate the ruins with which her country had done nothing for two thousand years. That night, an angry Fallaci left Pete's home.[34]

The next day, Conrad was at a meeting with NASA officials. His secre-tary interrupted saying that Fallaci was on the phone and insisted on speak-ing to him. So he spoke to her in the presence of four colleagues. She wanted to know whether he really meant what he had said. He bluntly informed her that he had meant every word. The brief exchange was far from pleasant. Fallaci used the word *fuck* several times—a habit she still has to this day. Pete fired right back. That was the last time Pete heard from Oriana for many years. There was one exception. He did receive a letter in which she informed *him* how bad *he* was.[35]

On the night of the dinner at his home, Conrad did show Fallaci his shovel from the moon trip, and there was a film of dust on it. The mother's references in the fairy tale accurately reflect Conrad's account. They also mirror her loss of friendship with Pete Conrad, for whom she had expressed deep admiration and affection. Fallaci simply transferred this autobiographi-cal data into her book, linked it to her moral, and called it a fairy tale. Fallaci's tendency to form attachments, swiftly broken, if she perceives what she labels betrayal, characterizes many of her relationships. She will intensely focus on an individual until a rupture occurs. In the case of Alekos Panagoulis, the Greek imprisoned and tortured for having opposed the military junta in Greece, a similar dynamic occurred. She became his mistress and was obsessed with him (although she denies the obsession). A definite rift did not transpire with Alekos, but he died before the opportunity for a probable separation could have occurred. Nevertheless, a great deal of tension existed in the relationship, especially toward the end. They violently fought and argued. During one physical fight, she received a blow to the stomach. Immediately after, she miscarried their child.[36]

The theme of doubt further reinforces the connection with autobiography. Both Fallaci and the mother have a difficult time deciding whether to place their children in a terrible world. The writer's greatest apprehension resembles the mother's; each does not fear death but what comes after it. "If one dies, it means one was born, that one emerged from nothingness, and nothing is worse than nothingness."[37] Since each human being eventually returns to a state of nonexistence, her major concern becomes a justification of life. An avowed atheist, Fallaci early rejected religion for its false promises and began a search to sustain and generate optimism.[38] Her conclusion is that the continuation of life is a qualitative and tangible reality, despite the nothingness awaiting people after death. This perception alone provides some general motivation for maintaining a positive attitude toward humanity's fate. As the mother's condition rapidly deteriorates at the end, she voices this outlook.

> A light is on. I hear voices. Someone is running, crying out in despair. But elsewhere a thousand, a hundred thousand children are being born, and mothers of future children: life doesn't need you or me. You're dead. Maybe I'm dying too. But it doesn't matter. Because life doesn't die.[39]

Despite heroic attempts to maintain a positive outlook toward the human condition, the writer obstinately sustains the pessimistic skepticism of *Letter to a Child Never Born* and rejects easy interpretations of her novel. "Those who write that it is a book about abortion are fucking idiots. It is not a book about abortion; it is a book about doubt—*essere o non essere*; to be or not to be."[40] Fallaci is even ambiguous about love as a generating force in life. The mother in the novel mirrors this view when she suspects that someone may have invented the notion of mutual affection as a way of keeping people well behaved and as a panacea for tragedy in life. The mother hates the word *love*, tries never to use it, and thinks of the child in terms of life rather than emotional attachment. She refers to her earlier relationships as "disappointing ghosts in a search that always failed" and learns that "nothing threatens your freedom as much as the mysterious rapture that a human being can feel toward another."[41] She uses a comparison to illustrate the illusory nature of emotional submission. "Like a dog floundering in the water you try vainly to reach a shore that doesn't exist, a shore whose name is Loving and Being Loved."[42] Fallaci's life inspires these negative conclusions. She has had intimate relationships with men who have fathered the infants she could not carry; nevertheless, she has not established meaningful bonds that have withstood the test of time.

Fallaci gives vent to the inclinations of her performing self in the form of three fables that concretely stage highlights from her personal life. Unable to write her memoirs directly and claim the title *novel* for her book, she camouflages autobiographical details under the guise of fables that underscore the mother's and Fallaci's shared belief in the hardness of life. In the first, a child loves a magnolia tree in the garden below her window and, on the adjoining terrace, views many articles of clothing hanging on a line to dry. One day a woman who ordinarily comes to collect them stops to admire the magnolia tree and meets a man who embraces her. They make love and fall asleep until another man arrives and angrily attacks them. He drives away his rival, cruelly beats the woman, and finally kills her by throwing her into the magnolia tree. The protagonist reveals that she learned the moral early in life. "I was that little girl. May God protect you from learning the way I learned that it is always the strongest, the cruelest, the least generous who wins."[43]

The second fable is about a child who loved chocolate and ate as much as she desired when living in a house full of light. One morning, she awakens in an apartment below sidewalk level and remembers feet walking by little windows, dogs urinating on their protective bars, very little sunshine, and no chocolate. Her mother's stomach grows fatter while her father stays in bed each day with a nagging cough. To earn money, her mother works at the home of a rich aunt, washing dishes and cleaning her rooms. When the rich aunt complains that she has received insufficient funds from a business affair, the child's mother replies that she would have felt like a princess with the amount in question. The rich aunt's response is humiliating. "To me it's barely enough for taxis. You don't mean to compare yourself to me!"[44] The child begins to weep, notices a big jar filled with chocolates wrapped in gold foil, but remains silent in obedience to her mother's stern eyes. The rich aunt opens the jar and begins throwing the candy to wealthy children playing on the terrace below. She also slowly eats a piece and savors its taste as the child silently watches. The narrator/mother in the novel explains that she could no longer eat chocolate after that day. She actually vomits if she forces herself to take a piece. She admonishes the unborn child to expect only injustice in life. "I mean the injustice that separates the haves from the have-nots. The injustice that leaves this poison in the mouth, while the pregnant mother brushes someone else's carpet."[45]

In the third fable, a little girl believes in a better tomorrow. Her priest, teachers, and father all indoctrinate her with a strong faith in the future. However, she soon rejects religion and the kingdom of heaven, as well as education's vision of human progress, and becomes a skeptic when sores cover her hands and feet. Nevertheless, she continues to believe in her father, who had battled arrogant men dressed in black during the preceding twenty years. These same men begin a war, leave one night in July, and then return in September with other arrogant men speaking German. The father speaks of friends and allies (even though they bomb the city) and helps prisoners escape. On a splendid day in August, the friends arrive—handsome, smiling, festive angels in uniform—and receive homage from all of the townspeople. They summon her father to headquarters, where he finds a man, bent over with his head on the ground, crying for his mother. The commander informs her father that the man has stolen a sack filled with food. The little girl never forgets his pointed face, carrot-colored mustache, and the little whip in his hand. "Let me inform you that your people have welcomed us by stealing."[46] The commander states that in his country thieves are shot. After the British leave, everyone in the city awaits the arrival of the humanitarian Americans but soon learns that they too rape women and behave as big bosses. The lesson of the fable stresses that tomorrow is never better and that empty promises fill a mind with illusions.

As in the case of the fairy tale, Fallaci's personal experience informs the structure and spirit of the three fables. In the first fable, the magnolia tree was the same that Fallaci enjoyed as a little girl from her fifth-floor apartment on Florence's Via del Piaggione. On the opposite side of her home, she enjoyed a breathtaking view of the city's cathedral. The mother's description of herself as a child could easily have been the author's self-portrait. "Once upon a time there was a little girl who was in love with a magnolia tree. The magnolia stood in the middle of the garden. The little girl used to look at it for days on end, leaning out of the window from the top floor of a house facing on that garden."[47] Fallaci has always loved the big white flowers of magnolias and detests the fact that they turn yellow so easily. A beautiful magnolia also graced the garden of the family home on Via Mercadente. She also looks out on a magnolia tree that her father planted in the front garden of her current home on Via Giovanni Prati.

In the second fable, the child's awakening in a horrible basement apartment is also taken from Fallaci's personal life. After living in the happy residence on Via del Piaggione, where she enjoyed light, sunshine, a magnificent view of Florence, and as much chocolate as she wanted, the young child moved with her family to the dreadful location in the Piazza del Carmine, where the tenor of life changed drastically. No magnolia tree graced the premises. Her father was sick with a fever and a nagging cough and, because he refused to register as a member of the National Fascist Party and carry their identification card, was persecuted by Fascists. Her parents had rented the basement apartment, a humiliating condition for Italians, who traditionally prefer to lease on the highest possible floors. There was no more light and sky. The fable captures this unhappy phase. "From the windows of her new room, which were placed almost at the ceiling and protected by a prison grating, all she could see were feet going back and forth." After passing dogs lifted their legs to urinate on the grating, the little girl's mother wept. "Oh, no, not that!"[48] Her father coughed and stayed in bed during the day. His face turned yellow and his eyes shone.

Even the third fable derives from Fallaci's personal experiences during the war years: her exposure to Catholicism, her developing skepticism, and her specific recollections from the Resistance, liberation, and occupation. The little girl voices a young Fallaci's memory of Italy's capitulation and the subsequent Fascist-Nazi forces returning to Florence. "September came and the arrogant men returned, with new ones who spoke German."[49] The girl's father resembles Fallaci's father; they both calm fears of betrayal by assuring their daughters they are no longer alone. "Friends were arriving, a whole army of friends who were called allies."[50] The narrator's words in the fable also bring to mind the British and American bombing of Florence that Fallaci emphasizes in many of her articles. "Next day the girl's city was bombarded by the friends who were called allies and a bomb fell right in front of her house."[51] The child's father again tried to allay her anxiety about Allied friendship. "The better to convince her he brought into the house two of those [Allied soldiers] who had dropped bombs." They had become German prisoners but escaped. When father and daughter helped them reach safety, they duplicated Edoardo and Oriana Fallaci's clandestine activities in the Resistance. "Together with her father, who was risking the firing squad for these men, she hid the friends and fed them and guided them to safe villages."[52]

The narrator even makes direct references to Edoardo Fallaci's arrest and torture, as well as his daughter's subsequent visit. "The girl visited him in prison and could hardly recognize him, he had been so tortured."[53] The narrator further connects the father to Edoardo Fallaci by alluding to his attempt to cheer up his family—an autobiographical detail about which Fallaci had earlier written. Finally, the fable underscores the father's popularity, a transparent connection to the prestige enjoyed by Edoardo after the liberation of Florence. "The girl's father, now freed, was greeted by everyone with great deference and in his eyes shone the light of one who has known the faith."[54] The three fables reflect such prominent associations with Oriana Fallaci's life that the book emerges as a camouflaged autobiography transformed by a literary journalist into a rich account and labeled a novel.

The relationship between incidents in the book and Fallaci's life—the mother's atheism, employment with a newspaper, miscarriage, views on the dubious value and hardness of life, attitudes toward American astronauts, and the references to her own childhood—provides insight into how the writer transforms her lived experience. Autobiographical details blend together to form and embellish a new entity. This tendency to combine particular memories and events as the basis for a redesigned, recreated reality characterizes how Fallaci wrote *Letter to a Child Never Born*. She observed, listened, spied, and stole from life to refashion the souvenirs into a new unity. Then, too, a particular moment in the history of the Italian abortion controversy provided additional motivation to initiate and bring the book to its conclusion.

When she began writing the book, Fallaci had no idea what type of structure it would take. She did not begin with what her uncle called *la scaletta* (a brief summary in outline form). Bruno believed that a novel first required a synopsis. With a typical twist of irony, Fallaci notes, he composed no books during his lifetime; she simply ignored his teaching. "If you put *la scaletta* together beforehand, you've already written the book."[55] According to Fallaci, the creative process is like giving birth to a child. New life appears after a long period of gestation; the fetus only leaves its mother's womb when it is ready. Incubation sometimes lasts five or six years. Fallaci consequently discusses a work only after its completion. "Because when spermatozoon enters an egg, a mysterious and confused process takes place and requires time to set it on fire." An artist may plan on using red for his painting but suddenly change to a different color. The masterpiece becomes apparent only after the final stroke. The entire operation moves slowly. "It is like yeast that causes bread to rise."[56]

Fallaci refuses to plan her chapters and believes that a new insight might change her design and previously planned format. She asserts that *Letter to a Child Never Born* created its own story and welcomed its author as an active participant. At a certain point, she stopped writing, revised, eliminated, rewrote, and then faltered, utterly confused. Very late in the process, an unexpected spark reignited her creative energy. She had imagined the mother delirious and then a trial in which she is charged with allowing the child to die. She came to a standstill. Filled with frustration, she told the incomplete story to friends at dinner. "What will happen during the trial? What will happen? I am bogged down in this trial; I am filled with despair." She even told the plot to her mother, who loved every detail, and to her adopted sister Elisabetta. "I can't go on because I do not understand who can accuse the mother." Tosca stared intently but said nothing. Her little sister spoke up quickly. "The baby will; it's obvious; he accuses her; he is the one who died! He accuses her of not allowing him to be born." That was another moment of conception. "You're right Elisabetta, good girl! It is the baby who accuses her!"[57] And then, with the directness, the simplicity, and the penetration of a child, Elisabetta summarized what the infant would say to the mother. Fallaci developed what her sister had provided at that dinner in Florence and finalized a key scene.

The trial is the mother's catharsis; it crystallizes the novel's themes, arguments, and characterizations. In a dream, the mother awakens in a snow-white room, seated in a cage; she stares at the seven members of the jury: the unfeeling male doctor, her friendly female physician, her employer, her feminist friend, the baby's father, and finally her own parents. Each speaks to the charge of murder, and the verdict is determined by a simple majority. The male doctor summarizes the classic pro-life argument that life begins at the moment of conception and reflects the miracle of creation. The female

physician argues as a feminist, choosing first the mother's safety. She faults
her colleague for refusing to extend the cult of life to whoever lives and calls
him a hypocrite for going to war and killing people, including children. The
child's father is a coward. He weeps and hesitates before accusing the mother
of guilt. The mother's woman friend attacks the father, reminding him that
he originally wanted an abortion and then remained away for the first two
months. She represents the feminist viewpoint, assailing a male-dominated
society in which men use women's bodies and relegate them to motherhood.
When the employer takes his turn, he provides the damaging evidence of a
motive for the crime. She feared that a rival colleague would take the business trip and therefore left her hospital bed to make the journey, utterly
without mercy for the child. The mother's disheartened, exhausted parents
defend individual choice; no one can enter another's conscience.

The unborn child finally enters the scene and asserts that everyone has
spoken truthfully but that only he can penetrate the essence of the question.
"Only I, Mother, can say that you killed me without killing me."[58] Because
the mother fails to communicate beautiful thoughts to her unborn child, she
can no longer save him. He understands that she tried to prepare him for
the horror of existence. He thus makes his first and final choice—a refusal
to be born. Why should he accept life if it involves so much torment? She
never tricks him by stating that he is created in the image of God, that he
would spend his earthly existence preparing to merit the reward of paradise.
Her only defense of life has been that birth assures the continuation of human existence. Developing to full term, therefore, appears to be an unreasonable act. "In my universe, which you call the egg, the purpose existed; it
was to be born. But in your world the purpose is only to die: life is a death
sentence. I don't see why I should have had to emerge from nothingness just
to return to nothingness."[59]

An experience similar to the unexpected conversation with her little sister further reinforced Fallaci's lack of faith in prefabricated story outlines.
A strong difference of opinion with her lover, Alekos Panagoulis, accounts
for the unanticipated ending in the book. In the first rendition, the mother
dies from complications after the miscarriage.[60] In the final rendering, she
lies in her hospital bed and utters words that leave the ending unclear.

> The cold goes away when I say that life exists, my drowsiness goes away, I
> feel I'm life itself. A light is on. I hear voices. Someone is running, crying

out of despair. But elsewhere a thousand, a hundred thousand children are
being born, and mothers of future children: life doesn't need you or me.
You're dead. Maybe I'm dying too.[61]

From the moment of her first meeting Alessandro Panagoulis in Athens
on Thursday, 23 August 1973, Fallaci regarded Alekos's home as her second
residence, even decorating it with Italian furniture. She completed the novel
in Florence at their shared apartment and, after receiving galley proofs from
her editor, decided to correct them at his residence in the Greek capital,
where the exiled Panagoulis had returned after the reestablishment of democracy. He had been elected a legislative deputy. His days in Parliament
allowed Fallaci sufficient private time to make all of the needed revisions.

Fallaci is fiercely protective of and secretive about anything she writes
and hid her manuscript under a pile of paper. Panagoulis found it anyway,
read it without her knowledge, and then made two suggestions. The first
dealt with making an already lyrical text completely lyrical.[62] He himself
had authored a book of poetry entitled *Vi scrivo da un carcere in Grecia*,
which she and several friends helped translate from Greek to Italian.[63] He
told his astonished mistress that her pages read like poetry and that she
should write every sentence as though writing a poem. "Last night I knew
you existed: a drop of life escaped from nothingness" (first line); "I was lying,
my eyes wide open in the darkness, and all at once I was certain you were
there" (second line). With typical brio, Fallaci expressed her amazement in
no uncertain terms. "You are an idiot."[64] Furthermore, how dare he read the
manuscript without her permission?

His second suggestion caused additional exasperation. He wanted the
main character to live.

"Barbarian, you killed that poor woman."
"I will kill whomever I want to kill."[65]

She became so indignant that she packed her things and checked into a
nearby hotel. The next morning, he called her on the telephone and, speaking
Italian with his thick Greek accent, tried to settle the dispute.

"If you agrrreeee to rretourn, I to do little amistizio. I give you a prezent."
"What kind of present?"
"A prezent buotiful wrrriiten, a prrezent; a vrze of poetry."[66]

If he had offered her a beautiful diamond, she would have refused—"Bah! I don't want your jewelry"—but she could never ignore a literary gift. She went back to him. Standing at the door with a big grin on his face, he proposed the ultimate solution. "If you do not kill that poor woman, I will give you the last three words of your book." And so, she continued her gradual capitulation and listened to the words—"Life does not die."[67] She liked it so much that she changed the final lines in her book from *You have died. Now I will also die*" to *"Maybe I'm dying too. But it doesn't matter. Because life doesn't die.*" Fallaci did not know how the last sentence would read when she began the book; she simply placed her faith in the future and refused to adhere to rigid guidelines.

Letter to a Child Never Born, which was successful from the moment of publication in 1975, is a mixture of social history, true confession, and fiction.[68] Readers recognize Fallaci in the person of the mother. They understand that she is the journalist expecting a child and debating whether or not to have an abortion. They see *her* thoughts, *her* information, and all the trimmings of *her* heart. They instinctively know that her book takes the place of children she will never have, that it receives the discipline she would have dedicated to child rearing. They receive it all in the form of entertaining, popular literature that communicates Oriana Fallaci's anguish and doubts toward life and death.

The Man or the Woman

10.

MORE OBVIOUSLY THAN *LETTER TO A Child Never Born*, *Un uomo* demonstrates Fallaci's conjoining of journalism, fiction, and autobiography. The 1979 book also widened the rift between the author and translators. Fallaci had first wanted John Shepley to translate *Un uomo* into the English *A Man* and to capture the Oracle-at-Delphi quality of Alekos Panagoulis's voice. But then her editor called Shepley to inform him that Simon and Schuster had big publicity plans for the novel and that they would choose a famous translator. They picked the "king of Italian translators," William Weaver. Shepley, though disappointed, was willing to absolve Fallaci of blame and to attribute his dismissal to the insistence of her editor. He did not go so far as to accuse her of reneging on her promise, but when he mentioned it in a phone conversation—"I understand you want a big-name translator"—she replied coolly that she did not need a translator's name to sell her books.[1] This conversation marked the beginning of the end of Shepley's rapport with the writer.

Around that same time, Shepley had agreed to translate Enzo Siciliano's biography of Pier Paolo Pasolini. Since Fallaci had not acknowledged responsibility for dropping him, she might have expressed satisfaction that he had found another important project to replace her own. Instead, she strenuously objected, even though Siciliano is considered a serious writer-critic in Italy. According to Shepley, Fallaci disliked the way Siciliano had used her interview with Pasolini and expressed no happiness for the translator's acquisition of a prestigious contract. As Shepley explained, she cursed Siciliano and absolutely did not want to see his book translated into English by anyone. Nevertheless, Shepley went ahead and honored his agreement with Siciliano. The biography of Pasolini was published by Random House in 1982.[2]

When Fallaci began to write *A Man* in 1976, she still felt allegiance to journalism, but a series of events helped sever formal ties with *Europeo*. Her lover, Alekos Panagoulis, died under suspicious circumstances in May of that year. Then her mother, Tosca, fought a long, agonizing, losing battle with cancer. After losing the most important people in her life, she took stock of her age, which was then over forty, and wondered whether to continue to dedicate herself in such a passionate manner to a profession entered as a compromise. In the midst of this soul-searching, the directors of *Europeo* initiated a new set of policies that disgusted Fallaci. What used to be one of Europe's most serious publications became sensational: bare breasts and buttocks, pubic hair, nude women in nuns' wimples, and naked couples on automobile seats. "It was like seeing a body smeared with shit. The body of *Europeo*, the journal to which I had given my life."[3] In addition, *Europeo* replaced Tommaso Giglio with another editor in 1976. Fallaci regarded the sudden termination of this erudite, highly respected professional as unjust. She resigned in protest and withdrew to her country home at Grevi in Chianti to compose her book about Panagoulis.

Having decided to quit her job, she devoted herself to the writing of her book with unprecedented discipline, laboring for three and one-half years. "I wouldn't even answer the phone; I didn't even hear it. I went on and on, isolated in myself. No food, no talk, no interruptions."[4] In the evening, she ate very little; smoking sixty cigarettes a day killed all desire for nourishment. Afterwards, she watched some television (she always appreciated a good Western) and ended the day with a newscast. "When I would at last go to bed, I'd suffer from insomnia, unable to stop thinking about the book. Even in sleep, I would go on dreaming about the book."[5] The routine sometimes proved frustrating. Seeing that Mao Zedong had died, that elections were taking place in America, and that Vietnam had invaded Cambodia, she

wanted to witness the electoral results or travel to the Far East. "It was the
life of Tantalus. But I couldn't do any of it—the book had to come first."[6]
Living only for Alekos Panagoulis, she committed her whole being to completing her task. "It is my death because each day it takes my life from me: it
devours me like a cancer."[7]

Despite Fallaci's use of the Italian word *romanzo* (novel), her book
exudes the personality and energy of journalism. In fact, her earlier writing
about Panagoulis became the foundation of the book. She may have changed
time sequences and taken liberties with names and places, but she still remains magnetically attached to real information and events.

Fallaci summarizes her entire relationship with Panagoulis in the introduction to her interview with him.[8] This chronological account of her three-
year private life with the Greek resistance hero emerges again as the content
of *A Man*. Meeting him at his home in Athens in August 1973, she writes,
she is immediately overwhelmed by the suffering he had experienced in
prison and by his refusal to cooperate with the military regime. She discusses
his poetry and her many subsequent visits to Greece, minutely describes his
constant harassment by government agents, and reveals that they had become lovers. As an expatriate in Italy, Panagoulis organizes resistance against
the government until civilian government is restored in the summer of 1974.
He then returns to Athens in August and successfully enters politics. He realizes that the real enemy is Minister of Defense Evanghelos Averoff-Tositsas,
and he skyrockets into fame as the man most threatening to the leaders of
the false and vacuous democracy. His tremendous pride militates against his
taking precautions and consequently facilitates his appointment with destiny.
Averoff-Tositsas has convinced the national judiciary to prohibit publication
of Panagoulis's evidence against him on the grounds of national security. The
hero's only option is publicly, histrionically to present his incriminating files
to Prime Minister Konstantinos Karamanlis during a parliamentary session.
This was to have occurred early Monday morning, 3 May 1976. On the way
to his mother's home in Glyphada, however, sometime between Friday evening and the early hours of Saturday morning, two cars begin to follow him
and, on Via Vouliagmeni, sideswipe him at a high rate of speed, hurling him
off the road. He died a short while later.[9]

Fallaci herself maintains that *A Man* contains true information but that
it is still a novel. "The facts are real, so this made the book difficult to write.
I do not use my own name in the book, but sometimes I use the word 'you'
to describe my own feelings." The entire account is a true story in which the

main words are those of Alekos. "I recall very well the things he told me, the way he expressed his political beliefs. My memory was still fresh when I started writing the book, and he often repeated himself about his ideas." She consequently made journalistic data the core of her book. However, Fallaci still clings to the title of *novelist* because she discarded some material and maintains that the whole truth would have been unbelievable. "I left out an attempt on his life in Rome because it would have diminished the impact of the final attempt in Athens when he died. In fact, there were many more attempts on his life. In a novel, the empty spaces count, too."[10]

Historical facts are the skeletal structure of the account, which points an accusing finger at high members of the government. However, since the author had strong suspicions rather than absolute proof, a certain amount of ambiguity characterizes the accusations. Even news articles and critics stopped short of directly pointing a finger at Averoff-Tositsas, the prime minister, or other members of his cabinet and simply stated that Panagoulis died under very mysterious circumstances. Greek journalist Georgios Bertsos sees Fallaci's evidence as inconclusive. She charges that Averoff-Tositsas personally threatened Panagoulis, but the documentary evidence against the defense minister consists mainly of cordial letters to members of the junta government, part of his policy to create a "bridge" between the colonels and a new democratic regime. "Averoff[-Tositsas] never denied his communications with the junta," says Bertsos. "None of Fallaci's arguments prove anything or reveal anything that we didn't already know."[11] Nevertheless, the novel's allegations so seriously indict high-ranking officials that, for politically aware readers, it would have been difficult to mistake identities. No member of Greece's former ruling party has ever challenged their accuracy or refuted in court her many damaging innuendos. Their silence lends validity to her accusations.

The form of *A Man* changed several times during the three-year period of its composition. She wrote the prologue later and completed a first draft that was almost three hundred pages longer than the final version. She compares it to an overdecorated outfit and calls it the infancy stage of what would become a revised and mature novel. Although parts of the longer manuscript pleased her, she eliminated 230 pages despite her editor's objections. "Do you realize that you are throwing a book away? There are people who would buy this book." The conversation took place on a cold winter evening at her country home as wood burned brightly in the fireplace. Recalling it, she grows pale with anger. Her editor began,

"Sooner or later, I will publish that part."

"You must be joking."

"No, I am not joking."

"You will never do anything with this because it is my book. If I do not wish to publish this part. . . . Look at what I am doing."[12]

She threw the pages into the blazing fire, provoking her editor to cry out, "Ahhhhhhhhhhh!!!!" Her impulsive gesture was an angry protest against the editor's arrogance. "When I do not like something, I burn it."[13]

The inspiration to write a novel about Alekos Panagoulis occurred during his funeral. On that day, she felt the creative impulse that would motivate her long and arduous task. Photographers and reporters from all over the world attended, as did a mass of mourning countrymen. Fallaci vividly described the crowd as a nightmarish monster that inundated her with affection, imploring her to write truthfully the hero's story. On the spot, she resolved to preserve his memory by narrating every detail of his harried existence and of their relationship.[14]

In the book itself, Fallaci comments on its genesis. During a private reception with Archbishop Makarios III subsequent to the attempted overthrow of his government in Cyprus, Panagoulis explains the nature of his research against the Greek regime. "Your Eminence, there is a great deal to be discovered about the coup on Cyprus. I am told that [Dimitrios] Ioannidis fell into a trap set for him by the CIA and by some Greek politicians." The Cypriot leader warns him that his search for evidence could result in his death. Later in the hotel, Fallaci expresses her concern about the risky nature of his investigation. "Alekos, did you hear what Makarios thinks?" Alekos's response alludes to the book that she would write.

"Don't forget it in the book."

"What book?"

"The book you will write after my death."

"What death? You're not going to die and I'm not going to write any book."

"I will die and you will write a book."[15]

Fallaci uses a wide variety of literary techniques in her attempt to transform biographical events into a rich novelistic account of Panagoulis's life. The narration summarizes his personal investigation of the country's corrupt government and preserves the memory of a charismatic figure, crushed by the Greek power structure. Panagoulis emerges as the prototype of the poet who declines to become the instrument of power, who rejects the efforts of those who purchase or force obedience, and who perseveringly fights alone for truth and freedom. He dies the victim of cunning leaders, docile servants, violent torturers, and indifferent compatriots. The book indicts tyranny in its portrayal of a modern hero, and, in the process, generates truth in a literary and journalistic experience.

The prologue introduces the funeral and uses a scene construction that cuts from one geographical or chronological site to the next, resorting as little as possible to straight-line narrative. Fallaci panoramically conveys his burial on Wednesday, 5 May 1976 by skillfully combining five main movements interspersed with personal reactions. She first delineates the onslaught of the populace toward the cathedral where the hero's body is laying in state and records the painful, angry cries—"Zi, zi, zi! He lives! He lives, he lives, he lives!" The writer then cuts to within the cathedral, focusing on a second series of situations—the crystal-covered coffin, bolted portals, and visits from such hypocritical servants of the power structure as government delegates, fraudulent opponents of the country's demagogues, political profit seekers, members of the clergy, and the Orthodox patriarch. The frightening collapse of the main doors introduces the third segment of the scenario: the onrushing crowd, its crushing weight around the catafalque, and heroic attempts to carry out the coffin create frenzy and despair. A creeping three-hour funeral procession through a sea of humanity constitutes the fourth key element of the description. The fifth emphasizes the arrival at the cemetery, the transportation of the body to the grave, the enigmatic silence that engulfs the concluding ceremony (despite the presence of tens of thousands of spectators), and then the crowd's spontaneous chants after the actual burial, "Alekos isn't dead . . . zi, zi, zi! He lives, he lives, he lives!"[16]

One of the most striking examples of description is the first incident Fallaci actually wrote—the scene in which Alekos dies in a car wreck. The protagonist's death occupies only one paragraph set off from the rest of the text and rendered as a triptych. A taxi driver first reaches the crash site, advances through a cloud of thick dust, and incredulously beholds the mass of twisted steel and crushed windowpanes on the narrow incline descending to an underground garage. The second part focuses on the act of pulling the broken victim from the tangled wreckage and dragging him to a nearby sidewalk. The final segment deals with a futile attempt to save him as bystanders grab his dislocated arms and severed legs, place him on the backseat of the taxi, and speed toward the nearest hospital. However, he dies en route after speaking his last words. "Oh Theos! Theos mou! Oh, God! My God!"[17] This brief and isolated description of the death scene began Fallaci's long and arduous process of writing a finished book and never evolved or underwent revision. She ordinarily revises and rewrites scrupulously but never changed that piece.[18]

The reproduction of Panagoulis's statements also stands as one of Fallaci's methodological mainstays; the character reveals himself, develops action, plot, and personality through the words he speaks. When accused of subversion, attempted assassination, possession of explosives, and desertion, Alekos denies nothing since it is all true. However, when his judges maintain that they have a signed confession, he jumps up, raises his index finger at them, calls them liars, and says: "I denounce you, I condemn you, for your torture, for your torture!"[19] Unremitting counteraccusations during his trial not only focus attention on abuses under the military regime but also reveal Panagoulis's refusal to bow to tyranny. Dialogues or tirades expose his defiant character.

Right from the start, Fallaci writes in the second person singular, addressing herself to Alekos, and sets a rhythm that remains constant. She speaks only to him, as though he is the other person in an intimate dialogue, and chooses to communicate with a dead man rather than to live readers, accenting the solitude that had united them. In the prologue, she explains his funeral (to him) and justifies her method by referring to the dead lover as her "only possible interlocutor."[20] She speaks as though he accepts and understands her because they had thought the same politically. The technique of direct address had already appeared in *Letter to a Child Never Born*, where the mother speaks directly to the baby. However, its use in *A Man*, because the book is much longer, is more sustained and launches a vast accusation against the power structure.[21]

After the protagonist is condemned to death before a firing squad, Fallaci captures the existential despair of a man in his minutes before execution. He fears dying in the rain and hopes they will aim straight for his heart rather than his face. Despite his plan to scream out a heroic slogan before they pull the trigger, he continues to experience nauseating anxiety. Philosophical disgust invades his entire being. The usual metaphysical questions are easy in comparison to comprehending a sudden cessation of existence.

As given in *A Man*, years after Panagoulis's stayed execution Fallaci asks Alekos what he had thought about during what he believed would be his last five minutes. His reference to three works—Fyodor Dostoyevsky's *Idiot*, Albert Camus's *Stranger*, and Níkos Kazantzákis's *Last Temptation of Christ*—summarizes his feelings. He had identified with Meursault prior to his execution and with Jesus the night before the crucifixion. He gets into an argument with her about Dostoyevsky's book. She insists that nothing similar happened in *The Idiot* while he maintains the opposite.[22] "You answered that I was wrong, that as a young man Dostoyevsky had been sentenced to death for a political crime and reprieved twenty minutes before being tied to the stake; in the book, it was Prince Myshkin who told the story."[23] Trying in vain to find the passage in one of the two volumes, he finally concludes that he might have made an error. However, Fallaci indicates that he had actually been right. After his death, she discovers the passage. He must have placed a piece of paper in the book at the appropriate page and then forgotten. Picking it up, she notices the underlined words about the seemingly unending and immensely rich last five minutes of life. Dostoyevsky's condemned character could have lived many lives in the final interlude. He divides the remaining minutes into saying good-bye to his friends, thinking about himself, and looking around for a last time.

One of the most intriguing aspects of *A Man* is the development of Death as a major character. It has the presence of a smile without a face and establishes the atmosphere of epic tragedy. Not by chance did Fallaci quote Socrates in the dedication. "The hour of departure has arrived, and we go our ways—I to die, and you to live. Which is better only the god knows." In *A Man*, Panagoulis repeatedly speaks of death, sings hymns to it, courts it as a lovely woman, runs after it, and finally throws himself into its arms. Even after his release from prison, his fascination with dying continues. Taking Fallaci to Egina, where authorities had almost executed him, he relives the agony of his final moments, as well as the unexpected stay of execution, and actually experiences nostalgia.[24] "Because a man who has been sentenced to death, who has lived three days and three nights waiting for death, will never be the same again. He will always carry death with him, like a second skin, like a frustrated desire."[25]

In addition to existentialist overtones, the informative details, humor, and portraits sustain the reader's attention. During his five years of unending psychological and physical torture in the military prison at Boyati, the protagonist never loses his independent spirit. The word picture of the jail warden, Zakarakis, begins with his physical features and leads to caustic observations and burlesque humor. The prisoner first sees Zakarakis standing in front of his cell on the prison grounds. "A big man of about fifty with a huge bald head and a great beak of a nose. . . . Porcine eyes, at once dull and malignant. Fat mouth, nasty. Heavy, shaky hands, hands that could plead or strike with the same ease."[26] His sycophancy earns Panagoulis's disrespect. "I know what you're here for. You're here to tell me I'm handsome and you like me and you want me to fuck you. It's an old story, everyone knows that all the servants of the junta are faggots."[27]

The most startling example of humor occurs when he begins a radio news bulletin each evening related to the warden's sex life. "Nicholas Zakarakis, commandant of this shit farm, is suffering from liver trouble. Rumor has it that his disease is a consequence of the violent fury that seized him when he was unable to rape a prisoner who doesn't like faggots." Succeeding announcements maintain the same harassing tone that attracts the attention of guards and prisoners alike. "Zakarakis is a liar. He doesn't have liver trouble; he has hemorrhoids. This prisoner knows the truth because that pig showed them to him. He also explained that he got them from the Turks when he was working as a whore in a brothel in Constantinople."[28]

Accurate melodramatic details sustain interest in the hero's story. With the passing of time, he stops trying to escape from his cement block and no longer misses people, open space, or blue skies. Yet his mind resists and gives birth to beautiful verses. "You had always written poems, ever since you were a boy, but it was in this period that your creative vein burst forth, irrepressible. Dozens and dozens of poems. Almost every day a poem."[29] Even after Zakarakis confiscates all of his paper and pens, he finds a way to write by cutting his left wrist with a razor blade, using a match or toothpick dipped in blood as a pen, and writing on a gauze-pad wrapper or an empty cigarette box. When Zakarakis allows him to have paper again, he copies every word, folds up the sheets into narrow strips, and smuggles them out into the world to tell the tale of a man who refuses to surrender.

The main justification for Fallaci's insistence on calling *A Man* a novel is her attempt to refashion reality and historical events. Her power of imagination achieves its greatest success in this regard by creating a mythological archetype. Panagoulis represents more than a historical hero and emerges as a poetic figure or as a protagonist in an ancient fable. His human qualities are revealed in the book when he expresses disillusionment with his personal ideals, pursues sensual appetites, physically fights with Fallaci, causes the loss of their child, and struggles against political tyrants. Dream sequences then elevate him to the status of a mythological hero who sees his destiny unfold in the darkness of sleep. The first vision consists of a beautiful seagull with silver feathers flying over a sleeping city, diving into the water, and capturing fountains of light. The entire populace awakens to celebrate what everyone considers a victory. However, the author injects the voice of doom. "But you knew they were wrong, all of them, and the seagull had lost."[30] The image of majesty then gives way to the macabre vision of fish tearing the august creature to shreds. The narrator tells readers that dreams about fish have always been a harbinger of bad luck for Panagoulis and indicates that he could not remove the image from his mind on the night of the military coup in Greece. This imbues the story with mystery, simplicity, symbolism, and despair.

The description of the hero's attempt on the life of George Papadopoulos and his stealthy flight to a hiding place resembles something that could have appeared in a spy thriller or war movie. The account takes on the flavor of epic irony when the searching police captain stumbles, falls from a rock, and unexpectedly sees the unsuccessful assassin in his hiding place. They literally stare at each other like two wide-eyed characters in a comedy of errors. The police official fears being shot with a pistol that the fugitive does not have; the hero, hidden in the rocks, wearing only his underwear, laments his failure. The fugitive becomes a prisoner. "With the ferocity of the fish attacking the seagull in your dream, they fell on you."[31]

Panagoulis's second vision reinforces the impression of an ancient fable; it relates to his life and focuses on the death of his brother. His sibling deserts from the Greek army as a protester, flees to Israel via Turkey and Lebanon, and is captured by Israelis in Haifa. They then turn him over to the captain of a Greek ship who is to deliver him to the junta in Athens. When the vessel reaches Piraeus, the police find the cabin empty and the porthole open. Alekos knows that he has not disappeared because the dream has revealed it.

> You were walking with George along a mountain path, a path over a precipice that dropped to the sea. Suddenly the mountain shuddered, an avalanche engulfed George. "George!" you cried, clasping him. "George!" But you hadn't been able to hold on to him. And George had fallen into the sea, among the fish.[32]

The dream sequence injects into the narrative the charm of a popular tale and the gloom of a tragic premonition.

Mythological dimensions are further developed when Fallaci characterizes the opening of Panagoulis's case in a Greek law court as the natural outcome of physical forces. "Nineteen days later, when November had come with the winds from the north, the trial began."[33] The judges of the military regime appear as mysterious and poetic puppets representative of the comic forces of evil in an infant's tale or the denizens of a surrealistic universe: "Choked in their bottle green uniforms with gold buttons and red insignia."[34] The same type of prose recalls the concise, striking rhythm of ancient ballads. "They took you to the island of Egina where you waited three days and three nights to be shot."[35]

The paragraph dealing with Panagoulis's affection for a cockroach in his Boyati cell adds to the prisoner's tragedy but also introduces a surrealistic dimension. "He had long hairy legs and erect antennae like two bristles, but the amazing thing about him was his wings." The absurd monologue directed at the winged creature—"Fly . . . Jump, at least! Jump!"—animates the narrative with the magic of legend.[36] Then, when the pathetic insect dies, crushed under a soldier's boot, the white pulp incites feelings of pity, as though the prisoner is on the verge of losing control or possibly experiencing the loss of his only meaningful companion.

> You said you almost felt they had crushed a creature with two arms and two legs, not a cockroach, and that the idea of losing him made the blood rush to your head because suddenly it brought back to you the awareness of your solitude, the image of the empty cell, furnished with a slop bucket and nothing else.[37]

In the final analysis, it matters little whether the protagonist of *A Man* lived in the real world, whether he supported a leftist, rightist, or centrist regime, or whether he courageously opposed power in favor of individual freedom. Panagoulis emerges from the book's pages as an exciting combination of such heroes as Odysseus and Roland—a magical warrior armed with his lance in pursuit of twentieth-century tyrants.

When she composed *A Man*, Fallaci confronted the problem of giving the structure and form of a novel to events that actually took place and of betraying neither her personal creativity nor the facts. She used every conceivable literary avenue, combining techniques from realism, the spy thriller, classical tragedy, and lyrical description. By observing the life of Alekos Panagoulis and selecting pieces with an artist's touch, she not only captures the deeper half of reality that a documentary of his life in the style of cold,

clipped, factual biography would have excluded but also reinvents his story
and structures it with literary skill in a classic example of journalistic literature. If she had written a straight historical account, she could not have taken
liberty with time sequence or even expressed philosophic viewpoints without
compromising the objectivity of her content. Despite her enterprising embel-
lishments, Fallaci proudly asserts the verisimilitude of the story.

Personal information abounds on many pages. She reveals so much
about herself that she could legitimately call her book *A Woman*. A lyrical
description of Tuscany provides an intimate look at where Fallaci lives at
Grevi in Chianti. She walks along beautiful paths, breathes the fragrance of
fresh mushrooms and broom brushes, hears the wind blowing from hills lined
with cypress and fir trees, fishes for "eels in the gullies where the streams
roll over stones slippery with moss, and hunts hare and pheasant in the
underbrush of red heather." During harvesttime, purple grapes swell on thick
clumps of vine leaves while ripe figs hang from branches "that quiver with
chaffinches and larks." In the woods, yellow and orange begin to mingle
with summer's monotonous green leaves. The whole environment contributes
to a renewed state of mind. "If you feel tired of yourself and need to find
yourself again, wash away your doubts, there is no better place than Tuscany
in autumn."[38]

Flaming red ivy covers her beautiful, huge house on the hill up to the
second-floor windows and the merlons of the little tower. Rose bushes unexpectedly blossom as though springtime has joyfully returned. Cascades of
tender blue wisteria flow over the terrace railings. Even the strawberry tree
in front of the chapel sprouts purple berries that blackbirds gluttonously
devour. White water lilies float majestically on the water basin. The entire
passage summarizes the impact of the scene as Fallaci retreats from the agitation of her lover's troubled life and offers to him the refuge of her country
home.

In Florence, Fallaci had secretly rented an apartment on a large, secluded piece of property to protect herself and Alekos from unwelcome and
dangerous attention. When spies discover their hideaway and observe their
every move, she desperately blocks Alekos as he goes to confront them. She
struggles and fights with him; she receives a blow in the abdomen; she loses
the child she is carrying.[39]

When Panagoulis returns to Athens on 13 August 1974 and receives an
unimpressive welcome from his fellow Greeks, Fallaci manages to make her
own movements and statements more important than his. She calls him from

New York and offers her analysis of the Greeks' poor showing. She attributes it to inadequate publicity in newspapers and emphasizes her scorn and anger toward Greeks for their indifference. She feels they betrayed Panagoulis. In one scathing passage, she castigates people who always go where they are told to go, do what they are told to do, think what they are told to think, "victim of every established authority, of every dogma, of every church, every fashion, every ism, absolved of all guilt and cowardice by the demagogues who care nothing about it."[40]

Her wholesale condemnation in *A Man* enraged some Greek readers. Journalist Georgios Bertsos, who was instrumental in uncovering the 1963 assassination of leftist Deputy Grigorios Lambrakis (a conspiracy immortalized in the movie *Z*), was one of Fallaci's more understanding Greek critics.

> She would have wanted Panagoulis to have felt the same bitterness toward the Greek people that she was feeling. But he was not that way. He became very bitter and disappointed, especially with many of his colleagues [in Parliament], but he never, never accused the Greek people as a whole.[41]

Fallaci's subsequent letter to Alekos not only expresses her support but encourages him to pursue his plans. In *A Man*, she projects an image of herself as his spiritual mentor, reminding him that he had come to terms with human indifference in his poetry. She even tells him the story of Washington Irving's character Rip Van Winkle, arouses Alekos from his lethargy, and motivates his entry into national elections. When Fallaci joins him in Athens, she focuses less on his emaciated face than on her reaction to his unkempt appearance. She tries to console him during their ride from the airport but, once at his office, turns attention to her second emotional shock. A death threat has been written on the door below his name. She again releases her explanation of events—that the authors of the message intended to intimidate him on the day of national elections.

So often in the book, Fallaci's personal journey far overshadows her lover's. In melodramatic language, she explains that entering Alekos's life was her destiny, a concept that she fully embraces despite her disbelief in God. "If you deny fate, life becomes a series of missed opportunities, a regret for what never was and could have been . . . and the present is wasted, twisted into another missed opportunity."[42] Fallaci tries to explain why she and Alekos failed to meet earlier and, with a contrite heart, retraces her travels as a correspondent. Destiny required her presence in different cities,

just as it did their meeting in Athens on a particular day and hour. She
believes that she had met him earlier in the faces of the many resistance
figures she had encountered, that her life had followed a predetermined plan
that would ultimately lead her to him.

> If fate did not exist, if I hadn't had to become an instrument of your fate,
> we would have to ask ourselves why I telegraphed you on that August day
> and then rushed to Athens with the urgency of someone obeying a long
> awaited summons and why the moment I arrived in your city I had the
> presentiment that something was about to crash down on me.[43]

The sound of his first greeting—"Hello, you've come"—sealed her fate and
entwined their destinies.[44]

Fallaci keeps the focus on her own person when she explains how happy
she was with Panagoulis at the beginning of their liaison. She describes her
pride as she wears a beautiful red dress and enters a restaurant with him.
All eyes are upon her standing next to him. He holds her hand and dedicates
his favorite poem, "Viaggio," to her. She spends one utopistic week with him
at the shore in Glyphada. After her period of contentment ends, she centers
on her wave of unhappiness and physical danger. Along the narrow, altitu-
dinous ride to the hilltop town of Iráklion, two men in a blue automobile
almost force Oriana and Alekos off the mountain road into a deep ravine.[45]

Fallaci reveals how she begins to lose her attraction and enthusiasm for
Panagoulis, as though something has broken in her after fourteen months of
living with him. She no longer desires to walk in his desert or to relieve his
solitude. The personality that she had loved crumbles into a new and unrecognizable identity. She travels without him to London, Paris, and New
York to overcome her emotional crisis and salvage their mutual affection.
She then allows herself to return after receiving his letter. Lying in bed with
him, however, her feelings turn to disgust. Alekos tells her that he will seduce
the wife of his former jailer as an act of revenge. He will thus execute the
plan he had formulated while in prison—to take her physically so many
times that she will urinate blood. He further offends Fallaci when he asks
her to buy him the car in which he plans to court his victim.

Fallaci again melodramatically abandons her lover. She waits until he
leaves for Parliament and then rushes to the airport. While awaiting her
flight to New York, she analyzes her feelings for him and makes it known to
the reader that she had never found Panagoulis physically appealing, even

judging him a little ugly right from the start, and that she had found his mannerisms irritating. Her attraction, she reveals, had been spiritual; she had longed for his soul, his thoughts, his feelings, and poetry rather than his body. Nevertheless, the writer adds, she is consumed by a passion for Panagoulis but stresses her disgust. Her lover suddenly appears before her in the terminal, demands she return to him, orders her to rise when he speaks to her, and jabs her with his keys, before threatening to kill her if she moves toward the airplane. At that point, Fallaci insists that the gods will curse her if she ever steps foot again in the filthy city of Athens. Alekos reacts angrily by striking her in the chest. After the second blow, she leaves anyway and tells him to drop dead.[46]

Fallaci makes a point of describing how she rediscovers her equilibrium in New York. She belongs to her own world, not his. She speaks English, a language he could not understand, and enjoys familiar sights. In the evening, she explains, after returning home to her tenth-floor apartment in Manhattan, she revels in the view of the glittering city—the beautiful skyscrapers and bridges across the East River. She appreciates her own career and gives no thought to unstable Greek politics. Above all, she is free of the imposing personality of Panagoulis.[47]

In spite of her new freedom, Fallaci allows Alekos to trick her into returning to Athens. Then, against his wishes, she leaves, argues with him again, and goes to Amherst in Massachusetts to give a lecture on the role of newspapers in the formation of a political conscience in Europe. Her time in the New England college town is like anesthesia. She forgets the world of political turmoil in Greece. Freshly mown lawns, green trees, red homes with white columns and blue shingle roofs, enchanting clouds, and a warm welcome from kind, hospitable people free her from all anxiety.[48] Then, after colleagues at *Europeo* and personnel at Agenzia Nazionale Stampa Associata (ANSA) in Rome verify Panagoulis's death, Fallaci takes on the role of bereaved widow. She calls a taxi and hurries to the airport. Flight attendants behave sensitively and seat her far from other passengers. They respectfully give her private time to grieve. At the airport in Athens, his friends await her arrival. Photographers shoot so many flashbulbs that Fallaci feels like the national widow of Greece.[49]

Fallaci used to believe that love ensnared its victims and was an invented story to placate the unhappy. However, she must have felt its power after the hero's tragic death. Recalling Alekos's words—"I'll die soon, and then you will be stuck because you will love me forever"—she concludes that he was right and that he has conquered her. "When he was alive, I gave all I had to him, but he was not an obsession. Now that he is gone, he is a ghost inside my brain. Evidently love does exist—and I am stuck."[50] In *A Man*, Fallaci acts as a kind of Sancho Panza, loving, following, and acting as the voice of reason to a quixotic master. In real life, she did the same and, after his death, became another Don Quixote who did something dangerous—she wrote *A Man*. Writing a book that indicted both Greek and Italian officials entailed risk. "Don't expect I could go unpunished. There have been political repercussions." While composing it, she slept with a loaded rifle at her bedside because many offended politicians to the right, center, and left had expressed their displeasure. Not belonging to a political party, she had no support system for protection, feared that someone would confiscate the manuscript or prevent its publication, and consequently had it secretly printed. The writer dismissed the threats with typical brio. "The more they persecute me, the more the people love me."[51]

From the beginning, *A Man* has been at the center of controversy. The book decidedly cooled the Greek publishing house Papyros, which relinquished Greek rights, while complaining that *A Man* was "a howl of a wounded animal."[52] The book enraged Panagoulis's mother, Athena, and younger brother Stathis, both of whom affirmed that it distorted the facts, as well as his political credo. They felt that the author exploited his name for her own self-interest and stained the memory of a hero of the Greek resistance. Fallaci immediately reacted with swift anger toward Alekos's family for daring to challenge her motives. She labeled their attitude scandalous and incredible. The book, she countered, denounces the murder of Alekos and his enemies. She rejected their accusations, reminding them that she spent the last years of his life with him and that her intentions were to preserve his memory and unmask his enemies. She ended by expressing contempt for both members of the family.[53]

Robert Scheer infuriated Fallaci when, during their interview, he insisted that, in the book, there is not a single moment in which Alekos feels responsible for another human being—not even for her. "He seemed to say he had a nobler goal than most people and any means could be sacrificed to it." Scheer particularly criticized Fallaci's slant that Alekos's life of resistance to dictatorship defined the way a man should live. Alekos actually considered bombing the Acropolis to demonstrate his point and even talked about taking American tourists as hostages. "And you seem to endorse that." Scheer lectured Fallaci about the problem of a means to an end. "To consider kidnapping innocent American tourists in order to resist, that's a form of terrorism, and it's an important subject in the world today." Despite her attempt to refute the attack—"You Americans don't know what that was, the Resistance"—Scheer continued to take the writer to task. "You have a condescending view of Americans, and that comes out in the book as well. You write: 'America is made up of the rejects of Europe.' That isn't true."[54]

According to Scheer, Fallaci was neither Alekos's accomplice nor his sister. Because of him, she took risks that she did not believe in and went along with crazy things. "You wrote that you thought maybe he was mad. You went along like some teeny-bopper, some sorority girl. You did what lovesick groupies have always done: you went along with his plans, no matter what you thought for yourself." Scheer accused Fallaci of making Panagoulis an example to other men around the world who resist authoritarian power. He was like a prism and measuring rod for everything she believed about courage, politics, and life itself. "The test of a man is never being a reformer, making the world marginally better. It's never being a parent, diapering a baby. You seem contemptuous of anyone who takes small steps."[55] He challenged her view of bravery and suggested that individual acts of terrorism, although courageous, alienate people and end up as self-defeating. Fallaci attempted to counter Scheer's onslaughts but failed and unleashed her frustration. She told him that he would make a very good dictator; she screamed at him that he would not let her talk; she admitted feeling helpless in talking to him. "Even if you were a more tolerant interviewer, I feel as if I'm speaking Chinese."[56] Scheer's relentless pounding brought Fallaci's frustration to a head. "I remember when I did a story about the astronauts, I took a battery of intelligence tests and they were exhausting, they give me headaches. This is what you are doing to me. This is what you do with your fucking interview."[57]

After the death of Alekos, Fallaci dealt with personal suffering and, through the narrative magic of her book, prevented Panagoulis from disappearing into oblivion. The historical man who died in 1976 at the age of thirty-eight would in fact soon evaporate from people's memories but would live as the protagonist of the writer's journalistic novel. Fallaci too would burst forth from the same pages as the heroine who stands up to a military regime and sustains her lover in his struggle against power. It is as much her story as it is his. Fallaci tells about the revolutionary guards in Iran who mistakenly confuse an Italian journalist for her. After seizing the frightened individual, they hold up their copies of A Man in an act of adulation. They even force the terrified visitor to address a huge rally and introduce her as the author of the book.[58] If statistics indicate anything, they certainly attest to the fact that both characters—Oriana and Alekos—survive in the minds of a vast public. The Italian critic Ranieri Schippisi recognized the dual thrust of the book and commented, "Not only does the character Panagoulis dominate but the anxious, sorrowful femininity of the woman who lived with him for the last three years of his irresistible, tragic, existence also emerges."[59] According to Fallaci, three million people have read the book in twenty different languages.[60] What first pushed the writer to her typewriter after Panagoulis's death was grief and rage. What sustained her through three years of self-imprisonment while writing in Tuscany was a determination that the man she loved not be forgotten. "He is not defeated. I talk for him."[61] In the process, Fallaci also wrote her own autobiography.

Tolstoy, Dostoyevsky,
and Fallaci

11.

● FALLACI REACHED THE HEIGHT OF HER writing career in 1990 with the publication of *Insciallah*, her most mature book.[1] Her use of the Arabic word *insciallah*, which means "as God wills," emphasizes her concern with human destiny and search for answers to the eternal questions. The book is the expression of a new image. Fallaci wanted the world to see her as a hermetic, literary writer, entirely devoted to the creation of art. She talks about this aspect of her performing self as if she felt the need to make certain her readers caught sight of the new Fallaci. At the same time, she claims the title of French and English translator of her own book. This performance brought her tension with translators to a head and framed her book's appearance in America with controversy.

Fallaci insists that a book is not only what it communicates but also how it communicates. She objects to unacceptable license in translations through lacunae or additions that betray the original. She believes that serious writers—not word merchants—spill their blood into each word. Translators who change, alter, or betray the text would do better to refuse the job in the first place. Fallaci acknowledges this concern as a fixation and makes no bones about the war between her and translators. God's punishment of Adam and Eve as they leave the Garden of Eden, she states, affects writers. "Ugly turds, idiots, carcasses, and rascals! You ate my apple? And now I am punishing you. From now on, you will speak different languages, and when you write a book, you will have to be translated. Get out!"[2] The bane of writers is a Babel of diverse tongues. She envies artists and musicians, who do not need translators.

Having a degree of fluency in English and French, as well as some knowledge of Spanish, Fallaci claims that she possesses the expertise to detect unacceptable liberties in any of these languages. She speaks of a triple heart attack after receiving what she claims were three unsatisfactory translations of *Insciallah*. To make corrections, she abandoned the editing of Bruno Fallaci's diary, as well as the preparation of her next book. She first rejected a Spanish translation and then accepted the services of a Chilean professor who redid the work to her satisfaction. The French version also displeased her, and she retranslated it into French under the pen name of Victor France.[3]

There are at least two possible explanations of Fallaci's use of the pen name Victor France. First of all, she has always possessed a penchant for flair and mystery. At the same time, a fear of exposure is not outside the realm of possibility. She might have lacked confidence in her French language skills. As it turned out, French critics praised the novel and perhaps facilitated Fallaci's willingness to say publicly that she was Victor France.[4] Then again, the media in France may have failed in their responsibility, since no one seems to have questioned whether she had the right to call herself the French translator.

Fallaci's French translation is, in fact, completely new in comparison to the first and builds on the first translation, which she rejected twice.[5] However, the writer never mentions the first translator. Educated as a native speaker of Italian, Fallaci's artistry expresses itself primarily in Italian. Consequently, she spent several months in Paris with the French representative of Rizzoli Editore redoing the original French translation.[6] In addition, the version finally submitted to the French publishing house, Gallimard, underwent more editorial revisions.

Fallaci then redid what she considered an unacceptable English translation. According to the writer later, its verbatim literalness accounted for its lack of polish and readability. She insists that it was horrible because it was word for word, that she rewrote it, and that no one could have rewritten it as she could. In her opinion, it reflected the translator's unfamiliarity with Italian—a condition that compounded the problem of restructuring sentences, adding words, and omitting entire expressions. In addition, as Fallaci claims, the impossibility of correctly communicating Italian dialects interspersed throughout the Italian version forced her to leave them out in the English translation.[7]

James Marcus, the original English translator, explained that Fallaci knew exactly how he wrote and that she praised the quality of his work. Whatever flaws there may have been in his translation, they were not due to "verbatim literalness," as Fallaci later suggested. Nobody—not even Fallaci, according to Marcus—suggested at the time that Marcus's translation was too literal. The decision to eliminate the various dialects (Sardinian, Sicilian, etc.) had been discussed before Marcus began his work; it was not something that Fallaci had to remedy in the retranslation. Fallaci even lauded Marcus's translation as it was in progress over ten months. After she rejected his rendition and structured another translation based on it, Marcus submitted his English translation and sections of Fallaci's version to a Poets Essayists Novelists (PEN) committee, consisting of impartial translators, who concluded that Marcus's work was superior to hers. PEN had no legal authority to force Doubleday to accept Marcus's rendition; nevertheless, when confronted with the possibility of a lawsuit, the American publishing house agreed to include the credit as a "translation by Oriana Fallaci from a translation by James Marcus."[8]

The real problem with Fallaci's "translation" of *Insciallah* into *Inshallah* is her command of English, which is sufficient for conversation but not for elaborate, incantatory prose. Her awkward English often contains maladroit phraseology, indicative of an obvious lack of formal training in the language: "Now that the story spreads out to give us characters so far kept in the shadows, other actors of the tragicomedy the Professor is using to write his miniature Iliad, a smile on the lips serves us better than a tear in the eyes."[9] During the Christmas Battle, the water tank disintegrates and five soldiers are torn to a thousand pieces: "Eagle covered his eyes and hell exploded along with the cries of the inhabitants then the shout of Bilal who wearing his patched multicolored jacket and pointing his Kalashnikov hurled himself into the conquest of the Tower."[10]

The soldier Nicolin suffers a nervous breakdown after one month in Beirut and whimsically bemoans his fate: "Why me, he sobbed, why not Marcello who was a volunteer and got balls?" The others cruelly refuse to offer any consolation: "Mommy, Mommy, my bottle! Give the baby his bottle." Luca alone befriends him in a gesture of infantile love: "Don't cry, Nicolin. You're not the only one who fell into this hitch."[11] In Fallaci's description of the Italian general, a soubrette sent to cheer up the troops howls from the stage: "General, you are a stud, you are a cake! Let's get together tonight!"[12]

In his review of *Inshallah*, Thomas Keneally reacts unfavorably to Fallaci's English and summarizes her deficiencies. "In company with her vigorous narrative comes dialogue that creaks and overreaches for effect in her translation, done from a first translation by James Marcus." The critic supplies one of Fallaci's unfortunate sentences: "When something big happens, something that changes the status quo or even provokes a tragedy, we don't wonder which weft of marginal and apparently trivial episodes has eased or determined its realization." He maintains that such observations repeatedly occur and "are often backed up in Angelo's thoughts by the frequently repeated formula for chaos devised by the physicist Boltzmann." According to Keneally, American readers would find some of the book's expletives unlikely; for example, "By Christopher Columbus and his mother's dirty underpants!"[13]

Fallaci formally commented on her frailty in English as early as 1976 during her lecture at Amherst College. In her exordium, she requested forgiveness; her English was far from being Shakespearean. She admitted that speaking her Fallaci English in front of teachers and students at an American college was irresponsible. At the same time, she stated that she had nothing else but her English to communicate with her audience. She asked her listeners to try to understand her when her pronunciation became unbearable, her choice of words inexact, and her phraseology extravagant. At the time, her honesty merited admiration. However, her later insistence on recognition as *Inshallah*'s legitimate English translator emerges as an attempt to force her image as translator champion into the public eye, no matter what.[14]

Ahdaf Soueif strongly objects to Fallaci's misuse of the Arabic language and maintains that her transliterations are almost invariably wrong.

"Tawaffi" the rabble yell when they want to say "Death to you," "kaofa aktòl," seems to signify "I'll kill him" (with a meticulous—and misplaced—accent) and "Hal tas ma'wai la'im?" is apparently how an Arab says "Do you hear me, you sheep?" Even the call to prayers, repeated five times a day and containing the basic creed of Islam, is quoted madly, hilariously in error. And why are the 'Isha prayers in *Inshallah* mysteriously conducted at midnight when everywhere else in the world they happen closer to 8 P.M.?[15]

Fallaci owes much of her international fame to English translations of her writings. She has always understood that Italian lacks the linguistic power of English in contemporary society and has bemoaned her inability to write a book in English. Following unfriendly critical reactions to *Inshallah*, she modified her views and claimed that Italian was much richer than English. Face to face with her Italian novel, Fallaci maintained that it could not have been translated because English lacks the richness and vocabulary required to do a proper translation. English was rich enough in verbs but lacked the linguistic variety of Italian.[16] She told a story of Norman Mailer, who had once said to her that reading Hemingway in English was like skiing on a field of snow. Fallaci disagrees and believes it is not great skiing. Mentally translating Hemingway into Italian, she found the words and, as she explained, really went skiing. She no longer regrets having to write in Italian.[17]

But the image of a refined, hermetic novelist comes to the forefront in spite of her weakness in English. Fallaci wants to tell about human beings and to compose a reinvented, universalized truth in which individuals everywhere identify and recognize themselves. "For years I've wanted it, for years I've waited for the occasion to do it, and the occasion has finally arrived," she says in *Inshallah* through the character the professor.[18] Her obsession to fashion a great work of literature finally emerges in this epic tale. "I began it! I'm working on it! Every night I shut myself in this office and work, work, work."[19] In 1985, the writer transformed a room on the first floor of her New York City home into a study with a desk, bookshelves, Xerox machine, typewriter, and then enclosed herself in it like a monk.[20] As Fallaci never tires of repeating, she took six long years to complete the arduous task, regarding everything in life as a function of the book.[21] She expounds on how she rewrote the entire work three times and labored persistently from ten to twelve hours, even on Saturdays, Sundays, Christmas, and Easter. Principal distractions consisted of occasionally glancing at New York pedestrians from the window of her study as she worked in the glow of a Tiffany lamp or occasionally buying cigarettes and groceries at the corner grocery store.[22]

In her book, she loses no opportunity to comment on her self-imposed physical and mental torture.

It is the atrocious solitude of a room that gradually becomes a prison, a torture chamber. It is the fear of the blank page that stares at you mockingly. It is the torment of the word that you don't find and, if you find it, it rhymes with the adjacent word. It is the martyrdom of the sentence that limps, of the metrics that fall apart, of the structure that staggers, of the page that bores, of the chapter that you must dismantle and remake, remake, remake until the words seem to you food that recedes from the famished mouth of Tantalus.[23]

Fallaci portrays herself as a disciplined novelist who has shed her identity as journalist and war correspondent. She yearns for recognition as a Dostoyevsky, a Tolstoy, or a Dickens. She publicly announced this same message during her interview on *All Things Considered*. "I have so many books to write. I cannot afford the luxury of going around doing other things."[24] Even at the height of her career, Fallaci performs for her public. Only this time, she acts the role of the refined, cultured novelist consumed by her literary passion.

Fallaci interrupted her cloistered style of life only twice: once in 1986, after the American bombing of Libya, and again in 1988, after calling her father in Florence to inquire about his health. In the case of military action by the United States against Qaddafi, she felt compelled to defend her adopted country, the United States, against the vicious attacks of many European allies in defense of the North African nation. The article reinforces the impression of a heroine fearing no dictator and courageously ready to condemn those who fear Qaddafi and are ready to appease him. Written for *Corriere della Sera* and then translated for the *Washington Post*, it suggests that the Italians, French, Spanish, Germans, Swedish, and some British have pretended not to understand the Libyan dictator and reminds them of his long list of international crimes. Sustaining the vehement attack, she reviews how the Italian government helped the terrorist Mohammed Abbas escape arrest by U.S. officials, even protecting him as he boarded a Yugoslavian airplane. She labels Qaddafi "a hyena that feeds herself on the dead: the new Mussolini of the Mediterranean." She then courageously brings the article to a close and cements her status as a morally righteous figure staring down an oppressive tyrant.

I know that Qaddafi's followers and servants will say that I must pay for this, that they will kill me, that they know how to find me and how to wait.

I know that music. I have heard it sung to me by others, in the past. My answer to them is the recommendation that I make to the French, to the Spanish, to the Germans . . . to anyone who has not understood Qaddafi or pretends to have not understood him. Do not be afraid to understand him and to say it out loud. "Beware of the man or woman who is afraid of the Qaddafis. I am not."[25]

Calling Edoardo from New York in 1988, she interpreted her father's feeble voice as an ominous sign and left at once for Florence. Immediately suspecting cancer, she had an X ray taken of his lungs. The results confirmed her fears. Cancer, the disease that had killed Tosca, had already spread in Edoardo and led doctors to predict that one to three months of life remained. Fallaci had interrupted her writing of *Un uomo* to care for her mother until she died. In like manner, she stayed at Edoardo's side until the end, tended to him like a nurse and mother, and then returned to *Insciallah*. Umberto Cecchi, a journalist colleague, periodically called for news but would receive the usual tearful response. "I feel like his mother. He has become so small. When I get him up for the bathroom, I don't feel tired. . . . And he leans on me like a newborn child."[26] She held him in her arms as he took his final breath at eighty-four years of age and then kept a vigil throughout the night of his wake on 9 February 1988. Alone in his room with all the windows open, she stoically bore the cold winter weather of Tuscany. As she gazed at her father, she remembered his desire that she deliver his funeral oration. In the solitude of the evening, she composed the farewell address (which she considers one of her most beautiful writings) and then delivered it the next day in the chapel at the cemetery in Florence.[27] Cecchi, who was in attendance for the service, calls it her finest piece of writing—"more beautiful even than her very beautiful *Insciallah*."[28]

Just as the loss of a child inspired *Letter to a Child Never Born* and Panagoulis's death led to *A Man*, strong emotional experiences resulted in the creation of *Inshallah*. She again compares these generating moments to the act of conception. "You never know why the egg of your mind gets fertilized by the spermatozoon of an idea. And we don't know why, among the dozens or thousands of ideas that you have, that one particular idea ovulates."[29] Two events were significant in the conceptualization of *Inshallah*. In 1982, Fallaci interviewed General Ariel Sharon, whose armies had just invaded Lebanon to crush Palestinian guerrilla forces. Before going to meet him, she went to the besieged city of Beirut and spent more than eight days under bombardment. "Don't ask me why I went because I don't know. I went to Beirut two or three times on my own at my own expense and I didn't know why. I only knew that I had to be there. I understood later what it was. It was *Insciallah* that began to have life."[30] Beirut was the last place that anybody with brains would want to be; the Israeli army had begun its onslaught. Daily battles at the racetrack, museum, and pine forest, as well as the havoc wreaked on houses, hospitals, newspaper offices, hotels, and embassies, left an indelible mark on her spirit. Even more unforgettable, however, were the atrocious human casualties, especially the dead, maimed children. "I would never have been able to write *Insciallah* if I had not seen the siege of Beirut."[31]

Once inside the city, Fallaci survived despite the bombings from Israelis, Syrians, and Palestinians. She stayed in a corner room on the sixth floor of the Hotel Alexandria, which bordered the infamous Green Line. Each night, she took a pillow and searched for an empty room on the second or third level. If none was found, she slept in the lounge near the bar. Once, during a severe shelling, she hurriedly left her quarters and dashed for the staircase moments before a shell burst through the window and exploded.

In 1983, a second influential event took place. On a sleepless October night at 2:30 A.M., she turned on her television at the exact moment of a special news bulletin. What she saw was a scene of mass destruction. Two suicide trucks in Beirut had completely destroyed American and French compounds, killing and wounding over 400 soldiers. The writer refers to this as the moment of conception of a new literary life within her, initiating a long period of gestation. It all happened as she rested comfortably in her canopy bed with no desire to start a new novel or travel to any foreign land. However, after hearing that broadcast in New York City, she could not fall asleep and, early the same morning, packed her bags, called the Ministry of Defense in Rome, and announced that she wanted to go to Beirut. The next day, she arrived in Italy and, 72 hours later, landed in the ravaged city. She had no idea why an inner compulsion urged her to go there again, what fruit her travels would bear, or how the word *Inshallah* would forever change her life. The names Charlie, Angelo, Condor, Ninette, Eagle One, and Crazy Horse occupied no place in her consciousness.

Much like an addict, Fallaci has always been attracted by the excitement of adventure. When there was an attempted coup d'état in Moscow, she had to be there. "I am poisoned by the power of an event, by being inside. I had to see Moscow in those days while they were throwing down the statues because I have the fever. I have it inside."³² This same fever motivated her trip to Beirut after viewing the news broadcast about the terrorist attacks. Upon arrival, she encountered a city torn apart by years of bloodshed, vendettas, and insoluble political controversy. Continuous bombing and mortars unleashed havoc every night but became a part of the daily routine. All of this hectic, dangerous movement and sense of urgency aroused the curiosity of colleagues, who questioned her motives and eagerly wondered which newspaper had successfully contracted her service. That she had gone at her own expense and had not given a thought to reporting would have struck them as absurd. They would have raised eyebrows had she told them that another sperm had fertilized another egg and made her go to Beirut.

Subsequent to the moment of inspiration, Fallaci returned to the Lebanese capital time and again and observed sights, sounds, and people that would soon make their way into her novel. On one of her journeys, she flew on an army transport plane from Pisa. Umberto Cecchi had boarded the same flight and tried to provoke a discussion. "Why are you going to Lebanon? A special assignment? An interview?" Rather than respond with a detailed explanation, she shrugged her shoulders, wrapped herself more tightly in an oversized army jacket, and laconically signaled an end to their conversation. "To look, to look again."³³ She then closed her eyes and, in Cecchi's opinion, pretended that she needed sleep. In retrospect, he understood that the search for a book had begun and that, on that flight from Pisa to Beirut, the embryo of the future *Inshallah* already existed. Reading its pages years later, rediscovering alive the many human beings he had thought dead, and experiencing again the tragedies inflicted by the war, he easily understood what had drawn her to Beirut.³⁴

After arriving in the city, Cecchi saw her again a few nights later on Aerodrome Street. Beirut resembled a dying beast whose death rattle echoed in suffocating voices, blasphemies, and bursts of machine-gun fire. A direct hit on a building had unleashed a conflagration that turned the sky above the old city orange. He elected to return to Italy, while she chose to stay longer, for a total of three weeks. During their conversation, she unexpectedly opened up by recalling their brief time together as medical students at the University of Florence.

> "As young people, we did not think about death, right? Not even in the dissection lab as we desecrated cadavers with our scalpels and our inexperience . . . Now, however, I think of it all the time. I bring it with me, I wear

it. Ever since I went to Vietnam. I was there for eight years; I went there; I returned there; and death never deserts my mind . . . How I hate it . . . I want this book to bear within it my hatred for death."

"What book?"

"The one I will write. I am pregnant with a book."[35]

She said nothing specific about her embryonic book but did express personal views about writing.

"It's like bringing a child into the world, you see, it's like dying less when one dies. One dies a lot less leaving children, and I have never had children. I have never succeeded. To die less I only have books. Do you not believe that leaving a book is like leaving a child?"[36]

Fallaci explains that, on one occasion, the Islamic Sons of God discovered her whereabouts and tried to kidnap her. Extreme fundamentalists had never forgiven her audacious interviews with the Ayatollah Khomeini and Muammar al-Qaddafi; they intended to avenge what they considered her blasphemous disrespect. Around six or seven in the morning, a journalist barged into her hotel room to sound the alarm. She jumped up in pajamas and quickly followed him to hide in his room, where she called for help from an Italian general, who sent a contingent of special forces that immediately surrounded the hotel and then provided an escort back to their base. From that moment on, Fallaci never left the company of soldiers and adhered to a disciplined, military routine.[37]

On her last trip to Beirut, Fallaci still did not know that she would actually write a book called *Inshallah*. She knew that Italian forces had already decided to leave Lebanon in a state of urgent secrecy and had no intention of becoming the victims of any suicide truck bomb as their French and American allies had been. In Cyprus, she boarded the *Ardito*, an Italian war cruiser whose mission it was to station itself on the open sea just off the coastline and then to protect the withdrawing soldiers with its cannons and missiles. It journeyed throughout the night and arrived early on the same morning. Rough seas prevented the ship from getting too close to shore and required the use of a landing craft, which high waves prevented from actually landing. A few meters from the beach, she had to jump into the water up to her shoulders. Holding a small bag above her head, she waded to dry ground where Italian marines greeted her and offered immediate military protection.

Their commanding officer, whom Fallaci later calls Sandokan in the book, patiently waited and, with folded arms, greeted her as Venus rising from the sea. The tardy arrival allowed her to witness the Italian retreat and consequently to create the final scene in the book when Arabs burn the donated food left by departing soldiers.[38]

After her final trip to Beirut, Fallaci returned to New York and, in the privacy of her study, plunged into the creation of the novel. Through her alter ego, the professor, she gives vent to her inherent first personism.

> I can tell that the story unfolds over an arc of three months (ninety days elapsing from a Sunday in late October to a Sunday in late January), that it opens with an allegory verging on a chronicle (the dogs of Beirut), that it sets out with the double slaughter, that it follows the conducting thread of [Ludwig Eduard] Boltzmann's mathematical equation $S = K\,Ln\,W$. And that I develop the plot through the hamletic squire of Ulysses: the one who searches for the formula of Life.[39]

Fallaci never tires of saying that each book writes its own story. Only late in the process does it take on a particular shape or reveal in which direction it chooses to go.

> It is not you who sends it forth; it leads us and carries itself. You cannot say to yourself before writing the book: I, Oriana Fallaci, want to write it in this manner. You cannot! It is as though you were to decide to remain pregnant. And you decide that your son will have blue eyes and black hair. It's none of your fucking business. He decides to have blue eyes or blond or black hair. You can't. He's in there deciding. It's the same thing with a book. . . . I will repeat this as long as I have breath. A book has an independent life of its own.[40]

Inshallah, a war novel, emerges as the spontaneous outgrowth of a Florentine childhood lived under the threat of daily bombardment and adult experience in bloody conflicts.

> You are lucky in this country, because your wars are always abroad. Since the Civil War, you don't see war. You don't know what it means . . . the alarms, AHOOO, AHOOO, AHOOO, and people running and the bombs falling, you have no idea about that. The air bombings, for me, were always the

most terrorizing things. You have no idea what it means to be occupied by the soldiers of another country. And with this book [*Inshallah*], I have been reliving this experience.[41]

Fallaci encountered life-threatening situations in which she experienced the sensation of not knowing whether she would be alive on the following day. She describes the inebriation of surviving battles in Vietnam. "Afterwards, one feels so alive. A thousand times alive. One feels a happiness without equal much more profound than that which love sometimes offers."[42] The frame of mind of U.S. Marines after a battle stands as a case in point.

> When they come out of combat or a bombing mission, they look extremely tired. . . . But at the same time, you see a kind of gaiety in them, a joyousness. They are excited, because they are alive. It is the feel of defeating death. And you get drunk on that feeling. You have that feeling once, you want it again.[43]

Beginning *Inshallah*, Fallaci had no need to research battle strategies or military jargon. She was already familiar with the details of carnage, slaughter, and combat. It was simply a question of acquiring ideas and an appropriate medium of expression. The novel deals not so much with the brute portrayal of fighting as with the inward dynamism of the human spirit—the feelings of individual soldiers in combat. Fallaci expresses in *Inshallah* that soldiers profoundly love the vitality, challenge, gamble, and mystery of war and lie when they say otherwise.[44] Death is constantly in the background and springs its trap when least expected. Because of that relentless uncertainty, characters in the book vibrate with a mental and physical vigor that peace fails to arouse.

Condor, the commander in chief; the bomb expert, Sugar; the pedantic Crazy Horse; the head of security, Sandokan; the lover of war, Pistoia; and more than one hundred other characters populate the book and live in the shadow of death. They all respond to the intoxicating influence of war and emerge as admirable, despicable, or simply human. The counterespionage expert, Charlie, struggles to prevent the arrival of the third suicide truck; the shy Eagle One discovers the French plan to abandon their crucial position at Shatila; the apprehensive Hawk struggles to overcome his fear of suffering or dying; Charlie's aide, Angelo, a handsome twenty-six-year-old sergeant from northern Italy, has a tempestuous affair with Ninette, the splendid, mysterious, and older Lebanese woman. A vast array of secondary figures also inhabits the novel. Gino, the ex-peasant parachutist, writes poems but then loses his fingers in a terrorist explosion; Martino, the homosexual interpreter, suffers the humiliating consequences of his presence in a macho environment; Fabio, friend of the American soldier John, loses his mind after discovering his pal's mutilated body; Rambo, the gutsy and taciturn giant, suffers the torturous memory of the death of his little sister; the nineteen-year-old Ferruccio experiences friendship, loss, and understanding in the debacle of combat. Women, children, and Lebanese characters further contribute to the Odyssean dimensions of the story. All the protagonists enter into the action one by one in the first two acts and then reassemble in the third act, when the Christmas Battle begins.

Inshallah, one of the few war novels ever written by a woman, contains three acts and a conclusion that resembles an epilogue to a play. The story takes place in Beirut in the 1980s when American, French, and Italian peacekeeping troops arrive in the Lebanese capital. It begins with the massacre of three hundred U.S. Marines and one hundred French legionnaires when two dynamite-laden trucks enter and decimate their compounds. The attack against Italian quarters inexplicably fails to take place and provides the basic thread to the subsequent action. The novel substantially narrates the wait for the third truck, which finally comes in the form of a motorboat assault against the ship leaving the city's harbor to take Italian soldiers home.

Fallaci wrote *Inshallah* as though she were a camera operator sighting with a powerful lens and then zooming closer before panning to an adjacent scene. She juxtaposes photographic frames, whether of the past or present. The description of Beirut prior to the war and then in its subsequent agony illustrates the method. Her recurrent, nostalgic evocation of the Lebanese capital as the "Switzerland of the Middle East" is analogous to a movie's theme song. The opening in chapter 2 evokes the lost utopian qualities of life in this former oasis. The passage accentuates the city's enchanting landscapes and the desire to recapture an earlier splendor. Beirut's actual condition contrasts sharply with its beautiful past. Looters have destroyed its splendid villas and Alexandrian mosaics. Soldiers have demolished the magnificent racetrack, shot prized purebloods, devastated the archaeological museum, trashed sumptuous hotels, reduced the grandiose Cité Sportive to shreds, and ruined churches, mosques, synagogues, and the banks that once paid dazzling profits. Bomb craters have obliterated wide two-lane avenues, concrete overpasses, and elegant *ronds-points*. Both the airfield and port are unusable. "And everywhere, rubble, rubble, rubble."[45] Most critical analysts have failed to understand her attempt to use film techniques, as well as the human longing for an earlier time of life, and have viewed the portrayal of the city as a simple journalistic commentary. "Since cretins are in the majority in Italy and the most stupid of them deal with literature, they did not understand that this section, which they labeled journalistic, represents a Proustian recall of past time."[46]

Fallaci employs a camera technique early in the novel when one thousand American soldiers and French legionnaires sleep quietly in their compounds. Kamikaze terrorists smash dynamite-laden trucks into these buildings, inflicting heavy casualties. The first "frame" depicts the premises before the explosion. The second frame then captures a view of rescuers, who recover mutilated bodies and load them on rescue vehicles. Fallaci acts like a movie director advancing into a chaotic thicket of hellish destruction, photographing relief crews that gather scattered body parts, assist the few survivors without limbs, without faces, or with faces reduced to soft slush, and cause many of the less seriously injured to perish as they attempt to clear away the wreckage.

During the Christmas Battle scene, the fighting lasts more than five hours and unfolds in a triple sequence: the background, the conflict, and finally the aftermath. The battle begins with the vivid picture of Rashid launching an eighty-millimeter Katyusha. The rocket brightly crosses from east to west like a comet leaving a tail of orange light, following a descending parabola to land gently on the water tank, which then disintegrates into a fan of silvery flames, gold particles, and black smoke. Its impact hurls a soldier clutching an M-16 into the darkness and knocks five others into a thousand pieces. The second frame depicts the Amal everywhere on the opposite side of Nasser Avenue, firing Kalashnikovs, revolvers, mortars, and Katyushas, which inflict most damage on Shatila itself, tearing apart houses, shanties, and hovels on the strip parallel to Nasser Avenue. The third frame depicts a hord of lamenting, groaning Amal breaking into Post No. 22's little square and then slipping onto the small road to the tower. Elated by the hate of their battle cry, they fill the road in disorderly waves and are massacred by Gassan's men. Plasticity characterizes the governmental retreat from the tower under protective cover. Smoke bombs—twelve every minute for ten minutes—ensure that suspended gas particles never thin out.

Auditory inclusions—informative messages or overheard conversations—enhance the broad panorama of ongoing action, reinforcing the impact of the many visual images. Sandokan announces to headquarters that "the shit-heads of the Sixth Brigade" have occupied the ditch along Avenue Chamoun between 27 and 28 and have dug in with 120 mortars. "That's not all! While coming here I ran into a column of the Sixth Brigade! Fifteen M113s with Brownings, twelve jeeps with 106mm recoilless guns, ten armored cars! They were moving down Ramlet el Baida."[47] Major officers then hear the tun-tun-tun of Brownings, the thunder of mortars, the crashing of cannon, all smothering Sandokan's hurried notice that the attack against Gobeyre and the tower had begun.

Only the swift juxtapositions of scene in her camera technique permit the presentation of the many elements that constitute the larger battle scene. Fabio and Matteo squat behind the wall of Camp No. 3 to protect themselves from crossfire. Calogero the Fisherman fearfully jumps out of his M-113 at Post No. 28, hurls himself down the nearby slope, turns onto the Street Without a Name, enters a field of Browning and 106-mm rifle fire (directed at Gobeyre), and continues in the direction of the littoral Ramlet el Baida. He searches for a boat to return to his small Sicilian island. Sandokan enjoys the spectacle of war at 27 Owl until a small severed hand hits his sandbag and causes a crisis of conscience. Bilal sings at the captured tower, continues to fight as most of his men lay dying, and suddenly feels the need to return home to see his family. Gassan, however, plans to wait for Bilal to reenter his neighborhood, Gobeyre. He drives his jeep onto Nasser Avenue, halts thirty yards before 22, aims straight down the road, and lowers the gun to dwarf's height. Remembering his father's murder by Shiite Muslims, he frames the unsuspecting Bilal in his sights and then releases a twenty-inch-long 106-mm missile that so disintegrates the victim that not even a piece of his patched jacket remains. Natale pursues Passepartout with a knife after he takes decorative feathers from his helmet and receives a hail of grenade fragments in the face, stomach, and legs.[48]

Fallaci's use of motion-picture devices not only influences the construction of visual scenes but also allows free entry into a character's mind by means of the flashback or stream-of-consciousness technique. Fallaci often focuses on a real situation that then provides the stimulus for a character to recall past experience or to generate personal reflections. As a young journalist and writer, she always delved into motivation and background. She greatly admires Marcel Proust but maintains that her use of the procedure results from a spontaneous, personal preference.

In the case of Lance Corporal Salvatore Belezza, Fallaci employs stream of consciousness as he waits in Colonel Falcon's office to receive his punishment for ineptly guarding the roof of the Italian ambassador's residence. He overhears a heated conversation with Condor; the angry statements act as a catapult, launching a host of considerations. He romantically imagines himself before a firing squad like Cavaradossi in Giacomo Puccini's *Tosca*. The thought of dying almost pleases him because it would force the Muslim girl, Sanaan, to repent of the cruel things she had said to him. She would commit suicide, just like the opera character Tosca, and jump from the Castel Sant'Angelo. Condor's loud statement interrupts his train of thought, "Colonel! I demand an exemplary punishment!"[49]

The irate words unleash a second round of reflections about Salvatore's desire for vengeance. He would take his revenge by telling everyone that the Italian ambassador's glass eye resulted from a car wreck in Cuba when he tried to imitate James Dean's drag race in *Rebel Without a Cause*; he would humiliate him by revealing that his fear of crucifixion by Druze kidnappers motivated the order that the military place a guard on his roof. Realizing that he never would have met the beautiful Muslim girl across the street if he had not been stationed there, he also remembers gratitude to Glass Eye for facilitating the encounter. He relives all of the details: her presence on the sixth-floor balcony, their first conversations, the time she agreed to go out with him, his lack of experience in physical love, the depth of his infatuation with her, and their many excursions.

The associative technique continues when Falcon angrily orders Salvatore into his office, humiliates him verbally, and acrimoniously accuses him of not listening. The chastisement inspires Salvatore's mental rebuttal. He simply cannot free himself from the memory of that unforgettable day at the beach. Sanaan, dressed in tight slacks and a sexy, transparent blouse, had kissed him on the mouth, rolled her tongue around his, and sensuously massaged his genitals. Stopping suddenly, she had abruptly ended their relationship. Falcon, continuing his reproof, interrupts his victim's mental fantasies: he should "uncork" his ears; he has "no balls"; he does not even have a "pinhead" between his legs. He will answer for such past crimes as insubordination, writing "amorous messages" on the walls, abandoning his guard post at the embassy, behaving as "a paranoid," as a "schizophrenic." Falcon's brief pause allows Salvatore time to assent mentally to the charges and then to rationalize his frantic behavior. He had never received another of Sanaan's kisses but, from his guard post each night, had observed her cousin—Ali—stealthily entering her bedroom and turning off the lights. On one occasion the girl's family had beaten her, calling her a whore. He had deserted his post and run to her rescue, but he had received a hostile reception as she opened her battered eyes. "Mind your own business, you fucking meddler. Go to hell."[50]

Falcon again intrudes into the soldier's thoughts by accusing him of screaming from the roof, of waking up the entire quarter, of making a laughingstock of the Carabinieri Corps, and of knocking out two of his squad leader's teeth because he had called Sanaan a trollop. Falcon sentences him to permanent separation from his little whore: thirty years in an Italian prison. Salvatore returns to his cot and responds to his sentencing by once again allowing his mind to drift like an oarless boat. An unexpected event then brings an abrupt end to his introspection. Sanaan visits with Ali in his car, sensuously fondles him, reveals that she carries his baby, and they drive away in a provoking embrace. Salvatore falls to the ground in a dead faint.[51] The entire episode illustrates the cinematic technique that captures the inner workings of the character's mind. An object or event provides memories from the recent or distant past; these inward considerations enable readers to understand each protagonist's history; phenomena then bolt subjects back to awareness of present time and space before again facilitating a return to their musings.

Movies influence Fallaci's emphasis on visible and tangible sensations. She enjoys good Westerns; they begin with a huge landscape or action scene. They always star adventurous heroes and leave little room for uncertainty. A camera filming a face, an entire body, two individuals, a group of people, a rugged terrain, or an earlier event corresponds to her creative technique in writing a novel.

Movie director Franco Cristaldi had agreed to film *Inshallah* for a television production but prematurely died in July 1992 at the age of sixty-seven. His death is one of the great tragedies in Fallaci's life. He understood the visual qualities of her book and maintained that it already had a script and could have easily evolved into a televised series. The only problems dealt with logistics and editorial considerations: the novel numbers more than seven hundred pages and contains an unending list of characters. Nevertheless, Cristaldi had committed himself to filming what he considered a palpably cinematic book.

Fallaci admires the American producer-director Steven Spielberg. In her opinion, he creates great movies based on literary technique. The written word is crucial to his creative process. During one of her spontaneous reflections, Fallaci recalled an acceptance speech he gave for an award. Quoting him by heart, she gave testimony to his influence. "It all begins with writing, rewriting, and rewriting, and rewriting, and finally rewriting again at least fourteen times. After you have written and rewritten, then you begin to think of a movie."[52] Fallaci suggested that Spielberg expresses himself as a writer through cinematic images, whereas she communicates as a movie producer through her writings.

Much to her surprise, the Italian editor of *Insciallah* stated that the novel struck him more like a concert than a movie. Fallaci acknowledged that the beginning of the novel emphasizes sound (stray dogs wander through the deserted streets of Beirut at night and unleash a barking fanfare), nevertheless, she desperately searched for images throughout the composition of her book. An attraction for cinema explains this preference, as does her beloved city of birth. Palaces and churches so saturate her that she refers to Florence as a movie theater that unceasingly projects the artistic designs of Cimabue, Giotto, and Ghirlandajo. The Renaissance mecca is a panoramic, seductive film that does much to explain why she stresses the visual in *Inshallah*. "Before TV and cinema, there is Florence with its frescoes and images everywhere on walls, walls which are never white. There are always paintings on the walls. And that's how I see things."[53]

On one occasion, before completing her novel, Fallaci invited two physicist friends to dinner at her Manhattan home and discussed the book with them. As Fallaci explained, both scientists believed that she had translated into literary terms the Ludwig Boltzmann formula: S equals K multiplied by L to the n power multiplied by W, which means that entropy equals Boltzmann's constant multiplied by the natural logarithm of the probability of distribution. After repeated explanations, she intuitively understood and let loose her enthusiasm. "For Christ's sake, this is the formula of death."[54] At that moment, the new idea inspired another version of the book and an additional Fallaci role: insightful philosopher and mathematician who inferred a tremendously important scientific equation.

She promoted her erudite self-portrait by rewriting the plot within the framework of Boltzmann's formula and infusing the new version of the book with a rationalism that had been missing from the preceding draft. Angelo's mathematical background takes on greater importance because, after the kamikaze attacks, he repeatedly reflects on death and how all things from the infinitely small to the infinitely great ineluctably tend toward a destructive state. Any foolish attempt by man to oppose this tendency and make order out of disorder increases rather than diminishes the universal disarray. Chaos absorbs the energy employed to defeat it. "It devours it, it uses it to arrive more quickly at its final goal which is the destruction or rather the complete self-destruction of the Universe. And it always wins. Always."[55] From the start, however, Angelo reflects Fallaci's own desire, despite her avowed atheism, to believe in life after death. He searches for an antidote to chaos and frantically struggles to reverse Boltzmann's formula.

> Oh, if one day he could discover the opposite and demonstrate that Death is an instrument of Life, food for Life, that dying is only a momentary standstill, a pause to rest, a short sleep that prepares us to be reborn, to live again, to die again yes but to be reborn again, to live again, to live and live and live forever![56]

In act 3, after Ninette's death, Angelo vindictively kills her assassin, Passepartout, in spite of his disbelief in revenge, which he had always considered a crude, visceral act dictated by the blindness of passion. Nevertheless, the idea of destroying his mistress's murderer attracts him; avenging her becomes a right to exercise in the name of logic, a rational gesture, an intellectually legitimate act, a morally creditable deed. Evening the score with someone who inflicts harm and pain suddenly appears to be highly reasonable. "Because it reestablishes a broken equilibrium, it makes order out of disorder, and through a positive act it erases the negative act of the individual who harmed you and robbed you and made you suffer."[57] Mathematicians call the technique *bringing the system back to its initial phase* and explain that it equals the operation of annulling the result of a problem by using the inverse of the procedure followed to get the desired result.

When Angelo aims his bullet at Passepartout's heart, he adheres to fallacious reasoning. In his mind, pulling the trigger reestablishes order and reaffirms life. He fails to understand that annihilating a person increases chaos, which feeds on death. His attitude—Passepartout killed Ninette and I do the same to him—represents a second intense reapplication of Boltzmann's formula, which states that any attempt to impose order onto disorder only augments a crisis because entropy feeds on these efforts. Boltzmann had already proven with his experiments on molecules that trying to reverse the process of eradication only accelerates destruction. The theory receives its confirmation in *Inshallah* in a tragic succession of irreversible events. Passepartout's homosexual lover, Rashid, retaliates to punish the perpetrators of what he views as an unpardonable crime. He delivers a death blow to Angelo and to the Italian force by ramming his explosives-laden motorboat into the retreating transport ship as it leaves Beirut harbor.[58]

Despite the failure to reverse Boltzmann's theory, the book carries on an ontological struggle against the nothingness that awaits each human being after death and reflects its author's existential anxiety. As the transport ship carrying troops back to Italy slowly leaves Beirut harbor, Angelo suddenly feels the weight of age and comprehends that the only hope for relief from despair lies in remote, primordial, unseizable time. Only distant epochs, whose traces dwell in the mind, provide the knowledge that never fails: the kind that comes from intuition and instinct. Suddenly switching his attention to the dock, he observes beastly pandemonium. Yelping, growling, barking, bawling, and thundering the sound of *Inshallah*, stray dogs pour through the deserted streets of the city, burst onto the dock, run toward the ship, and leap against closed hatches. Despite their filth, blood, encrusted sores, and broken bodies, they vibrate with such indomitable vitality that they seem healthy, intact, and splendid. The evidence emerges in their glorious survival even though they slaughter each other night and day. The entire concept crystallizes on the spot:

> Wasn't it because Chaos is Life not Death, because Life not Death is the ineluctable and irreversible tendency of all things, from the atom to the molecule, from the planets to the galaxies, from the infinitely small to the infinitely large? Wasn't it because it is Life that absorbs the energy of whatever and whoever tries to oppose its essence and process, it is Life that uses it to arrive more quickly at its final goal, and rather than being the destruction yet self-destruction of the Universe that goal is the construction yet self-construction of the Universe?[59]

In Angelo's mind, Boltzmann's formula and the mysterious word are suddenly the same thing: $S = K Ln W = Inshallah$. Having earlier tried to comprehend death with his intellect and not his instinct, he had blinded himself to viewing the act of dying as the instrument and food of life, as a momentary standstill, as a short sleep preparing humans for rebirth ad infinitum. Intuitively, he finally discovers his new certitude—one that no one would ever rationally prove. "Yet it was so: he felt it. He felt it, therefore he knew it, with every cell of his body and every pore of his skin and every fiber of his nervous system that it was so. That being alive means being immortal."[60]

No longer burdened by age, but rejuvenated by an immortal youth, Angelo places himself on the broadside of the ship, comprehends the enduring quality of life, and, in a highly dramatic conclusion, awaits the third suicide attack.

Despite a glimmer of affirmation, the inner core of the novel emphasizes Fallaci's familiar themes of doubt and apprehension. Optimism regarding the endurance of life in a generic sense actually camouflages basic pessimism, places a veneer of false hope on a tragic outlook, and amounts to an unconvincing attempt to communicate a positive message and, in the final analysis, a false truth. "I want to try to believe it, but I don't believe it because life has not been good to me."[61] Genuine human happiness always eludes her grasp; she fails to sustain lasting friendships; most of the people she loves have died; her dream of having a child remains unfulfilled. In addition, she claims that what society views as good luck and success matter little to her. She gives the impression of a damned person bearing the weight of destiny on her shoulders. "I have never been a happy woman; I am not a happy woman. I have good reasons for not being happy, and I have always had a very tragic life."[62]

Simply attributing all that occurs to cosmic forces by uttering with helpless resignation the word *Inshallah* fails to alleviate existential pathos. Fallaci summarizes this view through the professor, who says, "I too abhor the word destiny, the word Inshallah. Most people see it as a hope, a good omen, and identify it with their trust in the divine mercy. I see it as a submission, instead, as a renunciation of ourselves." Humans essentially ask a Heavenly Father, Omnipotent Lord, Jehovah, Allah, Brahma, Baal, Adonai, or whatever they call their Supreme Being to decide and choose for them. The professor views this attitude as unacceptable. "No thanks. I refuse to delegate my will and my mind to God. I refuse to renounce myself, to submit myself. A submitted man is a dead man before he dies, and I don't want to be dead before I die! . . . I want to be alive when I die!"[63]

Fallaci's image as a moralist emerges when she offers a practical solution to evil in society: the reinvention of traditional moral categories and clear definitions of good and evil. "It made sense when God and the Devil were alive and God vouched for Good by promising Paradise, the Devil vouched for Evil by threatening Hell. That is when the great religions of salvation determined our behavior."[64] She desperately calls for a change of ethical attitude and, despite her rejection of an Almighty, a Satan, and a belief in the beyond, defends arguments that take sin seriously. She supports the mes-

siahs who promise salvation or threaten damnation, repudiates the belittle-
ment of willpower, and issues a challenge to materialistic science.

> I defy them to produce Good in the pharmaceutical laboratories: to manu-
> facture an ointment or an unguent, a syrup, a pill, a suppository, an intra-
> venous or intramuscular injection. A vaccine that prevents us from raping,
> sodomizing, killing in our own cave or in the caves of others. A medicine
> that can be purchased at the drugstore.[65]

Fallaci is not a religious person and is convinced that the difference between
good and evil does not exist but rather depends on circumstances and the
moment, time and fate. Nevertheless, she plays the preacher in her book and
wears a good morality mask. Her message upholds the necessity of *making
believe* because human beings cannot live without feigning acceptance of
good and evil.

Still, chaos, metaphysical catastrophe, and the absurdity of death persistently loom in the background. No reinvention of moral categories successfully addresses the ultimate fate that awaits each person. Fallaci consequently changes her image once again and puts on the disguise of laughter.
Only a comedic frame of mind offers an illusive thread of hope and a scornful
rebuke to the monster of destiny. She comments on the connection between
catastrophe and amusement when the professor states that he must write his
novel "with a smile on the lips and a tear in the eyes." Although the tear
represents compassion for the suffering that humanity endures, the smile
implies a happy spirit. Without it, Fallaci reveals, she could never bear a
world in which foolishness, chaos, and masochism unfold. In a biting but
comic aphorism she attacks Condor's blunderous decision to send one-third
of the contingent on vacation before the Christmas Battle begins:

> Paradise is a place where the policemen are English, the cooks are French,
> the beer-brewers are Germans, the lovers are Italians, and everything is
> organized by the Swiss. Hell is a place where the policemen are Germans,
> the cooks are English, the beer-brewers are French, the lovers are Swiss,
> and everything is organized by the Italians.[66]

More than any other character, Crazy Horse provokes laughter. His
preparation for the Christmas Battle establishes an atmosphere of the ludi-
crous. He dusts off his jacket; combs his mustache; slaps on a few drops of

Napoléon's Preferred Cologne 4711; puts on his monocle, flak jacket, helmet, yellow gloves; cradles a riding crop beneath his armpit; and finally snaps on a codpiece. He then orders his driver to the front driveway rather than the rear and silences the chauffeur's objections. Arriving at the wrong site, he begins to tremble and loses precious minutes analyzing his trepidation, defining fear, lecturing his dumbfounded driver about the great Vicomte de Turenne's funeral oratio, interpreting valor, and expounding on Baruch Spinoza. Finally situated at the rear driveway, he is subjected to a paroxysm of protest to get the column moving, jumps on the first M-113, dismisses the gunner, removes his headgear, puts on a helmet, emerges to his waist from the hatch in front of the Browning, cuts off radio contact with the operations room, and leads the five armored vehicles toward the Street Without a Name as though the Battle of Waterloo awaited his arrival. When bullets graze his body, he ignores the pilot's entreaty to hunker down. Instead he reopens radio contact, raises himself even higher, adjusts his monocle, catches his breath, and emits the joyful phrase into the microphone, "Courage, my valiants! They're bullets, not shit, Lepic said!"[67] To complete the surreal fiasco, a unified chorus of "go-fuck-yourself-you-and-Lepic" emerges from each of the other M-113s.

Humor in the novel functions as a palliative to tragedy, as comic relief. Whether they consciously know it or not, characters spread their cheer in the form of drollery that makes the harshness of life more bearable. "This is especially true when I am overwhelmed with tragic chapters and need to rest and feel a smile. I put myself in place of a character so fed up with horrors and tragedy that he had to laugh."[68] At such moments, comic characters like Crazy Horse came into existence. Ironic twists and funny situations function as antidotes to the absurdity of man's fate and free *Inshallah* from perpetual pessimism.

Oriana Fallaci's earlier works differ from those of her later years. In the professor's three letters to his imaginary wife, he explains why he chooses the novel as his medium of communication. "It's a vessel into which one can simultaneously pour reality and fantasy, dialectics and poetry, ideas and feelings."[69] Rather than simply being replicated in a chronicler's report, reality undergoes the transforming power of imagination. During one visit to Beirut, the yelping, barking of dogs prevented Fallaci from sleeping. She later, in *Inshallah*, converts the incident into a symbol. This small episode illustrates how imagination transforms an experience into a significant element of the novel with both literal and figurative meanings. Certainly wild packs

haunted the quiet nights of Beirut. However, they also symbolize the continuation of life despite lacerations, disfigurement, and death.

Fallaci insists that she has created all of her characters and that, even
when inspired by real persons, they remain imaginary figures. Says the professor, "I listen, I spy, I steal from reality. Then I correct it, I reinvent it, I
re-create it to such a degree that often I no longer remember who the original
was."[70] The despotic Condor, who thinks he can defeat death, was modeled
after the head of the Italian forces in Beirut. However, the end product differs
so drastically from the original that they hardly resemble each other. The
same evolutionary process occurs with many of the other figures in the novel.
Assigning them a place and inserting them into the narrative structure, says
Fallaci through the professor, becomes an overwhelming task. "Certain
nights I feel like a sloppy puppetmaster who doesn't have enough fingers to
support the strings of his puppets. And I quiver."[71] Viewing life as a phan-
tasmagorical chaos of voices and faces and creatures whose actions link the
chain of events that determine human destiny, Fallaci must use the greatest
possible number of puppets to express her images. She creates protagonists
who represent aspects of her own life and thereby resembles Flaubert, who
stated that his main character Emma was himself. Fallaci, too, identifies with
the population of *Inshallah*. "I am any creature born out of my imagination,"
explains the professor, "all the creatures who exist thanks to my thoughts
and feelings, sucking those thoughts and feelings like a vampire sucks his
victims' blood."[72]

As Fallaci began to write, she expressed her overwhelming enthusiasm.
"A miniature *Iliad* is stirring around me," she states through the professor.
The many aspects of this early Greek masterpiece inform the structure and
content of *Inshallah* — "a modern *Iliad* where . . . I can locate almost all the
heroes of the divine poem."[73] By analogy, Helen is Beirut itself; Paris and
Menelaus represent the two halves of the contested city that degenerates from
a paradise to a hell of factions, groups, cells, hatreds, and strife. Condor,
with the ravenous energy of a lion who lacks a forest, spouts his rage at his
men and resembles Agamemnon. Charlie, the mustached giant who desires
to imitate Lawrence of Arabia, prefers the sophistries of intrigue to the cru-
dities of war making and embodies Ulysses. Sandokan is Achilles, an innocu-
ous pirate who hopelessly yearns for combat. Philoctetes is the mild Colonel
Falcon, who remains at the Rubino base convent on a hill to avoid confron-
tation. Pistoia, an amusing Don Juan, attracts beautiful Brissidas and Cres-
sidas and represents Ajax. His mania for coming to blows causes the Italian

military much woe. Crazy Horse, the aristocratic pedant of little wisdom but undoubted eloquence, oppresses his fellow men with Latin proverbs and Napoleonic anecdotes and symbolizes Nestor. Antenor is Eagle, a meek Neapolitan Jew who would sell Vesuvius and the Wailing Wall to avoid waging war. Diomedes is the meticulous technocrat Sugar, who lives for regulations and collects booby traps with the devotion of a philatelist. Bilal, the magnificent dwarf armed with a Kalashnikov and dressed in a patched jacket, sweeps the streets of the old city and represents Hector. Each of Fallaci's *Iliad* characters had existed as a real person but, under the influence of the Greek epic, was re-created.

Although *Inshallah* is based on the war in Lebanon, the annihilation of Italians at the end of the story never took place. The Christmas Battle is also a product of fancy, as are many characters. Those based on real people, no longer resemble their models. Lady Godiva is a case in point. Inspired by an actual event, Fallaci transformed her in the context of the plot. Hearing that a group of soldiers had an erotic doll with which they had sex, Fallaci cornered one of the men to ask about it and learned that some of the recruits had seen it advertised in the newspaper, ordered it, and then organized their orgies. The information served as a catalyst but assumes an independent life in the book. The original model for the White Stallion was a gray mare. During the Italian withdrawal from the Lebanese capital, gunfire from the enemy had wounded the animal, whose pasture was between the warring factions. An event on the last day of the author's visit left a lasting impression. The mare lay decapitated on the sidewalk, and the retreating convoy made a semicircle to avoid hitting the head. The incident as it appears in the book is significantly changed. The White Stallion allegorically reflects the author's life, which has not been happy but rather brought exposure to sorrow, death, and horror. According to Fallaci, unfriendly people have taken potshots at her in the same manner that enemy riflemen took aim at the defenseless animal.[74]

The mysterious personality of Ninette, almost born out of nothingness, further illustrates the reinvention of a character and Fallaci's craving to reveal herself in an additional form. She was born during a nightly visit by Fallaci to Italian checkpoints in Shatila and Sabra when two soldiers in a jeep had a brief exchange about their sergeant, who had become a certain Antoinette's lover. Fallaci then conceived the idea of Ninette, the character with whom Angelo would make love. Before starting her next draft, the writer still did not know anything about her. "The book had not yet told me who she was." She had already fallen in love with many of her characters—Zandra Sadr, Rashid, Mahomet, Bilal—but still had developed no attachment to Ninette. "And I need to be in love with my characters. If I am not, the character is fucked." The writer originally viewed her as a stupid, gorgeous woman but intuited that she had to have much experience.

> She had to be mature, older than Angelo because she had to know what he did not know—the formula of life. At that point, the Book with a capital *B*, pleased with my understanding and discovery, started slowly to reveal itself and to tell me more things about Ninette.[75]

Ninette's individuality becomes apparent during the Christmas Battle. The novel's developing structure asserts itself to make her death a practical necessity: Angelo could justify killing Passepartout only if the terrorist brutally assassinates her. If not, Rashid would not have to seek revenge against the retreating Italians in the deadly final scene. Passepartout's shooting of Ninette in cold blood leads to the scene in which he holds up the cross that he had taken from Ninette's neck. Seeing the pendant in his hands then motivates Angelo to pull the trigger of his rifle. The retreating contingent next tragically dies in a violent attack. Events mathematically trigger results: Passepartout kills Ninette; Angelo kills Passepartout; Rashid kills Angelo; everyone dies at the end.

At that point in her evolution, Ninette's story was incomplete. Fallaci then introduced more ideas (that Ninette's husband had been assassinated, that she had had a serious nervous breakdown) but still had to deal with a technical problem related to the behavior of individuals whose sorrow causes them to lose their minds. According to Ninette, the termination of love equals the death of a beloved and causes the same suffering, emptiness, and denial.

> Even if you expected it and caused it, wanted it out of self-defense or sagacity, when it happens you feel mutilated. You feel as if you're left with only one eye, one ear, one arm, one leg, one lung, half a brain, and you do nothing but invoke the lost half of yourself: the person with whom you felt whole, complete. You don't even recall his or her faults, the torments he or she inflicted on your soul, the sufferings you went through on his or her account.[76]

Ninette's voice recalls Fallaci's after the loss of Panagoulis; her husband was a replica of Alekos. The protagonist's regret derives from the memory of a beloved, of "an irreplaceable treasure," but it also suggests Fallaci's grief after her lover's death. Eventually, intense suffering passes, and refusal to accept the truth disappears. "You finally realize that the object of your dead love was neither an extraordinary individual nor an irreplaceable treasure, you replace him or her with another half or supposed half of yourself."[77] Ninette had substituted Angelo for her dead husband; Fallaci had embraced writing to fill the emotional void. However, each of their souls bears a disfiguring scar; they have both been changed by death. "Even if a love languishes without remedy, you keep it and you try to heal it. That's why, even if it is in a state of coma, you try to postpone the moment when it will breathe its last breath."[78]

Fully conscious of her fame at the time, Fallaci knew that her reading public would have easily recognized Ninette as an additional alter ego—over and above the professor. She thus makes a determined effort to downplay self-revelation by portraying Angelo as the main character. In addition, she depicts Ninette as mentally ill from her grief and a victim of manic depression. Mood disorders are apparent in her inexhaustive, excessive, and impulsive interest in other men, her increased sexual desire, and her attempt to replace her spouse with a lover. Her words—"We'll spend the night making love"—represent a reaction to stress, death, and life, as well as an attempt to forget by substituting a surrogate husband.[79] When she meets Angelo, who revives her husband like nobody else, she immediately desires him, tracks him down, and transforms him into the object of her maniacal need for love. After Angelo ends their affair and after her encounter at the Shiite clinic with injured survivors of the massacre, she reacts as a manic-depressive, subconsciously seeking suicide by exposing her cross in the Muslim neighborhood and going to meet Passepartout.

This cryptic character still leaves many questions about her background unanswered. "I didn't know who she was, what her real name was, and who her husband was, and who her mother and father were." At that point, Fallaci's downstairs tenant in her Manhattan home played an important role in the character's evolution. This monstrously obese lady with penetrating eyes—Bella Vanderlix—spoke to Fallaci one day. "Hi, I think I am your neighbor. How are you?"[80] She invited Fallaci to dinner and seduced her by revealing that she was an expert on the Arab world and had once been mar-

ried to a Saudi Arabian prince. From that point on, Fallaci hounded Bella
with questions about the novel she was writing.[81]

"Who is her husband?"
"It should be someone who is about to become the president of Lebanon."
"Good, good, I like that. But the father?"
"They killed the father."
"Why? She doesn't want to speak French in the book."
"Of course. Her father was killed by the French."
"For Christ's sake, why?"
"Because there was fighting."
"For God's sake, why was her father killed by the French?"
"I don't know."[82]

Vaguely remembering that the French had committed many ugly acts during
their mandate in Lebanon, Fallaci ran up the round wrought-iron staircase
leading to her apartment, consulted the *Encyclopédie Larousse*, and discovered that French police had massacred many Lebanese in 1947. Ninette's
father was born. This mathematician and statesman died in a volley of bullets by his country's so-called liberators as he stood at the head of a protest
march. "Bella, I know who her father is. The book told me. . . . He was
leading the march and the French police shot him."[83]

     In a further difficulty with Ninette's character, Fallaci wanted to know
why her husband was rich and famous and why the British had given husband and wife a tea party at the embassy. When Bella explained that both
he and his wife could have had gold mines in South Africa, like many rich
Lebanese, it became clear that the British were seeking their favor. When
Bella listed a series of Arabic names, Fallaci chose George Al Sharif as the
husband's name and created the highest magistrate of the Lebanese Supreme
Court, the man who could have saved his country had he not died in an
explosion after turning the ignition key of his Rolls-Royce. From that moment on, everything came easily. Fallaci placed the story of Sharif's assassination and Ninette's explanation that *Inshallah* means "As God wishes" in
the newspaper *Le Journal du Liban*. "No character has been as laborious as
Ninette. All the others were clear in my mind. She was the hardest."[84]

     Despite the autobiographical connection between Fallaci's obsession with
the death of Panagoulis and Ninette's with George Al Sharif, essential dif-

ferences separate the author from her character. She overcame the fixation, while the protagonist could not and committed suicide. The writer's love for life wins over the character's preference for death. Energetically accepting and living each day to its fullest constitutes the essential difference. The creation and evolution of Ninette exemplifies how a small occurrence can result in an entirely reinvented character. It also reflects Fallaci's compulsive need to reveal herself. Her hesitancy partially explains Ninette's enigmatic personality and the preponderance of male figures in the book. Reticence simply holds back the release of too much autobiographical revelation through a predominant female character. Ninette could have easily evolved into the novel's main figure but remains secondary; the book devotes many more pages to Angelo and the other soldiers.

In *Inshallah*, Fallaci forges an adventure and a portrait of people living in the chaos and violence of war. Into this horror, she pours all of the reshaped knowledge she had acquired in her vast array of experience, outstripping anything that journalism would have permitted. *Inshallah* falls within the tradition of war novels but rises above killing fields. Fallaci has done everything in her power to transcend cultural differences and wants her book to stand for all times and all places. She fulfills the dream that had begun many years earlier and finally writes freely about literature, the human condition, alternatives to cynicism, and life as the antidote to death—all within the confines of a war novel. She wants her not-so-miniature *Iliad*, with its nightmarish vision of massacres, dying cries of innocent victims, and Goya-like depictions, to take a position beside Tolstoy's *War and Peace*, Hemingway's *For Whom the Bell Tolls*, and Malraux's *Man's Hope*.

Critic Paul William Roberts maintains that he has not reviewed anything as good as *Inshallah* in eighteen years. "Fallaci's novel . . . is, beyond doubt, one of those few examples of writing that we eventually term classics of literature—beyond the reach of time and fashion. It left me trembling, drained and exhilarated."[85] In a letter to Fallaci's editor, the same critic calls *Inshallah* a masterpiece and one of the ten greatest novels ever written, even slightly better than *War and Peace*.[86]

> It seems scarcely believable that such a work has appeared in the cynical twilight of the second millennium. Anyone who cares about literature, about life, about the human condition cannot afford not to read this triumphant feat of literature and love, this antidote to cynicism and death.[87]

The critic Ahdaf Soueif takes a less laudatory position and reminds readers that Fallaci's literary reputation is not principally in the field of fiction. She claims that Fallaci is knowledgeable in military logistics but untrustworthy about people: the way they feel, speak, and act. She believes that Fallaci expresses a contempt for Arabs that had appeared in her introductions to the interviews with Yassir Arafat and Ahmed Zaki Yamani. She finds her *I-am-speaking-for-all-humanity* stance insidious and contradicted by the book's text. In Soueif's view, Fallaci's Arabs have no humanity; they are represented mainly as hysterical, mercurial, murderous extras. Their individuality is a caricature of lust, grief, hatred, or greed and, when granted metaphoric status, is represented by images of bats, snakes, and rabid dogs.

> The magnitude of error here is of such an order that one is moved to ask: What if an Arab were to write a book, call it "Speriamo," set it in Genoa, and fill it with Italians who . . . behaved in ways no ordinary Italian could fathom? And what if those Italians existed only to be outsmarted and pushed around by a squadron of Arab soldiers? Surely there would be an outcry, and at the forefront, probably, would be those who claimed to speak for a common humanity. Well, hasten the day when we Arabs can take a similar arrogance for granted and hope to get away with it.[88]

James Walton combines criticism and praise in his analysis. He first states that, in his view, a cast of more than sixty protagonists means that the characterizations are done "with broad brush strokes." However, he counters, "These [brush strokes] are applied with such energy that the characters live and move us." He chastises Fallaci for her tendency to sermonize. "The novel is constantly interrupted by little (and not so little) pontifications on love, friendship, courage, streetsweeping ("a noble trade") or whatever points she feels, usually wrong, we may not have fully understood from the narrative." According to Walton, she also practices literary deception. "One of the characters spends his time writing the novel 'we are reading' until he realizes that he is fictional himself, an invention of the shadowy female 'Saigon journalist' who has been hovering about the Italian camp." In the critic's view, the novel's wildest miss comes in its attempt to lay bare what Fallaci "shamelessly" calls the formula of life. He expresses disappointment when near the end it turns out to be the Arabic word of the title, *Inshallah*, which, as far as he can determine, translates as "whatever will be will be."

"So that is it—Doris Day was right all along." Walton's conclusion expresses both his praise and his criticism.

> The fact that *Inshallah* survives such major flaws is, then, a tribute to an indestructibility which, on occasions, rivals that of Beirut itself. Indeed, at times, I found myself thinking that it is only right that such an epic book should have such epic faults.[89]

Inshallah, the most developed, ambitious, and tragic of Fallaci's works, stands as the crowning achievement of her career. It is the sum of her personal experiences, the justification of her life as a writer, and the fulfillment of a dream that had begun when she read Jack London as a twelve-year-old child. Her themes of doubt, despair, and desperate search for life after death are familiar ones in the annals of fiction. However, Fallaci has made every attempt to repeat them in an innovative, fresh manner and, through the professor, makes a point of telling her readers, "And I know how to repeat the already said things in a way that they seem said for the first time: writing in my way."[90] Such Italian critics as Giancarlo Vigorelli, Bernardo Valli, and David Maria Turoldo enthusiastically praised the book. If Fallaci merits any claim to recognition by posterity as a great novelist, she rises or falls on *Inshallah*. The Italian woman from Florence is wildly extravagant, dissipated, and licentious with epic plot and historical detail in her war novel. For the first time, Fallaci the novelist far outweighs Fallaci the journalist. She has used all of her skill to enclose within *Inshallah* "the eternal story, the eternal novel of Man who at war manifests himself in all his truth."[91]

Facing the Alien

Conclusion. FALLACI'S RICH LITERARY

dramas fuse intimately with her personal ceremonials—a combination that thrusts her image before the public eye. The decision to make herself her own main character did not occur by chance. It was the product of reflection and deliberate choice. Fallaci has always hungered for dignity and power in her life and compares herself to Merlin the wizard. The power of this medieval figure consists of his intellectual creativity rather than military might. He is neither a king nor a skillful magician but a refined, cultivated, and highly intelligent individual whose brain power determines his course of action and earns his prestige. In the case of Fallaci, she suffered periods of poverty in her youth—a condition associated with weakness, infirmity, and subservience. At the same time, however, she possessed the haunting desire—characteristic of many underprivileged people—to acquire moral dignity and intellectual distinction. "It is not the richness of money but that of dignity that inspires power. He [a poor person] knows that he cannot have temporal, material, monetary, or social power. He therefore associates culture with the idea of power."[1]

Fallaci's father embraced politics; he even sketched and painted. Her mother's relatives included artists and sculptors. Both Edoardo and Tosca Fallaci indoctrinated their daughter with the notion of the special social status of writers. She then accepted that the highest honor in life and single most accessible power was *the book*. Her goal never focused on success as an actress, a singer, or a gymnast. She wanted to write, to put her own story into the hands of readers everywhere. This success would give her the intellectual authority toward which she aspired. "Because the immortality of the writer, that which he produces, remains alive when he dies. If you are obsessed with death, you are fascinated by books, by writing."[2]

Whether confronting a page of writing in *Inshallah*—novelist—documenting a historical phenomenon in the Mexico City articles—champion of the oppressed—or revealing the massive power of New York City in *Penelope at War*—wide-eyed visitor to America—Fallaci treats every occasion as a stage for creating a new version of herself, of generating her own mythical status. Her powerful performances and literary journalistic style, despite their narcissistic plea for attention, aggressively seduce readers into accepting her official image. Fallaci carves out her place as a notorious self-advertiser. Nearly everything she has ever written is an overt reconstruction and contemplation of her personal self-image.

Proof of her worldwide success can be found in her 1993 visit to Beijing to deliver a speech at the Academy of Social Sciences. The enthusiastic reception demonstrated how interested people were in the writer herself, as well as in her books. Students arrived by the busload, despite official resistance to their attending, and jammed the corridors of the meeting hall. During the question-and-answer period after her speech, Fallaci told Alberto Sinigaglia in an interview, a student of Italian spoke.

> I am not here to ask a question because I have been reading you ever since I know how to read, and I already know the answers. I am here to thank you in my name and on behalf of my fellow students. . . . I thank you, we thank you because through your books and your interview of Deng you have taught us two things which are the most important things in the world: courage and freedom. . . . Please do not die. . . . We need you very much.[3]

The student's comments are evidence of a phenomenon: connecting her books to her life, as though she not only speaks against tyranny and moral evil but also lives her convictions every day. In Fallaci's opinion, some authors write well and live badly; their actions betray what they write. She mentions Jean-Jacques Rousseau as a case in point. He eloquently composed an educational treatise but abandoned his own children. She specifically criticizes servants of the Fascist power structure in Italy, in particular the writers Elio Vittorini, Vasco Pratolini, and Benedetto Croce. "I live like I write. I have never given in."[4] During times of war and peace she claims to have remained faithful to her personal principles and to have struggled on behalf of freedom against all forms of totalitarianism. The Chinese student in Beijing sensed that writing is the mirror of her life and that she is not a liar when she encourages the new China to embrace principles of freedom. He understood the coherence of her life.

Perhaps, a soul divided, Fallaci views herself in terms of two distinct, contradicting temperaments. She is an adventurer who risks death, challenges tyranny, and never succumbs to the orthodoxies of fascism or communism—even when they are fashionable. At the same time, she is reflective, intellectual, interested in the arts, and capable of sitting at a table for years to complete a book. These two contradictory temperaments are like opponents forever at war. Nevertheless, Fallaci claims that the intellectual side of the person seated at a table is the stronger of the two. As a child, she was serious, thoughtful, calm, and studious; she spent long hours reading and writing stories. Then dreams of adventure overwhelmed her and affected her aspirations: she felt pulled in two opposing directions. She still wants to read and write quietly but is possessed by an insatiable desire to be where the action is. She can never travel to distant places without experiencing guilt (even while in helicopters over Vietnam); she feels uneasy, as though she is losing precious writing time. Enclosed within the privacy of a study, she often deprives herself of exhilarating escapades. She insists that her six years with *Inshallah* were hell; on the other hand, if she had been at Tiananmen Square, the Berlin Wall, or in Moscow, she would have felt guilty. Yet, from two different temperaments emerges a morally coherent person on whom Fallaci's spotlight continuously shines.

Fallaci now confronts her greatest challenge as she lives through what may be her final adventure—her battle with cancer. In the midst of hectic activity, on an unforgettable winter day, she discovered a lump at the base of her left breast. Feeling the bulge, she straightway came to a fatalistic conclusion. "Okay, that's a tumor. I'm finished."[5] In spite of her need for immediate medical treatment, she chose to do nothing. She had to meet a deadline and neglected her personal health. "I decided not to tell because if

I tell it, everybody would say, 'Oriana, you must go to the doctor.' I could not go to the doctor. I had to finish the translations of *Inshallah*. I lost six precious months."[6] She was like a soldier confronted with illness who could not cancel a mission.

In July 1992, after her surgery in Milan, Fallaci insisted on seeing what the surgeons had removed. When they replied that no one ever asks to view their cancerous flesh, she repeated her wish in no uncertain terms.

> "It's my stuff, I want to see it." So they came with this thing. Heh-heh. It was this big piece of Oriana. They came and I said, "I want to see him." And him was this little long white thing. I started talking to him: "You bloody bastard." Oooh, I hated him. I was insulting him. "You don't dare come back. Did you leave any children inside me? I will kill you! I will kill you! You will not win!" These doctors, they could not believe. They said, "Oh, my God. . . . "[7]

Cancer had become an insidious and unthinking but alert, plotting enemy. It had already killed her mother, Tosca, her father, Edoardo, and her sister Neera and had also invaded her sister Paola. She had always known that eventually the alien would strike her. This was her destiny. In her heart, she knew why fate never allowed her to die in Vietnam, Mexico City, or Bangladesh. She had a preestablished appointment with a higher power that had ordained she should die of cancer. Thus, when her surgeons held the cancerous flesh before her eyes, every fiber in her body yearned to inflict harm on this evil and formidable adversary: strangle it, spit at it, and curse it. "I feel I have a creature, an animal, inside. Ah, *si*, it's an intelligent thing. And he knows what I think. And so I cannot hide to him what I'm thinking, that I am pessimistic."[8]

Fallaci attributes the immediate catalyst of her malady to the Black Cloud that she encountered in Kuwait in 1991. She accuses it of hiding in her lungs and maintains that it asserted its presence almost a year later. Saddam Hussein had ordered the incineration of 635 Kuwaiti rigs that poured three million barrels of burning crude oil into the atmosphere each day. The immense mass of soot that rose from the flames was blowing in a northerly direction on the day Fallaci and three accompanying marines drove their vehicle eighty miles from Khafji. Suddenly, the wind changed its course, carried the cloud due south in their direction and, within minutes, engulfed their truck for a half hour. Their eyes teared; their throats burned; their chests hurt; and their stomachs strained to vomit. Covered with black pitch, the American driver summed up their feelings. "By God! If outside we're like that, what do we have inside our lungs?"[9]

Fallaci no longer draws a distinction between reality and imagination as she expresses her struggle with cancer, the monstrous creature inside of her that has become wholly independent of her will.

> In my subconscious, I have resigned myself. I say to myself that I must not
> give in because he will take advantage, but he already knows. I could say
> to myself that I will destroy him; he will not destroy me. But I don't believe
> it and he knows it. He knows it before I do.[10]

Any discussion of her cancer makes Fallaci angry. "I don't want to speak about being ill. It's my problem. I don't want to be pathetic. I don't want sympathy. That's the last thing I want."[11] Yet she is driven by an almost compulsive need to talk about it. "Oriana is an open book," she quotes her sister Paola as saying. "An open book, that is, written in Chinese or Sanskrit."[12] Fallaci expressed her displeasure toward Paul Hendrickson of the *Washington Post* for including too much about her illness in his laudatory and insightful "Oriana Fallaci, Forever at War."[13] Yet she freely unleashed a torrent of reflections during Hendrickson's interview. In Italy, her comments about her cancer appeared in the press as though she were waging a personal war. Even smoking a cigarette was an act of defiance. "Be careful, you piece of shit, I am blowing smoke in your face."[14] She also conversed about it in an uninhibited manner on Italian television.[15] She begrudges the sickness because it not only inflicts suffering but makes her feel disinclined to write during a period that should be the most fruitful in her life. She fears that the monster will snatch her away before completing her latest novel, a work of experience and wisdom that requires an understanding of oneself and others. "I was healthy when I was immature. As a mature person, I am sick. My monster derides and mocks me." She underwent surgery again in 1994, and the writer has a fifty-fifty chance of winning the battle. "My life at this point is a question mark. I don't know whether I'll have the time to write the next book."[16]

Before her first operation, Fallaci acted and talked as though she were immortal. Now she works hard to forget her illness and, through the power of her intellect, find a way to defeat her alien. During the summer of 1993, she recorded *Lettera a un bambino mai nato* on audiocassette. Her voice will live, even if her sickness robs her of life. The novel she now writes energizes her and, in a sense, keeps her alive. It will deride the alien by creating a child, albeit out of paper, that will live after she is gone. Her cancer will have no power over this offspring; it cannot invade its inner being. The writer thus madly races against time as though in a marathon race.

In her forthcoming book, which tells of fascism in Italy before, during, and after World War II, Fallaci again turns the full power of her creativity on herself. However, she reveals it all through the eyes of the child Oriana. Her readers will see her beloved Florence, intimate portraits of the parents she loved so much, Allied bombings, the Resistance movement, and the liberation. She will reveal the personal ideology that she embraced in her youth and account for her unswerving fidelity to it. At the same time, she will expose a side of herself never before shared—her humor. Fallaci knows how to make people laugh. She inherited her spirit of irony and good humor from her father and wants the world to see this side of her temperament. She owes it to a public that has seen mainly tragic, philosophical anxiety in her novels.

Fallaci consciously focuses on dying with dignity. Right before her father died, she held him in her arms and felt the need to speak to him.

> I was so desperate. It was a matter of seconds! He was suffering terrible pains and then I had an enlightenment. I said to him: 'For Christ's sake, what a marvelous man you are, what a courageous man you are! . . . You're great! Bravo! Bravo!' He opened his eyes and looked at me, and he had a smile. And he died. I hope I die like he did.[17]

Fallaci's struggle with cancer typifies the image building that characterizes her life. She simply cannot help but place her story before the public eye. On the one hand, her intense drive motivates the inception and completion of articles, interviews, and books in the best tradition of literary journalism. Yet they reflect the physical and spiritual journey of her existence. Her writings are one, long, continuous autobiography.

The last time I saw Fallaci, in New York in March 1993, she told me that her life had moved into a wait-and-see stage.[18] I disagree. She has actually initiated the high point of the Fallaci phenomenon, now unfolding as she completes the voyage of her life. Recalling how a young Italian police officer offered himself to save the people of his village from a German firing squad, she admires the courageous manner in which he met his end and remains determined to imitate his heroism by unflinchingly staring the alien down. In what may be her final role, Fallaci ferociously wages the battle and will until the countdown is over. She goes on writing and talking, fiercely resolved not to be upstaged even by death itself. La Fallaci will set the ground rules and, with great gusto, write the final chapter of her own myth.

NOTES

BIBLIOGRAPHY

INDEX

Notes

INTRODUCTION: IN SEARCH OF TRUTH

1. Santo L. Aricò, "Oriana Fallaci's Discovery of Truth in *Niente e così sia*," *European Studies Journal* 3, no. 2 (1986): 11–23.

2. Santo L. Aricò, "Breaking the Ice: An In-Depth Look at Oriana Fallaci's Interview Techniques," *Journalism Quarterly* 63, no. 3 (1986): 587–93.

3. Santo L. Aricò, "Oriana Fallaci's Journalistic Novel: *Niente e così sia*," In *Contemporary Women Writers in Italy: A Modern Renaissance*, edited by Santo L. Aricò (Amherst: University of Massachusetts Press, 1990), 170–82.

4. Interview with Fallaci, New York, Mar. 1993.

5. Robert Poirier discusses the concept of the writer as an exhibitionist. Although he never names Fallaci, his comments on literary peformance frequently describe her intrinsic mode of inserting herself as the center of her own writings. *The Performing Self* (New York: Oxford University Press, 1971).

6. Lord Raglan, *The Hero: A Study in Tradition, Myth, and Drama* (London: Watts & Co., 1936), 144.

7. Vigorelli's statement appears on the book jacket of *Inshallah* (the English title of the Italian *Insciallah*; all English translations are given in the bibliography). See also Bernardo Valli, "La piccola Iliade di Oriana," *La Repubblica*, 29 July 1990, 5; Giancarlo Vigorelli, "Guerra e amore nel 'suo' Libano," *Il Giorno*, 7 Aug. 1990, 5; David Maria Turoldo, "Viaggio nel vulcano 'Insciallah'," *Corriere della Sera*, 2 Aug. 1990, 5; Wolfgango Rossani, "La Fallaci come Flaubert," *Gazzetta di Parma*, 10 July 1990, 5.

8. Final interview with Fallaci, New York, Nov. 1993.

9. The letter is dated 16 Feb. 1994.

10. From a speech given by Fallaci in Cologne, Germany, Oct. 1986. Fallaci provided me with a copy of the speech. My translation.

11. Ibid.

1. FLORENCE

1. Interview with Fallaci, New York, Dec. 1991.

2. Ibid.

3. Ibid.

4. Ibid.

5. Ibid.

6. Ibid.

7. Ibid.

8. Oriana Fallaci, "Nota introduttiva," *Il richiamo della foresta*, by Jack London (Milan: Rizzoli Editore, 1953), iii. My translation.

9. Ibid., vii.

10. Ibid.

11. Douglas Foster, "Love, Death, and the Written Word: The Lonely Passion of Oriana Fallaci," *Los Angeles Times Magazine*, 10 Jan. 1993, 26.

12. Ibid.

13. Ibid.

14. Interview with Fallaci, New York, Dec. 1991. In the "Nota introduttiva" to *Il richiamo della foresta*, however, Fallaci states that she was twelve when she read *Call of the Wild* (vii).

15. Oriana Fallaci, "Nota introduttiva," viii.

16. Interview with Fallaci, New York, Dec. 1991.

17. Ibid.

18. Ibid.

19. Ibid.

20. Ibid. The examination of *maturità* occurred at the end of *liceo*.

21. Fallaci derides the boys in her class at the Liceo Galileo Galilei when she states that they seemed complacent about the tunnel vision of Italian curricula and that girls outshone them. "It was a mixed class—boys and girls. The boys—nothing; they all became lawyers, stupid lawyers, and stupid politicians." Interview with Fallaci, New York, Dec. 1991.

22. Foster, "Love," 24.

23. Ibid.

24. Interview with Fallaci, New York, Dec. 1991.

25. Mentioning Fallaci's name in academic circles often arouses negative reactions.

26. Interview with Fallaci, New York, Dec. 1991.

27. Ibid.

28. Ibid.

29. Paola Fallaci, "Una donna chiamata Oriana," *Annabella*, no. 35 (30 Aug. 1979): 22. All translations of Paola Fallaci's articles about Oriana are mine.

30. Ibid.

31. Interview with Fallaci, New York, Dec. 1991.

32. Patrizia Carrano, *Le signore grandi firme* (Florence: Guaraldi Editore, 1978), 74. My translation.

33. Ibid.

34. Ibid.

35. Ibid.

36. Ibid., 78–79.

37. Umberto Cecchi, "Una notte, cercando *Insciallah*," *Europeo*, no. 33 (18 Aug. 1990): 59. My translation. All translations of *Europeo* articles are mine.

38. Paola Fallaci, "Una donna," 23.

2. KIPLING, LONDON, HEMINGWAY

1. Oriana Fallaci, "Lettera sulla cultura," *Europeo*, no. 19 (10 May 1973): 36. To read the articles Oriana mentions, see Fallaci, "Giovanni Leone," *Europeo*, no. 17 (26 Apr. 1973): 42–51; "L'interrogazione," *Europeo*, no. 7/11 (15 Mar. 1973): 54–59; "Radiografia di un uomo," *Europeo*, no. 31 (5 Aug. 1971): 36–43.

2. Fallaci does what James E. Murphy summarizes in "The New Journalism: A Critical Perspective," *Journalism Monographs*, no. 34 (1974): 3.

3. Seymour Krim, *Shake It for the World, Smart Ass* (New York: Dial Press, 1970).

4. William L. Rivers, "The New Confusion," *The Progressive*, no. 35 (Dec. 1971): 28.

5. Carrano, *Signore*, 78–79.

6. Interview with Fallaci, New York, Dec. 1991. See also Paola Fallaci, "Una donna," 25.

7. The critic Umberto Cecchi discusses her use of the word *reporter* rather than *journalist* in "Una notte," 59.

8. Interview with Fallaci, New York, Mar. 1993.

9. Carrano, *Signore*, 79. Fallaci's early dispatches were not all crime stories. They also consisted of articles on the fashion magnates Christian Dior, Edward Marcus, and Irina Roublon. They included reports on movie stars making films in Florence or just visiting the city—Joan Fontaine, Joseph Cotten, Danielle Darrieux, and Alida Valli—and portraits of such renowned, scholarly figures as Director of the Royal Cancer Hospital of London Alexander Haddow and the Czech genius Ales Cerny. Human interest anecdotes ranged from the story of the courageous, one-hundred-year-old grandmother who lived on the top floor of her apartment building to the innovative teaching methods of Maria Maltoni in her one-room schoolhouse on a narrow country road. She also regularly attended judicial hearings and covered postwar trials in Florence.

10. Interview with Fallaci, New York, Mar. 1993.

11. Oriana Fallaci, "Malinconica storia del 'Conventino' asilo di artisti e di povera gente," *Il Mattino dell'Italia Centrale*, 2 Oct. 1949, 3. All translations from *Il Mattino* and other Italian newspapers are mine.

12. Oriana Fallaci, "La cupola senz'ali," *Il Mattino dell'Italia Centrale*, 11 Aug. 1951, 4.

13. Oriana Fallaci, "Ebbe fra le mani i piedi del re," *Corriere Lombardo*, 15–16 Feb. 1950, 3. *Il Mattino dell'Italia Centrale* syndicated the article, and many others, without ever telling Fallaci.

14. Oriana Fallaci, "Hanno ritrovato la vita gli 'sciuscià' snidati da Tombolo," *Il Mattino dell'Italia Centrale*, 12 Aug. 1950, 6.

15. Oriana Fallaci, "Le confessioni di Sergio Vanzini condannato a 57 anni di carcere," *Gazzetta Sera*, 29 Dec. 1950, 3.

16. Oriana Fallaci, "Le donne dell'U.N.E.S.C.O. vanno spesso dal parrucchiere," *Corriere Lombardo*, 15–16 June 1950, 6.

17. Oriana Fallaci, "Anche a Fiesole Dio ha avuto bisogno degli uomini," *Europeo*, no. 19 (6 May 1951): 1.

18. Ibid.

19. Interview with Fallaci, New York, Dec. 1991. She also commented on this emotional experience in an interview given to Paola Fallaci, "E spiccò il volo: Poi venne la tragedia," *Annabella*, no. 36 (6 Sept. 1979): 18.

20. Oriana Fallaci, "Queste cinque malattie minacciano ancora i nostri bambini" *Europeo*, no. 25 (17 June 1951): 7.

21. Oriana Fallaci, "Ritratto della donna inglese," *Il Mattino dell'Italia Centrale*, 24 Oct. 1953, 3.

22. Oriana Fallaci, "Si allenano molte ore al giorno per imparare l'inchino alla regina," *Il Mattino dell'Italia Centrale*, 12 Nov. 1953, 3.

23. Oriana Fallaci, "Una tazza di tè con l'Imperatrice," *Il Popolo Nuovo*, 1 Dec. 1954, 3. The article was also printed in *Il Popolo di Milano* on 30 Nov. 1954 and in *Giornale del Mattino* on 25 Nov. 1954.

24. Ibid.

25. Ibid.

26. Oriana Fallaci, "Storia di una valigia persa e ritrovata a Teheran," *Corriere del Giorno*, 2 Dec. 1954, 3. The same article was printed in *Libertà*, 4 Jan. 1955.

27. Oriana Fallaci, "I bimbi poveri di Teheran non accettano carezze dagli stranieri," *Giornale del Mattino*, 7 Dec. 1954, 3.

28. Oriana Fallaci, "La richissima e potentissima Soraya si annoia mortalmente nella sua torre d'avorio," *Giornale del Mattino*, 10 Dec. 1954, 3.

29. Oriana Fallaci, "Neppure un soldato a guardia del preziosissimo trono dello Scià," *Giornale del Mattino*, 15 Dec. 1954, 3.

30. Ibid.

31. Oriana Fallaci, "Il petrolio è l'arbitro della Persia," *Sicilia del Popolo*, 22 Dec. 1954, 3.

32. Carrano, *Signore*, 80.

33. Paola Fallaci, "E spiccò il volo," 19.

34. Ronald Weber, "Some Sort of Artistic Excitement," in *The Reporter as Artist: A Look at the New Journalism Controversy*, edited by Ronald Weber (New York: Hastings House, 1974), 17.

35. Interview with Fallaci, New York, Dec. 1991. For later examples of Fallaci's literary tendencies, intensive first personism, and participatory journalism, see her articles on the Gulf War for *Corriere della Sera*: "A [otto] 8.000 metri sulle ali della guerra," 17 Feb. 1991, 3; "Credevo di andare a salvare il Kuwait," 9 Mar. 1991, 6; "La nuvola nera, Chernobyl del Golfo," 26 Mar. 1991, 8.

3. LIGHTS, CAMERA, ACTION

1. Fallaci was with *Europeo* from 1953 to 1976. Her articles were also in *Europeo* in 1982 and 1991.

2. Interview with Fallaci, New York, Mar. 1993.

3. Ibid.

4. Ibid.

5. Interview with Fallaci, New York, Dec. 1991.

6. Interview with Fallaci, New York, Mar. 1993.

7. Fallaci continued to write articles as though they were short stories, using innovative means of making them more interesting. Examples of her literary journalism while at *Europeo* include "Il figlio nella Legione Straniera," *Europeo*, no. 47 (15 Nov. 1953): 18–19; "Betty

Cowell è in Italia con un amico e un'amica," *Europeo*, no. 14 (4 Apr. 1954): 20; "È finito per gli orfanelli il terrore di Mamma Rosa," *Europeo*, no. 5 (31 Jan. 1954): 14.

8. Thirty of Fallaci's articles appeared in *Europeo* in 1954, forty-four in 1955, and twenty-four in 1956.

9. Oriana Fallaci, "Ho odiato Marilyn come una moglie gelosa," *Europeo*, no. 5 (29 Jan. 1956): 16.

10. Interview with Fallaci, Florence, July 1992.

11. Interview with Fallaci, New York, Mar. 1993.

12. Oriana Fallaci, "Hollywood dal buco della serratura," *Europeo*, no. 33 (18 Aug. 1957): 14.

13. Oriana Fallaci, *I sette peccati di Hollywood* (Milan: Longanesi Editore, 1958), 78. My translation.

14. Fallaci discusses this heavy toll in "La paura è il prezzo della loro fortuna," *Europeo*, no. 34 (25 Aug. 1957): 14–20. Most of the information in *I sette peccati di Hollywood* appeared first in Fallaci's articles for *Europeo*.

15. Interview with Fallaci, New York, Mar. 1993.

16. Ibid.

17. Ibid.

18. Ibid.

19. Oriana Fallaci, "Dovetti confessargli l'orribile verità," *Europeo*, no. 35 (1 Sept. 1957): 29.

20. Ibid., 35.

21. Oriana Fallaci, "Davvero non vorrei essere la moglie di Gregory Peck," *Europeo*, no. 36 (8 Sept. 1957): 17.

22. Oriana Fallaci, "I tre grandi dalle tempie grige," *Europeo*, no. 40 (6 Oct. 1957): 44.

23. Oriana Fallaci, "La generazione dei ribelli in blu jeans," *Europeo*, no. 41 (13 Oct. 1957): 44–50; "Qualcuna più tardi finisce al manicomio," *Europeo*, no. 42 (20 Oct. 1957): 15–19.

24. Oriana Fallaci, "Serata d'addio con le gemelle Pierangeli," *Europeo*, no. 44 (3 Nov. 1957): 44–50.

25. Oriana Fallaci, "Un'ora fitta fitta col marito di Marilyn," *Europeo*, no. 48 (1 Dec. 1957): 27.

26. Ibid., 29.

27. During the years 1958, 1959, and 1960, she intensified her coverage of acting, cinema, royal marriages, and fashion in more than seventy-five articles.

28. Interview with Fallaci, Florence, July 1992.

29. Oriana Fallaci, "L'America vista da un'italiana," *Europeo*, no. 30 (25 July 1965): 37. The other issue numbers under the same introductory title are 31, 32, 33.

30. Fallaci's trip across the United States with Shirley MacLaine appears in five articles written for *Europeo*: "Partiamo alla conquista del West," no. 45 (7 Nov. 1965): 49–54; "Il sentiero dei Navajo," no. 47 (21 Nov. 1965): 74–78; "L'ultimo cow-boy," no. 48 (28 Nov. 1965): 76–84; "Paura a Mosca," no. 49 (5 Dec. 1965): 74–79; "Oltrarno in Alabama," no. 51 (19 Dec. 1965): 62–67.

31. Fallaci's two *Europeo* articles on teenagers are "I minorenni terribili," no. 7 (10 Feb. 1966): 49–57; "Inchiesta fra i teenager," no. 8 (17 Feb. 1966): 29–34. The three *Europeo*

articles on racism are "I franchi tiratori sparano," no. 31 (3 Aug. 1967): 20–23; "Che cosa volete dai bianchi," no. 32 (10 Aug. 1967): 37–43; "Sono pronto a uccidere," no. 33 (17 Aug. 1967): 26–29. The four humorous letters from America in *Europeo* are "L'AFTRA mi protege," no. 11 (16 Mar. 1967): 79; "La CIA starnutisce nel mio telefono," no. 12 (23 Mar. 1967): 81; "Mi hanno chiesto un uovo," no. 14 (6 Apr. 1967): 23; "Come si fuma una banana," no. 15 (13 Apr. 1967): 39.

32. Oriana Fallaci, *The Useless Sex*, translated by Pamela Swinglehurst (New York: Horizon Press, 1964), 7. All quotations are from Swinglehurst's translation, but see also *Il sesso inutile* (Milan: Rizzoli Editore, 1961).

33. Carrano, *Signore*, 76.

34. Fallaci, *Useless Sex*, 9.

35. Ibid., 15.

36. Ibid., 9.

37. See Oriana Fallaci, "Si risposano, non si uccidono" *Europeo*, no. 22 (29 May 1960): 48. Her photo appears on the first page, where she stands to the right of Jaipur Indian women in a rickshaw.

38. See review of *The Useless Sex*, by Oriana Fallaci, translated by Pamela Swinglehurst, *Economist* 213, no. 14 (1964): 715; review of the same work in the *New Yorker* 68 (19 Dec. 1965): 168; and Dorothy Nyren, review of *The Useless Sex*, translated by Pamela Swinglehurst, *Library Journal* 90 (1 Jan. 1965): 132.

39. Interview with Fallaci, Florence, July 1992.

40. Ibid.

41. The eight articles on the condition of women in the Orient were published in *Europeo* between 1 May 1960 and 26 June 1960 (issue numbers 18–22, 24–26).

4. ON CENTER STAGE

1. Oriana Fallaci, *Penelope at War*, translated by Pamela Swinglehurst (London: Michael Joseph, Ltd., 1966), 7. All quotations are from Swinglehurst's translation; but see *Penelope alla guerra* (Milano: Rizzoli Editore, 1962).

2. Ibid., 8.

3. Carrano, *Signore*, 76.

4. Ibid., 76–77.

5. Ibid., 77.

6. Ibid., 78.

7. Fallaci, *Penelope at War*, 12.

8. Ibid., 222.

9. Ibid., 168.

10. Ibid., 19.

11. Ibid., 18.

12. Ibid., 170.

13. Interview with Fallaci, New York, Dec. 1991.

14. Robert Scheer, "Playboy Interview: Oriana Fallaci," *Playboy* 28, no. 11 (Nov. 1981): 95.

15. In Carrano's interview with Fallaci, Fallaci discussed the loss of her virginity, *Signore*, 81.

16. Fallaci, *Penelope at War*, 23.

17. Ibid., 137.

18. Ibid., 148.

19. Ibid., 20.

20. Ibid., 21.

21. Ibid., 152.

22. Ibid.

23. Ibid., 15.

24. Ibid., 78.

25. Fallaci maintains that, during the Vietnam War, she strongly criticized American involvement but never lost her affection for the individual soldier.

26. Interview with Fallaci, Florence, July 1992.

27. Oriana Fallaci, *Gli antipatici* (Milan: Rizzoli Editore, 1963), 184. My translation.

28. Fallaci, *Penelope at War*, 206.

29. Ibid., 52.

30. Ibid., 23.

31. Ibid., 24.

32. Ibid., 26. An additional example of conversation used to reveal a person's character occurs during Giò's meeting with Florence, Richard's mother. It becomes evident that her domineering attitude and views on the lewdness of sex play a dominant role in her son's homosexual personality. See pages 61–64, 176–81.

33. Ibid., 27.

34. Ibid., 31.

35. See Michele Prisco, "Introduzione, *Penelope alla guerra*, by Oriana Fallaci" (Milan: Rizzoli Editore, 1962), ii. Prisco's introduction is not in Swinglehurst's translation. See also Santo L. Aricò, "Oriana Fallaci's Journalistic Novel."

36. A British publishing house later released the same work as *The Limelighters*, translated by Pamela Swinglehurst (London: Michael Joseph, Ltd, 1967), with nine of the original interviews and new ones with Sean Connery (Mar. 1965), Sammy Davis Jr. (Nov. 1964), Geraldine Chaplin (Nov. 1964), El Cordobés (Apr. 1965), Mary Hemingway (Mar. 1966), and Senator Robert Kennedy (Dec. 1964). Later, an American version was released: *The Egotists: Sixteen Surprising Interviews*, translated by Mihaly Csikszentmihalyi, Oriana Fallaci, and Pamela Swinglehurst (Chicago: Henry Regnery, 1968), and included new ones with Norman Mailer (Apr. 1967), Sean Connery (Mar. 1965), H. Rap Brown (Aug. 1967), Ingrid Bergman (Aug. 1967), Nguyen Cao Ky (Mar. 1968), Hugh Hefner (Feb. 1966), and Dean Martin (Aug. 1967). Quotations (including those from the preface) are from *Egotists*, unless otherwise indicated.

37. Fallaci, *Egotists*, ix.

38. Ibid., x.

39. Ibid., xi.

40. Fallaci, *Antipatici*, 69. My translation.

41. Ibid., 74.

42. Ibid., 57.

43. Fallaci, *Egotists*, 48.

44. Ibid., 111.

45. Ibid., 124.

46. Ibid., 193. But in *Antipatici* (84), the words are not as strong: *"Disgraziata. Screanzata. Ballista. Maleducata"* (Wretched person. Rude. Liar. Ill-mannered).

47. Fallaci, *Egotists*, 192.

48. Ibid., 209.

49. Ibid., 76-77.

50. Ibid., 97.

51. Ibid., 244.

52. Ibid., 136.

53. Fallaci, *Antipatici*, 337.

54. Ibid., 340.

55. Ibid., 341.

56. Ibid., 337.

57. Ibid., 338.

58. "Goring the Egotists," *Time* 92, no. 48 (29 Nov. 1968): 48.

59. Interview with Fallaci, Florence, July 1992.

5. REACHING FOR THE MOON

1. Oriana Fallaci, *If the Sun Dies*, translated by Pamela Swinglehurst (New York: Atheneum, 1966). All quotations, unless otherwise indicated, are from Swinglehurst's translation; but see *Se il sole muore* (Milan: Rizzoli Editore, 1965). She told me about other journalists' claiming her articles as their own in an interview, New York, Mar. 1993.

2. Review of *If the Sun Dies*, by Oriana Fallaci, translated by Pamela Swinglehurst, *Christian Science Monitor*, 17 Nov. 1966, 14.

3. Review of *If the Sun Dies*, by Oriana Fallaci, translated by Pamela Swinglehurst, *Library Journal* 91 (15 Dec. 1966): 80.

4. Fallaci, *If the Sun Dies*, 6.

5. Ibid., 7-8.

6. Ibid., 57.

7. Ibid., 18.

8. Ibid., 24.

9. Ibid., 27-31.

10. Ibid., 37.

11. Ibid., 38.

12. Ibid., 75.

13. Ibid., 76.

14. Ibid., 76-77.

15. Ibid., 84.

16. Ibid., 139.

17. Ibid., 140.

18. Ibid.

19. Ibid., 169–70.

20. Ibid.

21. The famous scientist later took offense at the chapter in which Fallaci indicates that he fathered the V-2 for Adolf Hitler before constructing the moon rocket for NASA. The writer, however, evidently felt it her duty, no matter how bitter it might be, to explain that the spaceship going to the moon was the child of his earlier invention that terrorized a good portion of England during the Second World War.

22. Fallaci, *If the Sun Dies*, 228.

23. Ibid., 230.

24. Ibid., 231.

25. Ibid., 237.

26. From a speech given by Fallaci, Cologne, Germany, Oct. 1986. Fallaci provided me with a copy of the speech. My translation.

27. Ibid.

28. Fallaci, *Se il sole muore*, 72–73. My translation.

29. Fallaci, *If the Sun Dies*, 124.

30. Ibid., 71.

31. Fallaci, *Se il sole muore*, 118. My translation.

32. Fallaci, *If the Sun Dies*, 91.

33. Fallaci, *Se il sole muore*, 126. My translation.

34. Ibid., 344–45.

35. Fallaci, *If the Sun Dies*, 283–84.

36. Ibid., 289.

37. Ibid., 293.

38. Ibid., 298.

39. Oriana Fallaci, *Quel giorno sulla luna*, edited by Alberto Pozzolini (Milan: Rizzoli Editore, 1970), 26. My translation.

40. Ibid., 36.

41. Ibid., 305.

42. Fallaci, *If the Sun Dies*, 307–8.

43. The later work is Fallaci's *Letter to a Child Never Born*, translated by John Shepley (New York: Simon and Schuster, 1976), 79; *Lettera a un bambino mai nato* (Milan: Rizzoli Editore, 1975).

44. Fallaci, *If the Sun Dies*, 316.

45. Conrad remembers that it was only A&W Root Beer stands on the moon and believes that Fallaci added the others. Telephone interview with Conrad, 26 Sept. 1994.

46. Fallaci, *If the Sun Dies*, 173.

47. Ibid., 179.

48. Ibid., 180.

49. Telephone interview with Conrad, 26 Sept. 1994.

50. Ibid.

51. The point is very important because Fallaci has always prided herself on the accuracy of her news reports.

52. Telephone interview with Conrad, 26 Sept. 1994.

53. Oriana Fallaci, "Il meteorite di Papà," *Europeo*, no. 35 (29 Aug. 1965): 38.

54. Ibid.

55. Ibid.

56. Ibid., 39.

57. Ibid., 40–41.

58. Ibid., 41.

59. Ibid.

60. After *If the Sun Dies*, Fallaci once more resumed a more normal schedule. She wrote a series on the royal families of Norway, Denmark, and Greece; interviewed more luminaries of show business; reported on the assassination of John Kennedy; and obtained a private audience with the former president's brother Robert Kennedy.

61. Her extensive analysis received a supplementary boost from the agreement signed between Rizzoli and Time-Life, on the basis of which *Europeo* became the only Italian publication with exclusive rights to the story of the moon's conquest. See Oriana Fallaci, "La più grande avventura del secolo," *Europeo*, no. 28 (10 July 1969): 44–51; "I nostri inviati sulla luna," *Europeo*, no. 29 (17 July 1969): 42–58; "Il giorno dopo," *Europeo*, no. 30 (24 July 1969): 43–56.

62. Jonathan Cott, "How to Unclothe an Emperor: The *Rolling Stone* Interview with Oriana Fallaci," *Rolling Stone*, no. 215 (17 June 1976): 68.

63. Fallaci, *Quel giorno*, 196. The actual article in which Fallaci describes the moon launch is "L'uomo sulla luna," *Europeo*, no. 31 (31 July 1969): 26–36. An additional article on the moon launch is "Di che cosa è fatta la luna," *Europeo*, no. 32 (7 Aug. 1969): 43–49.

64. Fallaci, *Quel giorno*, 197.

65. Ibid., 208–9.

66. Oriana Fallaci, "Conrad," *Europeo*, no. 47 (20 Nov. 1969): 40.

67. Ibid.

68. In the opening chapter of *If the Sun Dies*, Fallaci claims that everything in the book really happened and adds that she could have included things that she felt or thought.

69. Telephone interview with Conrad, 26 Sept. 1994.

70. Oriana Fallaci, "Ecco perchè ridevano come matti," *Europeo*, no. 49 (4 Dec. 1969): 34–35.

71. Telephone interview with Conrad, 26 Sept. 1994.

72. See Fallaci, *Se il sole muore*, 418–20, for her comments on the accident. Conrad's comments, which disagree with Fallaci's account, are from a telephone interview, 17 June 1994.

73. Fallaci, "Ecco perchè ridevano," 34.

74. Telephone interview with Conrad, 26 Sept. 1994.

75. The words are recorded by Fallaci in "Ecco perchè ridevano," 36.

76. Conrad regrets not having kept her many letters to him but remembers one very clearly. Fallaci needed a green card and asked him for a recommendation. "I had to write a nice letter to the United States Immigration Department and so I did." Conrad then played a joke on her by sending her a purported copy of that letter. "To Whom It May Concern, I am pleased to recommend Oriana Fallaci as a devout Communist who wants to become a capitalist and come to the USA to make a fortune." After receiving the false document, she called from New York. "Pete, I'm lying on the fucking couch trying to figure out how to pick out each of the few hairs on your head." Telephone interview with Conrad, 17 June 1994.

6. MOVIE SCREEN IN SOUTHEAST ASIA

1. Her three active, participatory, and personalized articles—all in *Europeo*—on the Hungarian revolution against the Soviet Union prefigured in capsule form her writings from Vietnam; see "Ho vissuto in Ungheria l'ultima notte della libertà," no. 46 (11 Nov. 1956): 30–33; "L'Ungheria è straziata come Maria Takacs," no. 47 (18 Nov. 1956): 29–31; "Questo è il racconto di uno dei deportati," no. 49 (2 Dec. 1956): 26–29.

2. Oriana Fallaci, *Nothing and Amen*, translated by Isabel Quigly (Garden City: Doubleday, 1972), 2. All quotations are from Quigly's translation; but see also *Niente e così sia* (Milan: Rizzoli Editore, 1969). The first Vietnam article written for *Europeo* was "Dio, non farmi morire," no. 2 (11 Jan. 1968): 25–36.

3. Fallaci, *Nothing and Amen*, 1.

4. Ibid., 3.

5. Ibid., 11.

6. Ibid., 14.

7. Ibid., 56.

8. The two interviews are also found in Fallaci, "È un prigioniero Vietcong," *Europeo*, no. 3 (18 Jan. 1968): 25–36.

9. Fallaci, *Nothing and Amen*, 142–47.

10. Ibid., 171.

11. Ibid., 176.

12. Ibid., 168–69.

13. Ibid., 112.

14. Ibid., 232.

15. For more information on the slain journalists, see Oriana Fallaci, "Non vogliono la pace," *Europeo*, no. 21 (23 May 1968): 34–41.

16. Fallaci, *Nothing and Amen*, 253.

17. Ibid., 253–54.

18. Ibid., 254.

19. Oriana Fallaci, "Ma come fate a bruciarvi vive," *Europeo*, no. 4 (25 Jan. 1968): 18. The information about Buddhist immolations is also found in *Nothing and Amen*.

20. The anecdotes are in Fallaci, "Le storie di Saigon," *Europeo*, no. 5 (1 Feb. 1968): 33–39. Other anecdotes are in "Addio Saigon," *Europeo*, no. 6 (8 Feb. 1968): 26–31.

21. Fallaci, *Nothing and Amen*, 98. See also Oriana Fallaci, "La rivoltella del generale Loan," no. 7 (15 Feb. 1968): 8–11.

22. Oriana Fallaci, "Sono tornata a Saigon in fiamme," *Europeo*, no. 8 (22 Feb. 1968): 28.

23. Fallaci, *Nothing and Amen*, 103–7. See also Fallaci, "Sono tornata a Saigon," 28.

24. Fallaci, *Nothing and Amen*, pp. 200–201. Her interview appeared first as "Ho intervistato il dittatore del Vietnam," *Europeo*, no. 12 (21 Mar. 1968): 21–27.

25. See Fallaci, "Eccomi tra le guardie di Mao," *Europeo*, no. 13 (28 Mar. 1968): 29–35; "Le storie di Hong Kong," *Europeo*, no. 14 (4 Apr. 1968): 29–35.

26. Fallaci, "Sono stata assalita dalla folla di Atlanta," *Europeo*, no. 16 (18 Apr. 1968): 38–41.

27. Fallaci, *Nothing and Amen*, 212.

28. Ibid., 213.

29. Ibid., 241.

30. Norman Sims, "The Literary Journalists," in *The Literary Journalists*, edited by Norman Sims (New York: Ballantine, 1984), 5.

31. Kidder quoted in Sims, "Literary Journalists," 5.

32. As an independent journalist, Fallaci has never bowed to the ideological imperatives of Marxists and has made independent judgments based on evidence. The other three journalists were committed Marxists.

33. Oriana Fallaci, "Oriana Fallaci nel Vietnam del Nord," *Europeo*, no. 13 (27 Mar. 1969): 20.

34. Ibid., 25. The atmosphere of a "big brother" police state was also apparent during Fallaci's interviews of the fifteen-year-old guerrilla Ho Thi-thu, the Catholic priest Father Jean-Baptiste, and Luu Quy-ky, head editor of one of five Hanoi newspapers; see Fallaci, "Oriana Fallaci nel Vietnam del Nord," 23–28.

35. See Oriana Fallaci, "Il Generale Giap mi riceve," *Europeo*, no. 14 (3 Apr. 1969): 25–30, as well as the full text of the interview in *Interview with History*, translated by John Shepley (New York: Liveright, 1976), 74–87; originally published as *Intervista con la storia* (Milan: Rizzoli Editore, 1974).

36. Oriana Fallaci, "Prigionieri nel Vietnam," *Europeo*, no. 16 (17 Apr. 1969): 21.

37. Oriana Fallaci, "Liberato il prigioniero americano," *Europeo*, no. 34 (21 Aug. 1969): 16–19. See also Oriana Fallaci, "Il prigioniero si rifiuta di vedermi," no. 41 (9 Oct. 1969): 26–31.

38. Fallaci's second article about Frishman, "Il prigioniero si rifiuta," contains the letter of protest. Between the first article, "Liberato," and the second, Fallaci wrote a documented history about Ho Chi Minh's life: "Storia di Ho Chi Minh," *Europeo*, no. 38 (18 Sept. 1969): 31–40.

39. Fallaci, "Il prigioniero si rifiuta," 30.

40. Ibid., 31.

41. Ibid.

42. Ibid.

43. Ibid.

44. Telephone interview with Frishman, 10 June 1994.

45. Ibid.

46. Ibid.

47. Fallaci, "Il prigioniero si rifiuta," 31.

48. Telephone interview with Frishman, 10 June 1994.

49. Ibid.

50. Information about Frishman's military career was obtained from the Navy Office of Information, Naval Historical Center in Washington, D.C.

7. SUPERSTAR ON A BALCONY

1. Tommaso Giglio and Renzo Trionfera, "Il servizio di Oriana Fallaci," *Europeo*, no. 42 (17 Oct. 1968): 5.

2. Oriana Fallaci, "Oriana Fallaci racconta: La notte di sangue in cui sono stata ferita,"

Europeo, no. 42 (17 Oct. 1968): 25–46; "Ecco il servizio che avevo perduto," *Europeo*, no. 44 (31 Oct. 1968): 30–33.

    3. Fallaci, "Oriana Fallaci racconta," 25.

    4. The first four photographs are in "Oriana Fallaci racconta," 24, 27, 28, 46. The photo of her in a black dress is in "Diario dal Messico," *Europeo*, no. 43 (24 Oct. 1968): 35.

    5. Fallaci, "Ecco il servizio," 30.

    6. Fallaci, "Oriana Fallaci racconta," 28.

    7. Oriana Fallaci, "The Shooting of Oriana Fallaci," *Look* 32 (12 Nov. 1968): 20.

    8. Fallaci, "Oriana Fallaci racconta," 28.

    9. Ibid., 30.

  10. Fallaci, "Shooting," 20.

  11. Fallaci, "Oriana Fallaci racconta," 30.

  12. Ibid., 33.

  13. Ibid., 35.

  14. Fallaci, "Shooting," 20.

  15. Ibid.

  16. Borg's account is given in "Massacro voluto dal governo," *Paese Sera*, 4 Oct. 1968, 1.

  17. Fallaci, "Oriana Fallaci racconta," 38.

  18. Ibid., 43.

  19. Ibid., 45.

  20. Ibid.

  21. Fallaci, "Conrad," 40.

  22. Telephone interview with Conrad, 17 June 1994.

  23. Fallaci, "Oriana Fallaci racconta," 46.

  24. Fallaci, "Diario dal Messico," 30.

  25. Ibid.

  26. Ibid., 33.

  27. Ibid.

8. PERFORMANCES OF A LIFETIME

    1. Many of Fallaci's interviews were published in *Intervista con la storia* and in *Interview with History*.

    2. See Lucinda Franks, "Behind the Fallaci Image," *Saturday Review* 8 (Jan. 1981): 18–19; Gloria Emerson, "Divine Troublemaker," *Vogue* 170, no. 11 (Nov. 1980): 332–35, 385–88; Thomas Griffith, "Interviews, Soft or Savage," *Time* 117, no. 12 (30 Mar. 1980): 47; David Sanford, "The Lady of the Tapes," *Esquire* 83 (June 1975): 102–5; Elizabeth Peer, "The Fallaci Papers," *Newsweek* 96, no. 22 (1 Dec. 1980): 90, 92; Bonfante, "An Interview Is a Love Story," *Time* 106, no. 16 (20 Oct. 1975): 69–73.

    3. Oriana Fallaci, "Tra i guerriglieri arabi," *Europeo*, no. 9 (26 Feb. 1970): 44.

    4. Ibid.

    5. Ibid., 45.

    6. Oriana Fallaci, "L'intervista con Arafat: L'uomo che è a capo dei guerriglieri arabi," *Europeo*, no. 11 (Mar. 1970): 23.

7. Ibid., 23. Another covert encounter occurred with Abu Lotuf, the real leader and creator of Al Fatah in 1956. During the exchange, Abu Lotuf addresses the tense situation between King Hussein and Palestinian forces in Jordan. See "Oriana Fallaci interroga il vero capo di Al Fatah," *Europeo*, no. 12 (19 Mar. 1970): 23–27.

8. Scheer, "Playboy Interview," 84–85.

9. Ibid., 84.

10. Ibid., 85.

11. Ibid., 95.

12. Ibid., 108.

13. Ibid.

14. Oriana Fallaci, "Perchè mettete le bombe sugli aerei?" *Europeo*, no. 13 (26 Mar. 1970): 27–31. The interview with Habash can also be found in *Intervista con la storia*.

15. Fallaci's open letter is quoted in *Intervista con la storia*, 166–67. Before leaving Jordan, Fallaci recorded an interview with Rascida Abhedo, the woman who exploded a bomb in a Jerusalem supermarket, causing the deaths of twenty-seven people, and who detonated another explosive in the cafeteria of Hebrew University. See "La donna della strage," *Europeo*, no. 14 (2 Apr. 1970): 26–33.

16. Oriana Fallaci, "Ceylon: Una tragedia sconosciuta," *Europeo*, no. 32 (12 Aug. 1971): 36–43; and "I draghi di Ceylon," *Europeo*, no. 33 (19 Aug. 1971): 36–47.

17. Oriana Fallaci, "Il vero volto della Tigre del Bengala," *Europeo*, no. 8 (24 Feb. 1972): 26–33. See also "Questa è l'amara verità," *Europeo*, no. 2 (13 Jan. 1972): 28–41.

18. Oriana Fallaci, "Sono entrata nel carcere a intervistare Debray," *Europeo*, no. 43 (22 Oct. 1970): 41–43; quoted page 42.

19. Scheer, "Playboy Interview," 83.

20. Ibid.

21. Oriana Fallaci, "Hussein of Jordan," in *Interview with History*, translated by John Shepley (New York: Liveright, 1976), 146. See also "A colloquio con Hussein," *Europeo*, no. 15 (9 Apr. 1970): 20–24.

22. Fallaci, "Hussein," 145.

23. Oriana Fallaci, "Lech Walesa: The Man Who Drives the Kremlin Crazy," *Washington Post*, 8 Mar. 1981, C1.

24. Scheer, "Playboy Interview," 88.

25. Telephone interview with Fallaci, 30 Aug. 1993.

26. Ibid.

27. Oriana Fallaci, "La verità sul golpe," *Europeo*, nos. 9–10 (8 Mar. 1982): 75.

28. Telephone interview with Fallaci, 30 Aug. 1993.

29. Ibid.

30. Ibid.

31. Oriana Fallaci, "Ali Bhutto," in *Interview with History*, translated by John Shepley (New York: Liveright, 1976), 199–201. See also "Bhutto risponde a Indira Ghandi," *Europeo*, no. 17 (27 Apr. 1972): 52–60.

32. Fallaci, "Ali Bhutto," 187–190.

33. Ibid., 187.

34. Ibid.

35. Oriana Fallaci, "An Interview with Khomeini," *New York Times Magazine*, 7 Oct. 1979, 31.

36. Ibid.

37. Scheer, "Playboy Interview," 82.

38. Ibid.

39. Telephone interview with Shepley, 22 June 1994; and interview with Shepley, Paris, 18 July 1994.

40. Oriana Fallaci, "Rivoluzione internazionale contro l'America," *Corriere della Sera*, 2 Dec. 1979, 2.

41. Ibid., 2.

42. Quotations from the second part of the interview are from the English, edited version, Oriana Fallaci, "Iranians Are Our Brothers," *New York Times Magazine*, 16 Dec. 1979, 120.

43. Ibid.

44. Ibid.

45. Ibid.

46. Oriana Fallaci, "William Colby," in *Intervista con la storia* (Milan: Rizzoli Editore, 1974), 441. (The Colby interview is not in Shepley's translation.) It was originally published as "Oriana Fallaci interroga il capo della CIA," *Europeo*, no. 11 (12 Mar. 1976): 30–36.

47. Fallaci, "William Colby," 443.

48. Ibid., 444.

49. Ibid., 445.

50. Ibid., 448.

51. Ibid., 452.

52. Ibid., 454.

53. Ibid., 461.

54. Ibid.

55. Alvaro Cunhal openly admitted that his Portuguese Communist Party viewed national elections as a game and consequently set back the efforts of European communism to prove its faith in the democratic process and to assume a shield of respectability. See Fallaci, "Alvaro Cunhal," in *Intervista con la storia* (Milan: Rizzoli Editore, 1974), 526–43.

56. Fallaci, "William Colby," 443.

57. Ibid.

58. Ibid. Fallaci hypothesized about the CIA's involvement in Panagoulis's death in "Perchè Panagulis è stato ucciso," *Europeo*, no. 20 (14 May 1976): 23–28; and in "Assassinato dal 'ragno'." *Europeo*, no. 30 (23 July 1976): 30.

59. Oriana Fallaci, "Oriana Fallaci intervista il General Sharon," *Europeo*, no. 36 (6 Sept. 1982): 11–12.

60. Ibid., 7.

61. "Introduction to the Playboy Interview: Oriana Fallaci," *Playboy* 28, no. 11 (Nov. 1981): 81.

62. Buckley quoted in "Introduction to the Playboy Interview," 81.

63. Peer, "Fallaci Papers," 90.

64. Oriana Fallaci, "Remembering Golda," *TV Guide* 30, no. 17 (24–30 Apr. 1982): 4. The original interview is in "Golda Meir," *Europeo*, no. 48 (30 Nov. 1972): 42–53; and is in

English as "Golda Meir," in *Interview with History*, translated by John Shepley (New York: Liveright, 1976), 88–122.

65. Fallaci, "Golda Meir," *Interview with History*, 112.

66. Ibid., 119.

67. Ibid., 117–18.

68. Fallaci, "Remembering Golda," 5–6.

69. Fallaci, "Golda Meir," *Interview with History*, 92, 122.

70. Ibid., 93.

71. Scheer, "Playboy Interview," 84.

72. Oriana Fallaci, "Deng: Cleaning up Mao's 'Feudal Mistakes'," *Washington Post*, 31 Aug. 1980, D1, D4–D5. Part 2 of the interview is entitled "Deng: A Third World War Is Inevitable," *Washington Post*, 1 Sept. 1980, A 1, A10–A11.

73. Fallaci, "Deng: Cleaning Up," D4.

74. "Ailé Selassie," in *Intervista con la storia* (Milan: Rizzoli Editore, 1974), 373 (my translation). The interview is not in Shepley's translation.

75. Ibid., 385–86.

76. Ibid., 389.

77. Ibid., 372.

78. "Henry Kissinger," in *Interview with History*, translated by John Shepley (New York: Liveright, 1976), 20. See also the original interview: "Kissinger rivela perchè non abbiamo ancora firmato l'accordo sul Vietnam," *Europeo*, no. 46 (16 Nov. 1972): 36–43.

79. Fallaci, "Henry Kissinger," 20–21.

80. Ibid., 24.

81. Ibid., 32.

82. Ibid., 33.

83. Ibid., 32–36.

84. Ibid., 37.

85. Ibid., 40.

86. Ibid., 41.

87. Ibid., 29.

88. Ibid.

89. Oriana Fallaci, "Lettera a Kissinger dopo il suo fallimento," *Europeo*, no. 14 (3 Apr. 1975): 32.

90. Ibid., 32–33.

91. Henry Kissinger, *White House Years* (Boston: Little, Brown and Company, 1979), 1409–10.

92. Ibid.

93. Scheer, "Playboy Interview," 105.

94. The letter is discussed in Scheer's interview of Fallaci, 105.

95. Ibid.

96. Ibid.

97. Ibid., 83.

98. Oriana Fallaci, "Mohammed Riza Pahlavi," in *Interview with History*, translated by John Shepley (New York: Liveright, 1976), 266. See also "Lo Scià di Persia," *Europeo*, no. 44 (1 Nov. 1973): 82–91.

99. Fallaci, "Iranians," 49.

100. Scheer, "Playboy Interview," 84.

101. Fallaci, "Interview with Khomeini," 29.

102. Scheer, "Playboy Interview," 100.

103. *Interview with History* contains the following interviews: Henry Kissinger, Nguyen Van Thieu, General Vo Nguyen Giap, Golda Meir, Yassir Arafat, King Hussein, Indira Gandhi, Zulfikar Bhutto, Willy Brandt, Pietro Nenni, Mohammed Riza Pahlavi, Dom Helder Camara, Archbishop Makarios III, Alekos Panagoulis. *Intervista con la storia* includes those interviews and interviews with Norodom Sihanouk, George Habash, Sirimavo Bandaranaike, Giulio Andreotti, Giorgio Amendola, Ailé Selassie, Ahmed Zaki Yamani, William Colby, Otis Pike, Mario Soares, Alvaro Cunhal, and Santiago Carrillo.

104. Fallaci, *Interview with History*, 9–10.

105. Ibid., 12.

106. Ibid., 11.

9. TO BE OR NOT TO BE

1. The letter from Fallaci to Shepley is dated 18 Nov. 1975 and is housed at the Boston University Library: Oriana Fallaci Collection (box 19, file 2). Oriana Fallaci granted me permission to research the special collection at Boston University. When I did my research there, her letter was on file in the library office.

2. Francesca Alliata Bronner, *Un soldato di nome Oriana*, RAI Radiotelevisione Italiana, Mar. 1993.

3. Interview with Fallaci, New York, Dec. 1991.

4. The character is the professor in *Inshallah*, translated by Oriana Fallaci from a translation by James Marcus (New York: Doubleday, 1992), 309.

5. Interview with Fallaci, New York, Dec. 1991.

6. Ibid.

7. However, Fallaci refuses to be categorized with purely popular-fiction writers. "I have no respect for these people who produce books like chickens produce eggs." Interview with Fallaci, New York, Dec. 1991.

8. Macdonald quoted in Weber, "Some," 23.

9. Interview with Fallaci, New York, Dec. 1991.

10. Lucia Chiavola Birnbaum, *Liberazione della donna: Feminism in Italy* (Middletown, Connecticut: Wesleyan University Press, 1986), 104; see 104–6 for a concise discussion of the abortion controversy in Italy in the 1970s.

11. Fallaci, *Letter to a Child*, 9.

12. Interview with Fallaci, New York, Dec. 1991.

13. Carrano, *Signore*, 90–91.

14. Fallaci, *Letter to a Child*, 12.

15. Ibid., 114.

16. Interview with Fallaci, New York, Dec. 1991.

17. Fallaci, *Letter to a Child*, 110.

18. Interview with Fallaci, New York, Dec. 1991.

19. Fallaci, *Letter to a Child*, 110.

20. Ibid., 68.

21. Ibid., 79–80.

22. Ibid., 80–81.

23. Ibid., 84.

24. Fallaci, *Quel giorno*, 22.

25. Fallaci, *Se il sole muore*, 126.

26. Fallaci, *Quel giorno*, 39. Fallaci did praise Aldrin for his walk in space.

27. Fallaci, "Conrad," 40.

28. Fallaci, "L'uomo sulla luna," 33.

29. See chapter 26 of *If the Sun Dies* for Fallaci's favorable reaction to Conrad.

30. Fallaci, *Letter to a Child*, 80.

31. See Fallaci, "Conrad," 43.

32. Fallaci, "Ecco perchè ridevano," 34.

33. Fallaci, *Letter to a Child*, 80.

34. Telephone interview with Conrad, 17 June 1994.

35. Ibid. My emphasis.

36. Oriana Fallaci, *A Man*, translated by William Weaver (New York: Simon and Schuster, 1980), 249–51. During the interview in Florence in July 1992, I asked Fallaci, "I beg your pardon if I ask you an indiscreet question, but in the book you have a fight with Alekos and you lose a child. Do you remember that?" Fallaci responded, "Yea. I am not going to answer that." She said further, "It's incredible how that episode scandalized many persons. . . . The book does not say that he killed the creature [fetus]. When a woman loses a child, she loses it for psychological reasons, for trauma's sake." She denies the obsession with Panagoulis in Harry Stein, "A Day in the Life of Oriana Fallaci," *Esquire* 91 (19 June 1979): 21.

37. Fallaci, *Letter to a Child*, 100.

38. Fallaci, *If the Sun Dies*, 20–26; also, interview with Fallaci, Florence, July 1992.

39. Fallaci, *Letter to a Child*, 114.

40. Interview with Fallaci, Florence, July 1992.

41. Fallaci, *Letter to a Child*, 20.

42. Ibid., 21.

43. Ibid., 45.

44. Ibid., 49.

45. Ibid., 50.

46. Ibid., 54.

47. Ibid., 44.

48. Ibid., 47.

49. Ibid., 52.

50. Ibid.

51. Ibid.

52. Ibid., 53.

53. Ibid.

54. Ibid.

55. Interview with Fallaci, New York, Dec. 1991.

56. Ibid.

57. Ibid.

58. Fallaci, *Letter to a Child*, 100.

59. Ibid., 103.

60. Interview with Fallaci, New York, Dec. 1991.

61. Fallaci, *Letter to a Child*, 114.

62. Interview with Fallaci, New York, Dec. 1991.

63. Aléxandros Panagulis, *Vi scrivo da un carcere in Grecia* (Milan: Rizzoli Editore, 1974). In *Interview with History*, she spells the name *Panagoulis*.

64. Interview with Fallaci, New York, Dec. 1991.

65. Ibid.

66. Ibid.

67. Ibid.

68. In Italy alone, seven hundred thousand copies were sold within two and one-half years. Within three years, the novel went into a fourteenth printing. As of 1997, sales figures approach the 1.5 million mark.

10. THE MAN OR THE WOMAN

1. Telephone interview with Shepley, 22 June 1994.

2. Ibid.

3. Carrano, *Signore*, 95.

4. Stein, "Day in the Life," 21.

5. Ibid.

6. Ibid.

7. Carrano, *Signore*, 96.

8. See Oriana Fallaci, "Alessandro Panagoulis," in *Intervista con la storia* (Milan: Rizzoli Editore, 1974), 612–53.

9. Ibid., 623. That there were two cars was established by an investigation after the accident.

10. Herbert Mitgang, "As Novelist, Miss Fallaci Still Deals in Real People," *New York Times*, 3 November 1980, C18.

11. Georgios Bertsos quoted in "Monument to a Martyr," *Time* 114, no. 12 (17 Sept. 1979): 31 (International Edition).

12. Interview with Fallaci, New York, Dec. 1991.

13. Ibid.

14. Interview with Fallaci, New York, Dec. 1991. See Fallaci, *Man*, 11–17.

15. Fallaci, *Man*, 323. All quotations are from Weaver's translation; but see also *Un uomo: Romanzo* (Milan: Rizzoli Editore, 1979).

16. Fallaci, *Man*, 16.

17. Ibid., 454.

18. In the book, after the death of Panagoulis, Fallaci discovers that one of the alleged assassins, Michael Steffas, a former Communist sympathizer, has expertise in open-circuit car racing; his skill in automobile collision and rear-front maneuvers would have proven invaluable in causing the fatal crash. Fallaci, *Man*, 445.

19. Fallaci, *Man*, 53–54.

20. Ibid.

21. As a student, Fallaci had discovered this technique in the *Iliad* and *Odyssey*. Commenting on its overuse, she refers to Hemingway: "One of the reasons why *Farewell to Arms*, in my opinion, is not a good book lies in its abuse of dialogue." Interview with Fallaci, New York, Dec. 1991.

22. Fallaci, *Man*, 67.

23. Ibid.

24. Ibid., 163–65.

25. Ibid., 166.

26. Ibid., 94.

27. Ibid., 95.

28. Ibid., 113.

29. Ibid., 126.

30. Ibid., 21.

31. Ibid., 33.

32. Ibid., 35.

33. Ibid., 51.

34. Ibid., 52.

35. Ibid., 62.

36. Ibid., 74.

37. Ibid., 75.

38. Ibid., 218.

39. Ibid., 249–50.

40. Ibid., 281.

41. Georgios Bertsos quoted in "Monument," 31.

42. Fallaci, *Man*, 141.

43. Ibid., 146.

44. Ibid., 148.

45. Ibid., 157–62, 185–90; also, interview with Fallaci, Florence, July 1992.

46. Ibid., 352–59.

47. Ibid., 361–63.

48. Ibid., 426, 434.

49. Fallaci, "Perchè Panagulis," 24.

50. Stein, "Day in the Life," 21.

51. Genevieve Stuttaford, "Oriana Fallaci," *Publishers Weekly* 218 (7 Nov. 1980): 7.

52. "Monument," 31.

53. Both the family's statement and Fallaci's rebuttal are summarized in "I familiari di Panagulis polemizzano con Oriana Fallaci," *Corriere della Sera*, 4 July 1979, 1. See also "Monument," 31; Kris Mancuso, "Oriana nella tempesta," *L'Ora*, 6 July 1979, 1.

54. Scheer, "Playboy Interview," 91.

55. Ibid., 92.

56. Ibid., 94.

57. Ibid., 108.

58. Fallaci revealed that the seized journalist was Miriam Mafai. Telephone interview with Fallaci, 30 Aug. 1993.

59. Ranieri Schippisi, "Un uomo (e una donna)," *Libertà*, 12 July 1979, 3.

60. Stuttaford, "Oriana Fallaci," 6.

61. "Monument," 31.

11. TOLSTOY, DOSTOYEVSKY, AND FALLACI

1. During the first year, the novel sold over 600,000 copies in Italy alone; see Oriana Fallaci, *Insciallah* (Milan: Rizzoli Editore, 1990).

2. Fallaci's tenth response in a written interview for a Spanish newspaper. On 6 Apr. 1992, Fallaci's assistant, Andrea Lorenzo Ingarao Zappata di Lasplassas, sent me, at Fallaci's request, the answers she had prepared. Her assistant could not find the questions but stated that Fallaci believed the responses alone would be helpful.

3. Ibid.

4. Such French critics as Jean-François Deniau, "L'Iliade à Beyrouth," *Le Nouvel Observateur*, no. 1445 (16 July 1992): 96–97, and Françoise Giroud, "Le regard sur la guerre d'une femme intrépide," *Le Journal du Dimanche*, no. 2736 (28 June 1992): 10, praised her novel.

5. Interview with Fallaci, Florence, July 1992.

6. Fallaci recommended that I contact the French representative of Rizzoli Editore in Paris to discuss the French translation of *Insciallah*. I did. Telephone interviews with Fallaci, 3 July 1992 and 16 July 1992.

7. Interview with Fallaci, Florence, July 1992.

8. Telephone interview with Marcus, 4 June 1994; I have also spoken with Marcus in Feb. and Mar. 1996 and have had written correspondence, as well.

9. Fallaci, *Inshallah*, 156. All quotations are from the Fallaci–Marcus translation unless otherwise indicated.

10. Ibid., 320.

11. Ibid., 294.

12. Ibid., 45.

13. Thomas Keneally, "Waiting for the Suicide Truck," *New York Times Book Review*, 27 Dec. 1992, 8.

14. A copy of Fallaci's 1976 lecture at Amherst College is housed at the Boston University Library: Oriana Fallaci Collection (box 21, file 2).

15. Ahdaf Soueif, "Lovers and Terrorists," *Washington Post Book Review*, 13 Dec. 1992, 5.

16. Interview with Fallaci, Florence, July 1992.

17. Ibid.

18. Fallaci, *Inshallah*, 149.

19. Ibid., 306.

20. Interview with Fallaci, New York, Dec. 1991.

21. Interview with Fallaci, Florence, July 1992.

22. Interview with Fallaci, New York, Dec. 1991.

23. Fallaci, *Inshallah*, 310.

24. National Public Radio, "Oriana Fallaci Interview," *All Things Considered*, 15 Nov. 1992.

25. Oriana Fallaci, "The Europeans' Qaddafi Cowardice," *Washington Post*, 27 Apr. 1986, C4.

26. Cecchi, "Una notte," 61–62.

27. Locals refer to the cemetery either as the Protestant or as the English cemetery; its formal name is Gli Allori (The Laurels).

28. Cecchi, "Una notte," 62. The complete text of Fallaci's "Addio a Edoardo Fallaci" is in *Europeo*, no. 33 (18 Aug. 1990): 63–64.

29. Nan A. Talese, "Oriana Fallaci: The D Interview," *D Magazine* 1, no. 2 (June–Sept. 1992): 9.

30. Telephone interview with Fallaci, 30 Aug. 1993.

31. Ibid.

32. Patricia Smith, "Oriana Fallaci," *Boston Globe*, 5 Jan. 1993, 64.

33. Cecchi, "Una notte," 60.

34. Ibid., 60–61.

35. Ibid., 61. Oddly, however, Fallaci told me that she did not remember him, that he had never studied medicine, and that she had never met him before the interview she gave him about *Insciallah*. Handwritten note by Fallaci, 2 Dec. 1993.

36. Ibid.

37. Interview with Fallaci, New York, Dec. 1991.

38. Ibid.

39. Fallaci, *Inshallah*, 306.

40. Smith, "Oriana Fallaci," 61.

41. Ibid.

42. Cecchi, "Una notte," 60.

43. Smith, "Oriana Fallaci," 61.

44. Fallaci, *Inshallah*, 104–5.

45. Ibid., 38.

46. Interview with Fallaci, New York, Dec. 1991.

47. Fallaci, *Inshallah*, 330.

48. Ibid., 338–46, 325–28, 381–82, 359.

49. Ibid., 172.

50. Ibid., 178–79.

51. Ibid., 179–83.

52. Interview with Fallaci, Florence, July 1992.

53. Ibid.

54. Interview with Fallaci, New York, Dec. 1991.

55. Fallaci, *Inshallah*, 33.

56. Ibid.

57. Ibid., 483.

58. Ibid., 599.

59. Ibid., 598.

60. Ibid.

61. Interview with Fallaci, New York, Dec. 1991.

62. Ibid.

63. Fallaci, *Inshallah*, 575.

64. Ibid., 578.

65. Ibid., 579.

66. Ibid., 306.

67. Ibid., 415.

68. Interview with Fallaci, New York, Dec. 1991.

69. Fallaci, *Inshallah*, 148–49.

70. Ibid., 306.

71. Ibid., 307.

72. Ibid., 308.

73. Ibid., 149.

74. Ibid., 265–71, 590; also, interview with Fallaci, New York, Mar. 1993.

75. Interview with Fallaci, New York, Mar. 1993.

76. Fallaci, *Inshallah*, 421–22.

77. Ibid., 422.

78. Ibid.

79. Ibid., 28.

80. Interview with Fallaci, New York, Mar. 1993.

81. Claudio Altarocca, in "Fallaci sola a New York col diavolo in corpo," *La Stampa*, 9 Aug. 1991, 15, gives Bella's last name as Vanderlip. Fallaci told me that Bella was a doctor; Altarocca states that she was doctor to the king of Saudi Arabia. Fallaci developed affection for her neighbor and wanted her name included in the biography. She told me that Bella developed cancer and returned to her native England where she died and was buried. Interview with Fallaci, New York, Mar. 1993.

82. Interview with Fallaci, New York, Mar. 1993.

83. Ibid.

84. Ibid.

85. Paul William Roberts, "Fallaci's Masterpiece: A Modern Day Iliad," *Toronto Star*, 12 Dec. 1992, D14.

86. Fallaci provided me with a copy of Roberts's letter. Roberts's laudatory review naturally pleases Fallaci, who calls Roberts "an intelligent and refined man." She met Roberts in Manhattan to have tea with him. Interview with Fallaci, New York, Mar. 1993.

87. Roberts, "Fallaci's Masterpiece," D14.

88. Soueif, "Lovers," 5.

89. James Walton, "Firepower," *Tablet*, 6 Mar. 1993, 5.

90. Fallaci, *Inshallah*, 150.

91. Ibid.

CONCLUSION: FACING THE ALIEN

1. Interview with Fallaci, New York, Mar. 1993.

2. Ibid.

3. Alberto Sinigaglia, "Oriana Fallaci a Pechino: il sogno della libertà," *La Stampa*, 26 Oct. 1993, 15.

4. Interview with Fallaci, New York, Mar. 1993.

5. Paul Hendrickson, "Oriana Fallaci, Forever at War," *Washington Post*, 24 Nov. 1992, E2.

6. Ibid., E1.

7. Ibid.

8. Ibid.

9. Oriana Fallaci, "Nuvola nera," 8. During my interview with Fallaci, Florence, July 1992, she again spoke with intense emotion about the experience.

10. Interview with Fallaci, New York, Mar. 1993.

11. Foster, "Love," 24.

12. Ibid.

13. Interview with Fallaci, New York, Mar. 1993.

14. Stefania Miretti, "Fumo contro l'alieno che è in me," *La Stampa*, 13 Mar. 1993, 15.

15. Fallaci spoke about her cancer during her RAI interview; see Bronner, "Soldato."

16. Interview with Fallaci, New York, Mar. 1993.

17. Foster, "Love," 43.

18. Interview with Fallaci, New York, Mar. 1993.

Bibliography

PUBLICATIONS BY ORIANA FALLACI

"Addio a Edoardo Fallaci." "Goodbye to Edoardo Fallaci." *Europeo*, no. 33 (18 Aug. 1990): 63–64.

"Addio Saigon." "Goodbye Saigon." *Europeo*, no. 6 (8 Feb. 1968): 26–31.

"L'AFTRA mi protegge." "AFTRA Is Protecting Me." *Europeo*, no. 11 (16 Mar. 1967): 79.

"Ailé Selassie." In *Intervista con la storia*, 368–89. Milan: Rizzoli Editore, 1974.

"Alessandro Panagulis." In *Intervista con la storia*, 612–53. Milan: Rizzoli Editore, 1974.

"Ali Bhutto." In *Interview with History*, translated by John Shepley, 182–209. New York: Liveright, 1976.

"Alvaro Cunhal." In *Intervista con la storia*, 526–43. Milan: Rizzoli Editore, 1974.

"L'America vista da un'italiana." "America Seen by an Italian Lady." *Europeo*, no. 30 (25 July 1965): 32–39.

"Anche a Fiesole Dio ha avuto bisogno degli uomini." "Even in Fiesole God Had Need of Men." *Europeo*, no. 19 (6 May 1951): 8.

Gli antipatici. Milan: Rizzoli Editore, 1963.

"Assassinato dal 'ragno'." "Assassinated by the 'spider'." *Europeo*, no. 30 (23 July 1976): 30.

"Betty Cowell è in Italia con un amico e un'amica." "Betty Cowell Is in Italy with a Boyfriend and a Girlfriend." *Europeo*, no. 14 (4 Apr. 1954): 20.

"Bhutto risponde a Indira Gandhi." "Bhutto Responds to Indira Gandhi." *Europeo*, no. 17 (27 Apr. 1972): 52–60.

"I bimbi poveri di Teheran non accettano carezze dagli stranieri." "Teheran's Poor Children Do Not Accept Caresses from Strangers." *Giornale del Mattino*, 7 Dec. 1954, 3.

"Ceylon: Una tragedia sconosciuta." "Ceylon: An Unknown Tragedy." *Europeo*, no. 32 (12 Aug. 1971): 36–47.

"Che cosa volete dai bianchi." "What Do You Want from White People." *Europeo*, no. 32 (10 Aug. 1967): 37–43.

"La CIA starnutisce nel mio telefono." "The CIA Sneezes in My Telephone." *Europeo*, no. 12 (23 Mar. 1967): 81.

"Città del Messico sconvolta da sei ore di violenta battaglia." "Mexico City Thrown into Disorder by Six Hours of Violent Battle." *Corriere Mercantile*, 4 Oct. 1968, 1.

"A colloquio con Hussein." "Hussein of Jordan." *Europeo*, no. 15 (9 Apr. 1970): 20–24.

"Come si fuma una banana." "How One Smokes a Banana." *Europeo*, no. 15 (13 Apr. 1967): 39.

"Le confessioni di Sergio Vanzini condannato a 57 anni di carcere." "Confessions of Sergio Vanzini Condemned to 57 Years of Prison." *Gazzetta Sera*, 29 Dec. 1950, 3.

"Conrad." *Europeo*, no. 47 (20 Nov. 1969): 38–48.

"Credevo di andare a salvare il Kuwait." "I Thought I Was Going to Save Kuwait." *Corriere della Sera*, 9 Mar. 1991, 6.

"La cupola senz'ali." "The Dome Without Wings." *Il Mattino dell'Italia Centrale*, 11 Aug. 1951, 4.

"Davvero non vorrei essere la moglie di Gregory Peck." "I Would Really Not Like to Be Gregory Peck's Wife." *Europeo*, no. 36 (8 Sept. 1957): 15–21.

"Deng: A Third World War Is Inevitable." *Washington Post*, 1 Sept. 1980, A1, A10–A11.

"Deng: Cleaning Up Mao's 'Feudal Mistakes'." *Washington Post*, 31 Aug. 1980, D1, D4–D5.

"Nel deserto già si respira odore di sangue." "The Smell of Blood Is Already Everywhere in the Desert." *Corriere della Sera*, 22 Feb. 1991, 5.

"Diario dal Messico." "Diary from Mexico." *Europeo*, no. 43 (24 Oct. 1968): 29–35.

"Di che cosa è fatta la luna." "What the Moon Is Made of." *Europeo*, no. 32 (7 Aug. 1969): 43–49.

"Dio, non farmi morire." "God, Don't Let Me Die." *Europeo*, no. 2 (11 Jan. 1968): 25–36.

"La donna della strage." "The Woman of the Massacre." *Europeo*, no. 14 (2 Apr. 1970): 26–33.

"Le donne dell'U.N.E.S.C.O. vanno spesso dal parrucchiere." "The UNESCO Women Go Often to the Hairdresser." *Corriere Lombardo*, 15–16 June 1950, 6.

"Dovetti confessargli l'orribile verità." "I Had to Confess the Terrible Truth to Him." *Europeo*, no. 35 (1 Sept. 1957): 28–35.

"I draghi di Ceylon." "The Dragons of Ceylon." *Europeo*, no. 33 (19 Aug. 1971): 36–47.

"Ebbe fra le mani i piedi del re." "He Had the King's Feet in His Hands." *Corriere Lombardo*, 15–16 Feb. 1950, 3.

"Ecco il servizio che avevo perduto." "Here Is the Article That I Had Lost." *Europeo*, no. 44 (31 Oct. 1968): 30–33.

"Eccomi tra le guardie di Mao." "Here I Am Amidst Mao's Guards." *Europeo*, no. 13 (28 Mar. 1968): 29–35.

"Ecco perchè ridevano come matti." "This Is Why They Laughed Like Crazy." *Europeo*, no. 49 (4 Dec. 1969): 34–40.

"È finito per gli orfanelli il terrore di Mamma Rosa." "The Orphans' Terror of Mamma Rosa Is Over." *Europeo*, no. 5 (31 Jan. 1954): 14.

The Egotists: Sixteen Surprising Interviews. Translated by Mihaly Csikszentmihalyi, Oriana Fallaci, and Pamela Swinglehurst. Chicago: Henry Regnery, 1968.

"Eleonora è triste per l'arresto dell'ingrato." "Eleonora Is Sad after the Arrest of the Ungrateful Beneficiary." *Europeo*, no. 49 (5 Dec. 1954): 8–9.

"È un prigioniero Vietcong." "He Is a Vietcong Prisoner." *Europeo*, no. 3 (18 Jan. 1968): 25–36.

"The Europeans' Qaddafi Cowardice." *Washington Post*, 27 Apr. 1986, C1–C4.

"Everybody Wants to Be Boss." *New York Times Magazine*, 28 Oct. 1979, 21–22, 26, 30, 37, 63–67.

"Il figlio nella Legione Straniera." "His Son in the Foreign Legion." *Europeo*, no. 47 (15 Nov. 1953): 18–19.

"I franchi tiratori sparano." "Snipers Are Shooting." *Europeo*, no. 31 (3 Aug. 1967): 20–23.

"Galtieri, discolpati." "Galtieri, Exonerate Yourself." *Europeo*, no. 26 (28 June 1982): 6–17.

"Il Generale Giap mi riceve." "General Giap Receives Me." *Europeo*, no. 14 (3 Apr. 1969): 25–30.

"La generazione dei ribelli in blu jeans." "The Generation of Rebels in Blue Jeans." *Europeo*, no. 41 (13 Oct. 1957): 44–50.

"Il giorno dopo." "The Day After." *Europeo*, no. 30 (24 July 1969): 43–56.

"Giovanni Leone." *Europeo*, no. 17 (26 Apr. 1973): 42–51.

"Golda Meir." *Europeo*, no. 48 (30 Nov. 1972): 42–53.

"Golda Meir." In *Interview with History*, translated by John Shepley, 88–122. New York: Liveright, 1976.

"Hanno ritrovato la vita gli 'sciuscià' snidati da Tombolo." "The Shoeshine Boys Dislodged from Tombolo Have Found Life Again." *Il Mattino dell'Italia Centrale*, 12 Aug. 1950, 6.

"Henry Kissinger." In *Interview with History*, translated by John Shepley, 17–44. New York: Liveright, 1976.

"Ho intervistato il dittatore del Vietnam." "I Interviewed the Dictator of Vietnam." *Europeo*, no. 12 (21 Mar. 1968): 21–27.

"Hollywood dal buco della serratura." "Hollywood Seen Through a Key Hole." *Europeo*, no. 33 (18 Aug. 1957): 14–20.

"Ho odiato Marilyn come una moglie gelosa." "I Hated Marilyn Like a Jealous Wife." *Europeo*, no. 5 (29 Jan. 1956): 15–16.

"Ho vissuto in Ungheria l'ultima notte della libertà." "I Lived in Hungary on the Last Night of Freedom." *Europeo*, no. 46 (11 Nov. 1956): 30–33.

"Hussein of Jordan." In *Interview with History*, translated by John Shepley, 140–51. New York: Liveright, 1976.

If the Sun Dies. Translated by Pamela Swinglehurst. New York: Atheneum, 1966.

"Inchiesta fra i teenager." "Survey of Teen-Agers." *Europeo*, no. 8 (17 Feb. 1966): 29–34.

Insciallah. Milan: Rizzoli Editore, 1990.

Inshallah. Translated by Oriana Fallaci from a translation by James Marcus. New York: Doubleday, 1992.

"L'interrogazione." "The Oral Test." *Europeo*, no. 7/11 (15 Mar. 1973): 54–59. *Interview with History*. Translated by John Shepley. New York: Liveright, 1976.

"An Interview with Khomeini." *New York Times Magazine*, 7 Oct. 1979, 29–31.

"L'intervista con Arafat: L'uomo che è a capo dei guerriglieri arabi." "Interview with Arafat: The Man Who Is Head of Arab Guerrillas." *Europeo*, no. 11 (12 Mar. 1970): 23–29.

Intervista con la storia. Milan: Rizzoli Editore, 1974.

"Iranians Are Our Brothers." *New York Times Magazine*, 16 Dec. 1979, 40, 116–24.

"Kissinger rivela perchè non abbiamo ancora firmato l'accordo sul Vietnam." "Kissinger Reveals Why We Have Not Yet Signed the Agreement on Vietnam." *Europeo*, no. 46 (16 Nov. 1972): 36–43.

"A Kuwait City nei giorni del rancore." "In Kuwait City During the Days of Rancor." *Corriere della Sera*, 6 Mar. 1991, 5.

"Lech Walesa: The Man Who Drives the Kremlin Crazy." *Washington Post*, 8 Mar. 1981, C1, C4–C5.

"Lettera a Kissinger dopo il suo fallimento." "Letter to Kissinger after His Failure." *Europeo*, no. 14 (3 Apr. 1975): 32–33.

Lettera a un bambino mai nato. Milan: Rizzoli Editore, 1975.

"Lettera sulla cultura." "Letter on Culture." *Europeo*, no. 19 (10 May 1973): 34–39.

Letter to a Child Never Born. Translated by John Shepley. New York: Simon and Schuster, 1976.

"Liberato il prigioniero americano." "American Prisoner Freed." *Europeo*, no. 34 (21 Aug. 1969): 16–19.

The Limelighters. Translated by Pamela Swinglehurst. London: Michael Joseph, Ltd., 1968.

"Ma come fate a bruciarvi vive." "But How Can You Burn Yourselves Alive." *Europeo*, no. 4 (25 Jan. 1968): 17–26.

"Malinconica storia del 'Conventino' asilo di artisti e di povera gente." "Melancholic Story of the Conventino Shelter for Artists and Poor People." *Il Mattino dell'Italia Centrale*, 2 Oct. 1949, 3.

A Man. Translated by William Weaver. New York: Simon and Schuster, 1980.

"Il meteorite di papà." "Father's Meteorite." *Europeo*, no. 35 (29 Aug. 1965): 36–41.

"Mi hanno chiesto un uovo." "They Asked Me for My Egg." *Europeo*, no. 14 (6 Apr. 1967): 23.

"I minorenni terribili." "The Terrible Minors." *Europeo*, no. 7 (10 Feb. 1966): 49–57.

"Mohammed Riza Pahlavi." In *Interview with History*, translated by John Shepley, 262–87. New York: Liveright, 1976.

"Neppure un soldato a guardia del preziosissimo trono dello Scià." "Not Even One Soldier Guards the Most Precious Throne of the Shah." *Giornale del Mattino*, 15 Dec. 1954, 3.

Niente e così sia. Milan: Rizzoli Editore: 1969.

"Non vogliono la pace." "They Do Not Want Peace." *Europeo*, no. 21 (23 May 1968): 34–41.

"I nostri inviati sulla luna." "Our Correspondents on the Moon." *Europeo*, no. 29 (17 July 1969): 42–58.

"Nota introduttiva." "Introduction." In *Il richiamo della foresta. The Call of the Wild*, by Jack London, i–xxvi. Milan: Rizzoli Editore, 1953.

Nothing and Amen. Translated by Isabel Quigly. New York: Doubleday, 1972.

"La nuvola nera, Chernobyl del Golfo." "The Black Cloud, Chernobyl of the Gulf." *Corriere della Sera*, 26 Mar. 1991, 8–9.

"Oltrarno in Alabama." "Beyond the Arno in Alabama." *Europeo*, no. 51 (19 Dec. 1965): 62–67.

"Un'ora fitta fitta col marito di Marilyn." "An Intense Hour with Marilyn's Husband." *Europeo*, no. 48 (1 Dec. 1957): 26–29.

"Oriana Fallaci interroga il capo della CIA." "Oriana Fallaci Questions the Head of the CIA." *Europeo*, no. 11 (12 Mar. 1976): 30–36.

"Oriana Fallaci interroga il vero capo di Al Fatah." "Oriana Fallaci Questions the Real Head of the Al Fatah." *Europeo*, no. 12 (19 Mar. 1970): 23–27.

"Oriana Fallaci intervista il General Sharon." "Oriana Fallaci Interviews General Sharon." *Europeo*, no. 36 (6 Sept. 1982): 6–21.

"Oriana Fallaci nel Vietnam del Nord." "Oriana Fallaci in North Vietnam." *Europeo*, no. 13 (27 Mar. 1969): 18–30.

"Oriana Fallaci racconta: La notte di sangue in cui sono stata ferita." "Oriana Fallaci Relates: The Night of Bloodshed in Which I Was Wounded." *Europeo*, no. 42 (17 Oct. 1968): 25–46.

"A [otto] 8.000 metri sulle ali della guerra." "8.000 Meters High on the Wings of War." *Corriere della Sera*, 17 Feb. 1991, 3.

"Partiamo alla conquesta del West." "We Are Leaving to Conquer the West." *Europeo*, no. 45 (7 Nov. 1965): 49–54.

"Paura a Mosca." "Fear in Moscow." *Europeo*, no. 49 (5 Dec. 1965): 74–79.

"La paura è il prezzo della loro fortuna." "Fear Is the Price of Their Fortune." *Europeo*, no. 34 (25 Aug. 1957): 14–20.

Penelope alla guerra. Milan: Rizzoli Editore, 1962.

Penelope at War. Translated by Pamela Swinglehurst. London: Michael Joseph, Ltd., 1966.

"Perchè mettete le bombe sugli aerei?" "Why Do You Put Bombs on Airplanes?" *Europeo*, no. 13 (26 Mar. 1970): 27–31.

"Perchè Panagulis è stato ucciso." "Why Panagoulis Was Killed." *Europeo*, no. 20 (14 May 1976): 23–28.

"Il petrolio è l'arbitro della Persia." "Petroleum Is Iran's Arbitrator." *Sicilia del Popolo*, 22 Dec. 1954, 3.

"La più grande avventura del secolo." "The Greatest Adventure of the Century." *Europeo*, no. 28 (10 July 1969): 44–51.

"Prigionieri nel Vietnam." "Prisoners in Vietnam." *Europeo*, no. 16 (17 Apr. 1969): 18–25.

"Il prigioniero si rifiuta di vedermi." "The Prisoner Refuses to See Me." *Europeo*, no. 41 (9 Oct. 1969): 26–31.

"Qualcuna più tardi finisce al manicomio." "Someone Later Winds Up in a Mental Institution." *Europeo*, no. 42 (20 Oct. 1957): 15–19.

Quel giorno sulla luna. That Day on the Moon. Edited by Alberto Pozzolini. Milan: Rizzoli Editore, 1970.

"Questa è l'amara verità." "This Is the Bitter Truth." *Europeo*, no. 2 (13 Jan. 1972): 28–41.

"Queste cinque malattie minacciano ancora i nostri bambini." "These Five Illnesses Still Menace Our Children." *Europeo*, no. 25 (17 June 1951): 7.

"Questo è il racconto di uno dei deportati." "This Is the Story of One of the Deportees." *Europeo*, no. 49 (2 Dec. 1956): 26–29.

"Radiografia di un uomo." "X Ray of a Man." *Europeo*, no. 31 (5 Aug. 1971): 36–43.

"Remembering Golda." *TV Guide* 30, no. 17 (24–30 Apr. 1982): 4–6.

"La richissima e potentissima Soraya si annoia mortalmente nella sua torre d'avorio." "The Very Rich and Powerful Soraya Is Mortally Bored in Her Ivory Tower." *Giornale del Mattino*, 10 Dec. 1954, 3.

"Ritratto della donna inglese." "Portrait of Englishwomen." *Il Mattino dell'Italia Centrale*, 24 Oct. 1953, 3.

"La rivoltella del Generale Loan." "General Loan's Revolver." *Europeo*, no. 7 (15 Feb. 1968): 8–11.

"Rivoluzione internazionale contro l'America." "International Revolution Against America." *Corriere della Sera*, 2 Dec. 1979, 1–2.

"Lo scià di Persia." "The Shah of Iran." *Europeo*, no. 44 (1 Nov. 1973): 82–91.

Se il sole muore. Milan: Rizzoli Editore, 1965.

"Il sentiero dei Navajo." "Path of the Navajo." *Europeo*, no. 47 (21 Nov. 1965): 74–78.

"Serata d'addio con le gemelle Pierangeli." "A Good-bye Evening with the Pierangeli Twins." *Europeo*, no. 44 (3 Nov. 1957): 44–50.

Il sesso inutile. Milan: Rizzoli Editore, 1961.

I sette peccati di Hollywood. The Seven Sins of Hollywood. Milan: Longanesi Editore, 1958.

"The Shooting of Oriana Fallaci." *Look* 32 (12 Nov. 1968): 20.

"Si allenano molte ore al giorno per imparare l'inchino alla regina." "They Train Many Hours a Day to Learn How to Curtsy Before the Queen." *Il Mattino dell'Italia Centrale*, 12 Nov. 1953, 3.

"Si risposano, non si uccidono." "They Marry Again, They Do Not Kill Themselves." *Europeo*, no. 22 (29 May 1960): 48–55.

"Sono entrata nel carcere a intervistare Debray." "I Entered Jail to Interview Debray." *Europeo*, no. 43 (22 Oct. 1970): 41–43, 48–51.

"Sono pronto a uccidere." "I Am Ready to Kill." *Europeo*, no. 33 (17 Aug. 1967): 26–29.

"Sono stata assalita dalla folla di Atlanta." "I Was Attacked by a Crowd in Atlanta." *Europeo*, no. 16 (18 Apr. 1968): 38–41.

"Sono tornata a Saigon in fiamme." "I Returned to Saigon in Flames." *Europeo*, no. 8 (22 Feb. 1968): 25–31.

"Storia di Ho Ci Minh." "Ho Chi Minh's Life." *Europeo*, no. 38 (18 Sept. 1969): 31–40.

"Storia di una valigia persa e ritrovata a Teheran." "Story of a Lost and Found Suitcase in Teheran." *Corriere del Giorno*, 2 Dec. 1954, 3.

"Le storie di Hong Kong." "Hong Kong Stories." *Europeo*, no. 14 (4 Apr. 1968): 29–35.

"Le storie di Saigon." "Saigon Stories." *Europeo*, no. 5 (1 Feb. 1968): 33–39.

"Una tazza di tè con l'Imperatrice." "A Cup of Tea with the Empress." *Il Popolo Nuovo*, 1 Dec. 1954, 3.

"Tra i guerriglieri arabi." "Among Arab Guerrillas." *Europeo*, no. 9 (26 Feb. 1970): 34–45.

"I tre grandi dalle tempie grige." "The Three Great Ones with Gray Temples." *Europeo*, no. 40 (6 Oct. 1957): 44–51.

"L'ultimo cow-boy." "The Last Cowboy." *Europeo*, no. 48 (28 Nov. 1965): 76–84.

"L'Ungheria è straziata come Maria Takacs." "Hungary Is Torn Apart Like Maria Takacs." *Europeo*, no. 47 (18 Nov. 1956): 29–31.

Un uomo: Romanzo. Milan: Rizzoli Editore, 1979.

"L'uomo sulla luna." "Man on the Moon." *Europeo*, no. 31 (31 July 1969): 26–36, 41, 60–62.

The Useless Sex. Translated by Pamela Swinglehurst. New York: Horizon Press, 1964.

"La verità sul golpe." "The Truth about the Military Coup." *Europeo*, nos. 9–10 (8 Mar. 1982): 67–82.

"Il vero volto della Tigre del Bengala." "The Real Face of the Tiger of Bengal." *Europeo*, no. 8 (24 Feb. 1972): 26–33.

"William Colby." In *Intervista con la storia*, 441–66. Milan: Rizzoli Editore, 1974.

WORKS BY OTHER AUTHORS

Altarocca, Claudio. "Fallaci sola a New York col diavolo in corpo." "Fallaci Alone in New York with the Devil in Her Body." *La Stampa*, 9 Aug. 1991, 15.

Aricò, Santo L. "Breaking the Ice: An In-Depth Look at Oriana Fallaci's Interview Techniques." *Journalism Quarterly* 63, no. 3 (1986): 587–93.

———. "Oriana Fallaci's Discovery of Truth in *Niente e così sia*." *European Studies Journal* 3, no. 2 (1986): 11–23.

————. "Oriana Fallaci's Journalistic Novel: *Niente e così sia.*" In *Contemporary Women Writers in Italy: A Modern Renaissance,* edited by Santo L. Aricò, 170–82. Amherst: University of Massachusetts Press, 1990.

————, ed. *Contemporary Women Writers in Italy: A Modern Renaissance.* Amherst: University of Massachusetts Press, 1990.

Birnbaum, Lucia Chiavola. *Liberazione della donna: Feminism in Italy.* Middletown, CT: Wesleyan University Press, 1986.

Bonfante, J. "An Interview Is a Love Story." *Time* 106, no. 16 (20 Oct. 1975): 69–73.

Bronner, Francesca Alliata. *Un Soldato di nome Oriana.* RAI Radiotelevisione Italiana Interview. Mar. 1993.

Bruner, Jerome S. "Myth and Identity." *Myth and Mythmaking,* edited by Henry A. Murray, 276–87. New York: George Braziller, 1960.

Carrano, Patrizia. *Le signore grandi firme. The Ladies with Great Names.* Florence: Guaraldi Editore, 1978.

Cecchi, Umberto. "Una notte, cercando Insciallah." "One Night, Searching for *Inshallah.*" *Europeo,* no. 33 (18 Aug. 1990): 59–62.

Chalon, Jean. "Oriana Fallaci: Une amazone à Beyrouth." "Oriana Fallaci: An Amazon in Beirut." *Le Figaro,* 2 June 1992, 1.

Colombo, Furio. "Chi ha paura di Oriana?" "Who Is Afraid of Oriana?" *Europeo,* no. 33 (18 Aug. 1990), 54–58.

Cott, Jonathan. "How to Unclothe an Emperor: The *Rolling Stone* Interview with Oriana Fallaci." *Rolling Stone,* no. 215 (17 June 1975): 44–47, 66, 68.

Deniau, Jean-François. "L'Iliade à Beyrouth." "The Iliad in Beirut." *Le Nouvel Observateur,* no. 1445 (16 July 1992): 96–97.

Dossena, Giampaolo. "Brivido al Premio Campiello." "Shivers at the Campiello Award." *La Stampa,* 24 May 1980, 1.

Emerson, Gloria. "Divine Troublemaker." *Vogue* 170, no. 11 (Nov. 1980): 332–35, 385–88.

Fabbretti, Nazareno. "L'ultima lettera di Oriana Fallaci." "Oriana Fallaci's Last Letter." *Gazzetta Del Popolo,* 7 July 1979, 1.

Fallaci, Paola. "Una donna chiamata Oriana." "A Woman Whose Name Is Oriana." *Annabella,* no. 35 (30 Aug. 1979): 17–25.

————. "E spiccò il volo: Poi venne la tragedia." "And the Flight Took off: Then Came Tragedy." *Annabella,* no. 36 (6 Sept. 1979): 16–25.

————. "I familiari di Panagulis polemizzano con Oriana Fallaci." "Panagoulis' Family Polemizes with Oriana Fallaci." *Corriere della Sera,* 4 July 1979, 1.

Ferrara, Giovanni. "Una donna testimonia per un uomo." "A Woman Testifies for a Man." *Il Giorno,* 11 July 1979, 1.

Foster, Douglas. "Love, Death and the Written Word: The Lonely Passion of Oriana Fallaci." *Los Angeles Times Magazine,* 10 Jan. 1993, 20–26, 43.

Franks, Lucinda. "Behind the Fallaci Image." *Saturday Review* 8 (Jan. 1981): 18–19.

Giglio, Tommaso, and Renzo Trionfera. "Il servizio di Oriana Fallaci." "Oriana Fallaci's Work as a Journalist." *Europeo,* no. 42 (17 Oct. 1968): 5.

Giroud, Françoise. "Le regard sur la guerre d'une femme intrépide." "A Fearless Woman's Look at War." *Le Journal du Dimanche,* no. 2376 (28 June 1992): 10.

"Goring the Egotists." *Time* 92, no. 48 (29 Nov. 1968): 48.

Griffith, Thomas. "Interviews, Soft or Savage." *Time* 117, no. 12 (30 Mar. 1980): 47.

Hendrickson, Paul. "Oriana Fallaci, Forever at War." *Washington Post*, 24 Nov. 1992, E1–E2.

"Introduction to the Playboy Interview: Oriana Fallaci," *Playboy* 28, no. 11 (Nov. 1981): 77–78.

Keneally, Thomas. "Waiting for the Suicide Truck." *New York Times Book Review*, 27 Dec. 1992, 8.

Kissinger, Henry. *White House Years*. Boston: Little, Brown and Company, 1979.

Krim, Seymour. *Shake It for the World, Smart Ass*. New York: Dial Press, 1970.

Ley, Willy. Review of *If the Sun Dies*, translated by Pamela Swinglehurst. *New York Times Book Review*, 5 Feb. 1967, 49.

Mancuso, Kris. "Oriana nella tempesta." "Oriana in the Storm." *L'Ora*, 6 July 1979, 1.

"Un massacro voluto dal governo." "A Massacre Wanted by the Government." *Paese Sera*, 4 Oct. 1968, 14.

Merck Manual of Diagnosis and Therapy. Rahway, NJ: Merck Sharp & Dohme Research Laboratories. 1987.

Miretti, Stefania. "Fumo contro l'alieno che è in me." "I Smoke Against the Alien in Me." *La Stampa*, 13 Mar. 1993, 15.

Mitgang, Herbert. "As Novelist, Miss Fallaci Still Deals in Real People." *New York Times*, 3 Nov. 1980, C18.

"Monument to a Martyr." *Time* 114, no. 12 (17 Sept. 1979): 31 (International Edition).

Murphy, James E. "The New Journalism: A Critical Perspective." *Journalism Monographs*, no. 34 (1974): 1–38.

Murray, Henry A. *Myth and Mythmaking*. New York: George Braziller, 1960.

National Public Radio. "Oriana Fallaci Interview." *All Things Considered*. 15 Nov. 1992.

Nyren, Dorothy. Review of *The Useless Sex*, translated by Pamela Swinglehurst. *Library Journal* 90 (1 Jan. 1965): 132.

Ostellino, Piero. "Il romanzo di Oriana." "Oriana's Novel." *Supplemento del "Corriere della sera"* 7, no. 29 (21 July 1990): 16–26.

Panagulis, Aléxandros. *Vi scrivo da un carcere in Grecia. I Am Writing to You from a Greek Jail*. Milan: Rizzoli Editore, 1974.

Peer, Elizabeth. "The Fallaci Papers." *Newsweek* 96, no. 22 (1 Dec. 1980): 90, 92.

Poirier, Robert. *The Performing Self*. New York: Oxford University Press, 1971.

Prisco, Michele. "Introduzione." *Penelope alla guerra*, by Oriana Fallaci, i–iii. Milan: Rizzoli Editore, 1962.

Raglan, Lord. *The Hero: A Study in Tradition, Myth, and Drama*. London: Watts & Co., 1936.

Review of *If the Sun Dies*, by Oriana Fallaci, translated by Pamela Swinglehurst. *Christian Science Monitor*, 17 Nov. 1966, 14.

Review of *If the Sun Dies*, by Oriana Fallaci, translated by Pamela Swinglehurst. *Library Journal* 91 (15 Dec. 1966): 80.

Review of *The Useless Sex*, by Oriana Fallaci, translated by Pamela Swinglehurst. *Economist*. 213, no. 14 (1964): 715.

Review of *The Useless Sex*, by Oriana Fallaci, translated by Pamela Swinglehurst. *New Yorker* 68 (19 Dec. 1965): 168.

Rivers, William L. "The New Confusion." *The Progressive*, no. 35. (Dec. 1971): 1–28.

Roberts, Paul William. "Fallaci's Masterpiece: A Modern Day Iliad." *Toronto Star*, 12 Dec. 1992, D14.

Rossani, Wolfgango. "La Fallaci come Flaubert." "Fallaci Like Flaubert." *Gazzetta di Parma*, 10 July 1990, 5.

Sanford, David. "The Lady of the Tapes." *Esquire* 83 (June 1975): 102–5, 154–60.

Scheer, Robert. "Playboy Interview: Oriana Fallaci." *Playboy* 28, no. 11 (Nov. 1981): 77–108.

Schippisi, Ranieri. "Un uomo (e una donna)." "A Man (and a Woman)." *Libertà*, 12 July 1979, 3.

Sims, Norman. "The Literary Journalists." In *The Literary Journalists*, edited by Norman Sims, 3–25. New York: Ballantine, 1984.

Sinigaglia, Alberto. "Oriana Fallaci a Pechino: Il sogno della libertà." "Oriana Fallaci in Beijing: The Dream of Liberty." *La Stampa*, 26 Oct. 1993, 15.

Smith, Patricia. "Oriana Fallaci." *Boston Globe*, 5 Jan. 1993, 61, 64.

Soueif, Ahdaf. "Lovers and Terrorists." *Washington Post Book Review*, 13 Dec. 1992, 5.

Stein, Harry. "A Day in the Life of Oriana Fallaci." *Esquire* 19 (19 June 1979): 21–22.

Stuttaford, Genevieve. "Oriana Fallaci." *Publishers Weekly* 218, no. 19 (7 Nov. 1980): 6–7.

Talese, Nan. "Oriana Fallaci: The D Interview." *D Magazine* 1, no. 2 (June–Sept. 1992): 8–9.

Turoldo, David Maria. "Viaggio nel vulcano 'Insciallah'." "Voyage into the Vulcano 'Inshallah'." *Corriere della Sera*, 2 Aug. 1990, 5.

Valli, Bernardo. "La piccola Iliade di Oriana." "Oriana's Little Iliad." *La Repubblica*, 29 July 1990, 5.

Vigorelli, Giancarlo. "Guerra e amore nel 'suo' Libano." "War and Love in 'Her' Lebanon." *Il Giorno*, 7 Aug. 1990, 5.

Walton, James. "Firepower." *Tablet*, 6 Mar. 1993, 5.

Weber, Ronald. "Some Sort of Artistic Excitement." In *The Reporter as Artist: A Look at the New Journalism Controversy*, edited by Ronald Weber, 13–26. New York: Hastings House, 1974.

Winters, Laura. "Combat Duty." *New Yorker* 68 (28 Dec. 1992–4 Jan. 1993): 59–60.

Wolfe, Tom. "Why They Aren't Writing the Great American Novel Anymore." *Esquire* 78 (Dec. 1972): 152–59, 274–80.

Zamjatin, Evgeny. *Tecnica della prosa. Prose Technique.* Translated by Maria Olsoufieva. Bari: DeDonato Editore, 1970.

Index

Abbas, Mohammed, 199
abortion: Fallaci on, 160–61, 162–63, 173
Action Party, 19
Adams, Constance, 44
Aeneid (Virgil), 17
Agnoletti, Enzo Enriquez, 21
Agony and the Ecstasy, The (film), 38
Ajeta, Marquis d', 28
Aldrin, Edwin "Buzz," 90, 165
Alighieri, Dante, 17
"American Official, The" (Fallaci), 103
Amin, Idi: and Fallaci's interview with
    Qaddafi, 139, 140
Angeli, Pier, 45, 46, 48
Angelico, Fra, 10
Angelo (*Insciallah*), 205; and Boltzmann's
    formula, 212–14
Annabella, 7
antisemitism: of Fallaci, 146
apprehension: as theme in *Insciallah*, 214
Arafat, Yassir, 128, 129, 133, 223
Armstrong, Neil, 84, 92–93, 165
Asham, Abu, 127
association, Proustian, 63, 208
associative technique. *See* stream of con-
    sciousness
auditory techniques: in *Insciallah*, 207–8
Aumont, Jean-Pierre, 46
autobiography (*see also* Fallaci, Oriana),
    176; in *Insciallah*, 221–22; in *Lettera a
    un bambino mai nato*, 164–65, 166,
    167–71; in *Penelope alla guerra*, 54, 55–
    59, 60, 61; in *Se il sole muore*, 71–73
Averoff-Tositsas, Evanghelos, 178, 179

Bani-Sadr, 132–33
Banti, Anna, 57

Barile, Paolo, 21
Baxter, Anne, 45
Bazargan, Mehdi, 138
Bean, Alan, 84–85
Beirut: as inspiration for *Insciallah*, 201–2,
    203
Belezza, Lance Corporal Salvatore (*Inscial-
    lah*), 208–9
Benedetti, Arrigo, 32
Bergman, Ingrid, 39
Bertsos, Georgios, 188; on death of
    Panagoulis, 179
Betrothed, The (film), 39
Bhutto, Zulfikar Ali, 136–37
Bill (*Penelope alla guerra*), 56, 59, 61, 62
Birch, Michael, 101
Bligh, Lady Rose, 33
Blyth, Ann, 45
Boccaccio, Giovanni, 17
Boltzmann's formula: in *Insciallah*, 211–14
Bonjour Tristesse (Sagan), 54
Borg, Ian, 121
Borman, Frank, 90
Botticelli, Sandro, 10
Bradbury, Ray, 73–74
Brando, Marlon, 46
Breschi, Lorenzo, 31
Brinckmann, Paul, 45
Bronner, Francesca Alliata, 158
Brothers Karamazov, The (Dostoyevsky), 47
Brown, H. Rap, 67
Brunelleschi, Filippo, 10
Buchanan, Frank, 19
Buck (*The Call of the Wild*): Fallaci and,
    13, 14
Buckley, William F., Jr., 143
Burning Daylight (London), 14

Callas, Maria, 39
Call of the Wild, The (London), 6, 13–15
camera technique: in *Insciallah*, 207, 208
Cancogni, Manlio, 43
Cantwell, John, 101
Cao Ky, Nguyen, 68, 105
Carità, Mario, 20, 77
Carson, Johnny, 48–49
Casini, Nello, 31–32
Castor, Anna, 83
Castro, Fidel, 142
Catholic Church (*see also* religion): and
     abortion, 163; and funeral of Nello
     Casini, 31–32
Cecchi, Umberto, 23, 200, 202
Central Intelligence Agency (CIA), 140
Cernan, Eugene, 85, 90
Chacko, Sarah, 30
Chaffee, Roger, 84, 90
Chaplin, Geraldine, 68
characterization, 63–64; in *Insciallah*,
     217–18
Charlie (*Insciallah*), 205
"Children of Saigon, The" (Fallaci), 102
Christian Democrats, 32
Christmas Battle (*Insciallah*), 206, 215, 218
CIA. *See* Central Intelligence Agency
Cimabue, Giovanni, 10
Clift, Montgomery, 46
Cocchi, Cesare, 32
Codignola, Tristano, 21
Colby, William, 126, 140–42
Collier's, 40, 60
Collins, Joan, 40
communism (*see also* Communist Party):
     and Fallaci's coverage of Vietnam War,
     107–8
Communist Party (Italian): Fallaci on, 66;
     and funeral of Nello Casini, 31–32
Condor (*Insciallah*), 205
Connery, Sean, 43
Conrad, Charles "Pete," 85–86, 88–89, 93–
     96, 123, 165–66, 243n. 52, 244n. 76
Contemporary Women Writers in Italy
     (Aricò), 3
Cooper, Gary, 40
Corriere della Sera, 32
Cotee, Gotha, 77
Cotten, Joseph, 41, 42, 43

Crain, Jeanne, 45
Crazy Horse (*Insciallah*), 215–16
Crime and Punishment (Dostoyevsky), 13,
     16–17
Cristaldi, Franco, 39, 210
Cronin, A. J., 22
Cronkite, Walter, 92
Crusades, The (film), 44
Cunhal, Alvaro, 142, 249n. 55
Cunningham, R. Walter, 90
Curly (*The Call of the Wild*), 14

Dak To, battle of (*see also* Vietnam War),
     98–99
Dalai Lama, 106
Damone, Vic, 46, 48
Dante. *See* Alighieri, Dante
da Vinci, Leonardo, 10
De Amicis, Edmondo, 13
Death: as character, in *Un Uomo*, 183
de Beauvoir, Simone, 40
Debray, Régis, 132
De Crescenzo, Neil, 143
DeMille, Cecil B., 43–45, 48
Deng Xiaoping, 4, 146–48
description, 80–81; in *Un Uomo*, 181–82
de Sica, Vittorio, 40
dialogue: Fallaci's use of, 62
Dickens, Charles, 6, 11; and Fallaci com-
     pared, 29, 30, 34
Didion, Joan, 107
Dinitz, Simcha, 145
Divine Comedy (Dante), 17
Don Quixote (Doré), 13
Doré, Gustave, 12–13
Dostoyevsky, Fyodor, 6, 11, 60
doubt: as theme, in *Insciallah*, 214; as
     theme, in *Lettera a un bambino mai
     nato*, 167
Dunaway, Faye, 159

Eagle One (*Insciallah*), 205
Eatwell, Nigel, 19–20
El Cordobés, 68
Empress Soraya, 34–35
Engels, Friedrich, 147
Epoca, 36
Espinosa, Gabriel, 122
È stato così (Ginzburg), 69

Europeo, 8, 32, 153; Fallaci's alliance with,
    177; Fallaci's articles on Hollywood for,
    38–48; Fallaci's celebrity interviews in,
    65–70; Fallaci's coverage of U.S. space
    program for, 75–77, 81, 82–86, 88–90,
    92–93, 244n. 61; Fallaci's coverage of
    Vietnam War for, 97, 102–3
"Execution, The" (Fallaci), 102
Ezcurra, Ignacio, 101, 102

Fabio (*Insciallah*), 206
Fables (La Fontaine), 12
Fallaci, Bruno, 15, 22, 36, 57, 161
Fallaci, Edoardo, 10, 11, 13, 18, 24, 69,
    99, 226; and autobiography in *Lettera a
    un bambino mai nato*, 171; death of,
    200; and Italian Resistance, 19–20, 77–
    78, 79–80; opposition to space program
    of, 72–73, 86
Fallaci, Oriana (*see also specific works*), 3–
    9; articles on Hollywood by, 38–48; at-
    tachment to United States of, 59–60;
    autobiographical writing of, 71–73, 164–
    65, 166, 167–71, 221–22; and cancer,
    228–31; celebrity interviews by, 65–70,
    237n. 9; as character within her own
    narratives, 73–74, 80–81, 133, 211,
    218–20; childhood of, 10–11, 17–19;
    coverage of Mexican student protests by,
    116–25; coverage of Vietnam War by,
    97–115; early articles on Iran by, 33–
    36; as exhibitionist, 235n. 5; formal edu-
    cation of, 21–24; Giò as (*Penelope alla
    guerra*), 55–59, 60, 61; interviewing
    techniques of, 126–27, 134, 143, 144,
    148, 150, 156–57; and Italian Resis-
    tance, 19–21; literary influences on, 13–
    17; literary journalism of, 25–26, 27–
    32, 37, 94–96, 238–39n. 7; love of
    books of, 11–13; narrating persona of,
    175, 187–91, 204–5, 225, 226–27; rela-
    tionship with translators of, 138–39,
    158–59, 176–77, 194–98; reportage on
    U.S. space program of, 75–77, 81–86,
    88–93; on romantic love, 14, 55, 167–
    68, 190–91; on status of women, 48–52;
    treatment of Arabs by, 223
Fallaci, Paola, 5, 7, 12
Fallaci, Tosca, 7, 10–15, 18–19, 22; death

    of, 177; illness of, 78; as model for Giò's
    mother (*Penelope alla guerra*), 54–55;
    on status of women, 49–50, 60, 73, 226
fascism, 11, 20, 70; Fallaci's hatred of, 59–
    60; and Islam compared, 155–56
Fasolo, Margherita, 21
Fattori, Giorgio, 49
Fedi, Father Bruno, 29
Fellini, Federico, 67
feminism (*see also* women, status of): of
    Fallaci, 56–57
Ferruccio (*Insciallah*), 206
fiction: Fallaci on, 61
Fisher, Eddie, 48
Fisher, Warren, 47
Flaubert, Gustave, 6, 15, 60
Fleurs du mal (Baudelaire), 60–61
Florence, 10; influence of, on Fallaci, 211
Foglianti, Francesca, 30
Fonda, Jane, 48
Ford, Glenn, 41
For Whom the Bell Tolls (Hemingway), 222
France, Victor (*see also* Fallaci, Oriana),
    195
Francesco (*Penelope alla guerra*), 61, 62, 63
Franciosa, Anthony, 47
Freeman, Faith, 91–92
Freeman, Theodore, 83–84, 86, 88
Freni, Carmelo, 28–29
Frishman, Robert Franchot, 109–15
From Here to Eternity (film), 46
Furno, Carlo, 21

Gable, Clark, 33, 47
Gandhi, Indira, 3; and Fallaci's interview
    with Zulfikar Ali Bhutto, 136–37
Gandhi, Mahatma, 51, 126
Garbo, Greta, 39
Garcia Barragan, Maximino, 121
Gardner, Ava, 33, 40, 46
Garland, Judy, 46
Garson, Greer, 41, 42
Gassman, Vittorio, 40
Genina, Augusto, 40
Giap, General Vo Nguyen, 108, 150
Giglio, Tommaso, 116, 160–61, 177
Gino (*Insciallah*), 206
Ginzburg, Leone, 69
Ginzburg, Natalia, 68–70

Giò (*Penelope alla guerra*), 54, 62–64;
    Fallaci as, 55–59, 60, 61
Giotto, 10
Glenn, John, 82, 83
Gli antipatici (*The Egotists: Sixteen Surpris-
    ing Interviews; The Limelighters*)
    (Fallaci), 65, 70, 241n. 36
Goldwyn, Samuel, 44
Gone with the Wind (Mitchell), 60
Gordon, Richard, 89–91
Gramsci, Antonio, 15
Grant, Cary, 46
Greatest Show on Earth, The (film), 44
Greene, Graham, 40
Guaita, Maria Luigia, 21
Guiducci, Armanda, 57

Habash, George, 130–31, 133
Haile Selassie, 3, 25, 148–49
Hawk (*Insciallah*), 205
Hefner, Hugh, 67
"He Had the King's Feet in His Hands"
    (Fallaci), 28–29
Hemingway, Ernest, 5, 6, 198
Hendrickson, Paul: interview with Fallaci
    by, 229
Hitchcock, Alfred, 41, 68
Holden, William, 45
Homer, 17
homosexuality, Fallaci's attitude toward,
    128–30, 134–35
Hong Kong: Fallaci's coverage of, 105
Hopper, Hedda, 42
Hué, Battle of (*see also* Vietnam War):
    Fallaci's coverage of, 100–101
humor, 87–88; in *Insciallah*, 215–16
Hungarian revolution, 245n. 1
Hussein, King, 133–34, 144
Hussein, Saddam, 228

Idiot, The (Dostoyevsky), 16, 183
Iliad (Homer), 17; influence of, on Fallaci,
    217–18
Illustrated Bible (Doré), 12–13
image, Fallaci's creation of (*see also* Fallaci,
    Oriana), 107, 110, 116, 123, 126, 154–
    55, 194, 199, 211
India: Fallaci's coverage of, 105–6

Insciallah (*Inshallah*) (Fallaci), 4, 6, 15,
    22, 48; Boltzmann's formula in, 211–14;
    characterization in, 217–18; characters
    in, 205–6; form of, 206–10; humor in,
    215–16; inspiration for, 200–202, 203;
    narrative persona in, 204–5; Russian lit-
    erary influence on, 16–17; translation
    of, 194–98
interviewing technique, Fallaci's, 126–27,
    134, 139, 143, 144, 148, 150, 156–57
Intervista con la storia (*Interview with
    History*) (Fallaci), 70, 156–57, 251n.
    103
Ioannidis, Dimitrios, 180
Iotti, Nilde, 66
Iran: Fallaci's articles on, 33–36
Iron Heel, The (London), 14

Johnson, Van, 45
journalism (*see also* literary journalism),
    25, 26, 64; and literature compared, 4,
    37, 107, 159, 178–79
journalistic activism, 97, 106–7
"journalit," 26
Justice and Liberty organization. *See* Resis-
    tance, Italian

Karamanlis, Konstantinos, 178
Katju, Jaishree, 51
Kaur, Rajkumari Amrit, 51
Keneally, Thomas: on translation of *Inscial-
    lah*, 197
Kerwin, Joseph, 91
Khan, Tikka, 137
Khomeini, Ayatollah Ruhollah, 4, 132, 138,
    139, 155–56, 203
Kidder, Tracy, 107
Kim (Kipling), 15
King, Martin Luther, Jr., 105
King of Kings, The (film), 44
Kipling, Rudyard, 6, 15–16
Kissinger, Henry, 3, 25, 126, 150–54
Kramer, Jane, 107
Krim, Seymour, 26

La Malfa, Ugo, 21
Lambrakis, Grigorios, 188
Lancaster, Burt, 45

Laramy, Ronald, 101
Lasky, Jesse, 44
Last Temptation of Christ, The (Kazantzakis), 183
Lebanon. *See* Beirut
Lenin, Vladimir Ilich, 147
Leone, Giovanni, 25
Lessico famigliare (Ginzburg), 69
Lettera a un bambino mai nato (*Letter to a Child Never Born*) (Fallaci), 3, 10, 158–75, 229–30
literary journalism, 5, 107, 159; of Fallaci, 25–26, 27–32, 37, 89, 94–96, 102–3, 238–39n. 7
Little Lady of the Big House, The (London), 14
Loan, General Nguyen Ngoc, 104
London, Jack, 6, 13–15, 19, 22
Look, 40
Loren, Sophia, 46
Lotuf, Abu, 248n. 7
love: Fallaci on, 14, 55, 167–68, 190–91
Lovell, James, 91
Lovell, Marilyn, 91
Loy, Myrna, 30
Luce, Clare Booth, 141
Lussu, Emilio, 21

Macbeth (Shakespeare), 17
Macdonald, Dwight, 160
MacLaine, Shirley, 48, 49, 239n. 30
Magnani, Anna, 39, 67
Maharishi Mahesh Yogi, 105
Mailer, Norman, 198
Makarios III, 180
Malraux, André, 6
Mansfield, Jayne, 45
Man's Hope (Malraux), 222
Manzoni, Alessandro, 11, 60
Maraini, Dacia, 57
Marco Polo (film), 39
Marcus, James: and translation of *Insciallah*, 196
Martine (*Penelope alla guerra*), 56–57, 61, 62, 63, 64
Martin Eden (London), 22
Martino (*Insciallah*), 206
Marx, Karl, 147

Mattino dell'Italia Centrale, Il, 8, 47; Fallaci's early work for, 26–32, 33
Mazandi, Joe, 34
Mazim, Abu, 127–28
McCone, John A., 142
McDivitt, James, 89, 90
McPhee, John, 107
Mehta, Anjani, 51
Meir, Golda, 3, 144–46
Melville, Herman, 6, 15
Merchant of Venice, The (Shakespeare), 12
Metamorphoses (Ovid), 17
Mexico: Fallaci's coverage of, 116–25
Michelangelo, 10
Miller, Ann, 45
Miller, Arthur, 47, 48
Mineo, Sal, 46
Minh, Le Vanh, 100
Minnelli, Vincente, 45
Miranda, Rogelio, 132
Molière, Jean-Baptiste Poquelin, 12
Mondadori, Giorgio, 36
monologue, interior, 62–63
Monroe, Marilyn, 40–41, 47
Montalban, Ricardo, 45
Montessori, Maria, 30
moon launch (*see also* space program, U.S.), 92–93, 94–95
moralism: Fallaci and, 214–15
Moreau, Jeanne, 68
Mori, Paola, 41
Morning Chronicle, 29
movies: influence of, on Fallaci, 210
Ms., 57
Mussolini, Benito, 21
Mutiny of Elsinore, The (London), 14

Nacion, La, 101
narrative, 107, 117, 175, 225; in Fallaci's novels, 64; in *Insciallah*, 204–5; in *Un Uomo*, 180–81, 182, 187–91
National Aeronautics and Space Administration (NASA). *See* space program, U.S.
Nazione di Firenze, 26
Nenni, Pietro, 144
Neway, Germane, 149
Neway, Mengistu, 149
New Journalism, 25

New York Times, 40
Niente e così sia (*Nothing and Amen*)
    (Fallaci), 3, 97, 116
Ninette (*Insciallah*), 205, 218–20
Niven, David, 41
Nixon, Richard M.: and Fallaci's interview
    with Kissinger, 150, 151, 152, 154
Novak, Kim, 45
Nyerere, Julus Kambarage, 139–40

O'Brien, Margaret, 45
Odyssey (Homer), 17
Oliver Twist (Dickens), 29
Ovando, Alfredo, 132

Paget, Debra, 45
Pallottelli, Duilio, 48, 50, 51, 52
Panagoulis, Alexandros "Alekos," 4, 14, 16,
    55, 161, 167, 221; death of, 253n. 18;
    and *Un Uomo*, 176–93
Panteri, Gastone, 26–27
Papadopoulos, George, 185
Parsons, Louella, 41, 42, 45
Pasolini, Pier Paolo, 176–77
Passani, Véronique, 45
Passepartout (*Insciallah*), 212
Pavan, Marisa, 45, 46
Peck, Gregory, 41, 45
Peckson, Geronima, 30
Peer, Elizabeth, 144
PEN. *See* Poets Essayists Novelists
Penelope alla guerra (*Penelope at War*)
    (Fallaci), 62–65, 66, 70; autobiographi-
    cal traits of, 54, 55–59, 60, 61
Pensées (Pascal), 102
People's War; People's Army (Giap), 108
Perkins, Anthony, 46
Petrarch, 17
"Petroleum is Iran's Arbitrator" (Fallaci), 35
PFLP. *See* Popular Front for the Liberation
    of Palestine
piccole virtù, Le (Ginzburg), 69
Pigott, Bruce, 101
Pistoia (*Insciallah*), 205
Pius XII, Pope, 31
Plainsman, The (film), 44
Plato, 17
Poets Essayists Novelists (PEN), 196
Poirier, Robert, 235n. 5

Popular Front for the Liberation of Pales-
    tine (PFLP), 130
Porter, Cole, 41
Power, Tyrone, 47
Pozzolini, Alberto, 96
Presley, Elvis, 46
Pride and the Passion, The (film), 46
Prisco, Michele, 64
privacy: Fallaci and, 39–40
"Prostitute, The" (Fallaci), 103

Qaddafi, Muammar al-, 3, 139–40, 145,
    155, 199–200, 203
Quil giorno sulla luna (*That Day on the
    Moon*) (Fallaci), 96

Rahman, Mujibur, 131–32, 136, 137
Rakowski, Mieczyslaw, 135–36
Rambo (*Insciallah*), 206
Rashid (*Insciallah*), 212
religion: Fallaci and, 74, 214–15
Resistance, Italian, 19–21, 69
resistance movement, Palestinian, 127
Rhodes, Richard, 107
Richard (*Penelope alla guerra*), 56, 57, 58,
    59, 61–64
Ridomi, Christiano, 36
Rivers, William L., 26
Roberts, Paul William, 222
Rockwell, Norman, 60
Rosen, Herb, 74–75
Rossani, Wolfgango, 6
Rosselli brothers, 21
Rousseau, Jean-Jacques, 227
Russell, Jane, 45

Sadat, Anwar al-, 144
Sagan, Françoise, 25, 65
Saigon, First Battle of (*see also* Vietnam
    War), 104
Saigon, Second Battle of (*see also* Vietnam
    War), 101–2
Salgari, Emilio, 13
Salvini, Guido, 40
Sam, Nguyen Van, 99
Samson and Delilah (film), 44
Sandokan (*Insciallah*), 205
Sartre, Jean-Paul, 40
Saturday Evening Post, 40, 60

Saturn V (*see also* space program, U.S.),
     78, 79, 88, 93
Scheer, Robert, 57; interview with Fallaci
     by, 128–29, 130, 132, 134–35, 143–44,
     146, 191–92
Schippisi, Ranieri, 193
Schirra, Walter "Wally," 83, 93
School of Space Medicine (*see also* space
     program, U.S.), 81–82
Schwieckart, Russell, 90
Se il sole muore (*If the Sun Dies*) (Fallaci),
     7, 12, 165; autobiographical nature of,
     71–72
Serra, Michele, 38, 49
sesso inutile, Il (*The Useless Sex*) (Fallaci),
     48, 51–52
sette peccati di Hollywood, I (*The Seven
     Sins of Hollywood*) (Fallaci), 41, 42, 47–
     48
Shah of Iran (Mohammed Riza Shah
     Pahlavi), 155
Shanti Baba, 105
Sharon, Ariel, 142–43, 200
Shearer, Norma, 41
Shepard, Alan, 82–83, 165
Shepley, John, 138–39, 158–59, 176–77
Shroff, Veena, 51
Shukla, Leela, 51
Siciliano, Enzo, 176
Sims, Norman, 107
Sinatra, Frank, 33, 46
Sketches by Boz (Dickens), 29
Slayton, Donald "Deke," 75–77, 82
Smith, Paul, 87–88
Socrates, 17
Solidarity, 134
Soueif, Ahdaf: criticism of Fallaci by, 223;
     on translation of *Insciallah*, 197–98
space program, U.S. (*see also specific astro-
     nauts*): Fallaci's reportage of, 75–77, 81–
     86, 88–93, 244n. 61
Spielberg, Steven, 210–11
Squaw Man, The (film), 44
Stalin, Joseph, 147
Steffas, Michael: and death of Panagoulis,
     253n. 18
Stranger, The (Camus), 183
"Stranger, The" (Fallaci), 102–3
stream of consciousness: in *Insciallah*, 208–9

student movement, Mexican: Fallaci's cover-
     age of, 116–25
Sugar (*Insciallah*), 205

Tale of Two Cities, A (Dickens), 29
Taming of the Shrew, The (Shakespeare), 12
Taylor, Elizabeth, 48
Tecnica della prosa (Zamyatin), 6
Ten Commandments, The (film), 44
terrorism: Habash on, 130–31
Tet offensive (*see also* Vietnam War), 103
Thi-an, Huyn, 99–100, 110–11
Thieu, Nguyen Van, 150
Tho, Le Duc, 151
Tierney, Gene, 46
Togliatti, Palmiro, 36, 66
Tolstoy, Leo, 6, 11, 60
totalitarianism, 20
translators, Fallaci's relationship with, 138–
     39, 158–59, 176–77, 194–98
Traquandi, Nello, 21
Trionfera, Renzo, 116
truth: Fallaci on, 102
Turoldo, David Maria, 6, 224
Twelfth Night (Shakespeare), 12

UNESCO. *See* United Nations Educational,
     Scientific, and Cultural Organization
Union Pacific (film), 44
United Nations Educational, Scientific, and
     Cultural Organization (UNESCO), Fifth
     Conference of, 30–31
United States: attitude toward Vietnam War
     in, 103; Fallaci's attachment to, 59–60
United States Information Service (USIS), 87
Uomo, Un (*A Man*) (Fallaci), 16, 42, 57,
     188–93; form of, 179–80, 181–83, 186–
     88; mythological elements in, 184–86
USIS. *See* United States Information Service

Valentino, Rudolph, 46
Valianti, Leo, 21
Valley of the Moon, The (London), 14
Valli, Bernardo, 6, 224
Vanderlix, Bella, 257n. 81; and *Insciallah*,
     220–21
Verghese, Jamila, 51
Verne, Jules, 13
Viale, Giovanni, 122

Victor Emmanuel III, 28
Vietcong (*see also* Vietnam War): Fallaci's
    attitude toward, 99–101, 102, 106, 107
Vietnam War, 3; Fallaci's coverage of, 97–
    115; and Fallaci's interview with Kissin-
    ger, 151; murder of journalists during,
    101–2
Vigorelli, Giancarlo, 6, 224
Visconti, Luchino, 39
von Braun, Wernher, 78–79
"Voyage to Iran" (Fallaci), 35

Walesa, Lech, 126, 134, 135
Wallace, Mike, 154
Walton, James: criticism of Fallaci by,
    223–24
War and Peace (Tolstoy), 13, 16, 222
war novel, *Insciallah* as, 204–5, 222
Weaver, William, 176
Weber, Ronald, 37
Welles, Orson, 41–43

White, Edward, 85, 90
White Fang (London), 14
Winters, Shelley, 47
Winter's Tale, The (Shakespeare), 12
Wolfe, Tom, 107
women, status of: Fallaci on, 48–52; Golda
    Meir on, 144–45
World War II, 19, 69; and Fallaci's attach-
    ment to the United States, 59–60;
    Fallaci's recollections of, 74–77, 79–80
Wuthering Heights (Brontë), 12
Wyszynski, Cardinal Stefan, 135

Yamani, Ahmed Zaki, 223
Young, Loretta, 45

Z (film), 188
Zamyatin, Yevgeny, 6
Zinnemann, Fred, 46
Zukor, Adolph, 44

SANTO L. ARICÒ received his Ph.D. from Fordham University in Romance languages and teaches French and Italian at the University of Mississippi. He has written *Rousseau's Art of Persuasion in "La Nouvelle Héloïse"* and edited *Contemporary Women Writers in Italy: A Modern Renaissance*.